BROTHERS IN ARMS

PERRY PIERIK

Brothers in Arms

Romania, Nazi Germany and operation 'Barbarossa'

Aspekt Publishers

"What is happening here is only the vengeance of the past"
- Jan Romein in *Machten van deze tijd*

Brothers in arms
© Perry Pierik
© 2023 ASPEKT Publishers
Amersfoortsestraat 27, 3769 AD Soesterberg, The Netherlands
info@uitgeverijaspekt.nl - http://www.uitgeverijaspekt.nl
Cover design: Snegina Uzunova
Translation: Isabel Oomen

ISBN: 9789464870121
NUR: 680

All rights reserved. No part of this publication may be reproduced, stored in a retrieval system or transmitted in any form or by any means, electronic, mechanical, photocopying, recording or otherwise, without the prior permission of the publisher.

Table of contents:

Introduction	7
Romania and Nazi Germany from the geopolitic perspective of the Third Reich	11
From King Carol II to Marshal Antonescu	25
The oil of Ploesti	51
The Romanian Holocaust	61
Operation 'Barbarossa'	73
The storming of Crimea	97
Turning point Stalingrad	107
Retreat from Kuban bridgehead	123
Mius and Wotan-Stellung	135
Between Dnieper and Bug	141
Drama Sebastopol	147
From Odessa to the Pruth	153
The decisive breakthrough at Jassy	161
The collapse of the Antonescu regime	185
Wrestling with the demons of the past	207
Endnotes	223
Literature	249
Documents/Archives	259
Internet links	264
Abbreviations	265
A word of thanks	266

Introduction

Between 1940 and 1944, Nazi Germany and Romania were brothers in arms. German historian Eberhard Jäckel, who studied Hitler's politics, concluded that Nazi Germany actually had two main goals: the conquest of 'Lebensraum' and the destruction of European Jewry. In both areas, Romania, under Marshal Ion Antonescu, was to play an important role. Romania was one of the biggest allies in terms of the number of troops that assisted Nazi Germany during Operation *'Barbarossa'*; the German invasion of the Soviet Union in June 1941. In doing so, Romania was the only country where the Germans hardly had to lift a finger to get the Holocaust going.

As time passed and the odds of war turned against Hitler, Romanian politics also turned. The Holocaust was toned down during 1942 in the areas taken by Romania. Many Jews from Romania's core country were spared. The initial enthusiasm at the front changed into an increasingly critical attitude and reticence. As soon as the Romanians had taken Odessa and seen their *'historical claims'* fulfilled, the enthusiasm to move further east declined considerably. The German general Von Manstein called this the traditional fear of Russia that the small Central European states suffered from.

But these fears proved justified. The summer conquest of 1942 started ahead, but en- route towards the Volga, Hitler split the 'Heeresgruppe Süd' (the Army Group South) into two army groups, one of which went into the Caucasus and the other continued on its way. Both armies were ultimately not strong enough for their task. At Stalingrad, things went completely wrong. Large army groups were surrounded and two Romanian army groups were almost completely destroyed.

From then on, there was a growing distance between the Romanians and the Germans. The long retreat began, with rivers running at right angles to the Soviet advance providing some support. Things became dramatic in Crimea, once so proudly taken in Romanian-German cooperation. Sebastopol was besieged by the Red Army and the garrison had to be rescued via a laborious evacuation by sea.

In August 1944, the front cracked around the town of Jassy and the German-Russian front broke apart. This also affected the political situation.

The young Romanian king deposed Marshal Antonescu and a new chapter of communist rule began for Romania. Germany lost its most important brother-in-arms. Hitler was vindictive as ever and, in anger, gave the order to bomb the *Royal Palace*. Villainous Romanian fascists were brought out of concentration camps to form an exil government. It was all to no avail. The war in Romania was lost and the German army fell back towards Budapest.

The dramatic story of Romania in World War II is told chronologically and introduced by a somewhat more general chapter on Germany's geopolitics in the region. Romania was a link for Germany in a long road to 'Lebensraum' in the east and hugely important due to the oil fields of Ploesti. Nazi Germany was an opportunity for Romania to recapture lost territories that had been taken from them during the interwar period. Romania had taken a curious turn in this regard, from 'Entente' power in the First World War, to ally with Nazi Germany in the Second World War. All this had to do with the West's failed appeasement policy and the convenient way Berlin had played out and controlled Romania. Each had their own agenda, but what they had in common was hatred of Jewry and communism, which stood for more or less the same thing within National Socialist ideology and propaganda.

History became an altar of blood for the population, ravaged by pogroms and an authoritarian regime; for Jews and gypsies and for the soldiers at the front as well.

That Romania remained on the side of Nazi Germany for so long had everything to do with circumstances. Berlin and Bucharest had a stranglehold on each other. Hitler could not do without Romanian oil and for Antonescu there was no turning back. He had tied his future to the outcome of the war and hoped until the last moment that the Red Army could be stopped. Hitler, for his part, showed relative humility towards Romania. The Führer personally had a great admiration for the incorruptible, anti-Semitic Antonescu and wanted to keep him on board.[1] Additionally, Romania's fall would affect neighbouring countries, above all Bulgaria and Turkey. It was therefore important to keep Bucharest on the German side.

But neither diplomacy nor the armed forces could turn the odds of war. History was written on the battlefield. Partly because of the unwise strategy of Hitler, who for instance held on to the Cowan bridgehead (the last territorial remnant of the attack in the Caucasus and later the Crimea) for far too long. Thus the main front lacked the troops needed to anticipate Soviet superiority with (mobile) reserves. As a result, the German forces had to try to save their lives time and again. Consequently, the Germans fell back from line to line with unprecedented discipline, but ultimately losing. The Romanians were sucked into this story. Time and time again, Hitler promised Antonescu that the German army would now hold out, but practice proved more recalcitrant.

My personal interest in this brotherhood of arms stems from earlier works that focused on the southern part of the Eastern Front as well, such as the book *Hungary 1944-1945, the forgotten tragedy*, published in 1994. After that, I also dealt with Stalingrad and Crimea, as well as with islamitic volunteers in German military service, who were recruited both in the Caucasus and the Balkans. This did impress upon me the massiveness of the tragedy that had taken place there, which goes way beyond Stalingrad, which most people are unaware of. The rest of the story was more or less unheard and unknown. Romanian participation was taboo for many years even in Romania itself. Typical was the fact that Gerhard Schröder - the German Chancellor from 1998-2005 - shared in his memoirs that he had never known his father because he had been killed in Romania. About the how and why he did not know anything. In addition, there is relatively little literature on the subject.

Extensive monographies could be written on the various chapters and themes in the book. The aim of this book is to achieve a first exploration for the Dutch-speaking region. A certain focus here is on a number of lesser-known military sites. For example, the retreat from the *Mius Front* and the *Wotan-Stellung* to Romania has been worked out in some detail. This is to show that this front was of great importance for the Romanian army and that not everything was limited to Stalingrad. The book further includes the liberation of Crimea by the Red Army.

As source material, a lot of archive material was used. Here, the German archives were consulted above all, as they now contain the best military data on this period. These include the *NARA Archive*, various *T-rolls*, as well as files from the *Bundesarchiv* and material released through the German-Russian digitisation programme of historical sources; *Germandocsinrussia*. Literature was used as well. All are included in the source list.

Writing this book earned me some new Romanian friends who were kind and patient enough to answer my questions. My thanks to them are included in the acknowledgements.

Dr Perry Pierik Soesterberg 2021

Romania and Nazi Germany from the point of view of Third Reich geopolitics

'The war should absolutely have been avoided. Germany should have obtained 'Lebensraum' without fighting, but we have no diplomats'
   (From a conversation overheard by the OSS from German officers, September 1944)

Hitler's 'Südost-Politik', which included Romania, was a part of German geopolitics. In the years after World War II, German geopolitics was sometimes referred to as a pseudo-scientific philosophy of renovation. The terms 'Heim ins Reich' (all Germans within a border) and 'Lebensraum' (Germany's territorial claim to the East) were seen as a dangerous spiritual engine behind Hitler's drive for conquest. Yet geopolitics in the years following World War I was no small obscure event. Precisely because of the disappointing outcome of the war, which was perceived as dramatic and as a great injustice (the *Versailles Peace Treaty* with the German *'all-guilt'* was perceived as a *'diktat'*), this science was able to take off. At the end of the nineteenth century, these already were the first developments in the field. Friedrich Ratzel is generally regarded as one of the first scientists who devoted himself to what was then called police geography. The ideas were characterised by a strong social Darwinian character, assuming the *'rise and fall'* of civilisations and empires. Not individual humans were central to this line of thinking, but the political form of human life in interaction with the spatial environment. Here, the issue constantly focused socially Darwinistically between survival or demise or, as the important geopolitical representative Karl Haushofer put it; it is about the eternal *'und um das ganze'*. Prof Albrecht Penck, attached to the Berlin Institute for *'Meereskunde'*, argued as early as World War I that the Great War was a struggle against 'Deutschtum' itself.[2]

That people were so sharp on the ball was due to the consequences of the First World War. In line with Swedish geopolitician Rudolf Kjellén, who died in 1922, the state was perceived as a 'Lebensform', which had to *survive*. A state was therefore not something *'abstract'* or *'dead'*, but was formed by the 'Volksgemeinschaft' and was subject to natural laws and natural influences. States were *'born'* too. Dr Richard Hennig and Dr Leo Körholz proclaimed this in their standard work *Einführung in die Geopolitik* from 1935. With regard to the newborn states, they were of course indirectly referring to the consequences of the *Treaty of Versailles* and other peace treaties after November 1918, from which new states had emerged. The list of new states was considerable, and made the idea of *'living states'* more understandable according to the ideas of the time. Since 1900, these included Albania, Ukraine, Finland, Estonia, Latvia, Lithuania, Poland, Czechoslovakia, Yugoslavia, Iceland and Ireland, and even Danzig was listed as a *'state'*. Politics - the interaction of the 'Volksgemeinschaften' - were closely monitored in this process. That states were not only *'born'* but also *'collapsed'* showed the *'youngest'* state of the time, Manchuria, which was soon *'swallowed up'* by Japan.[3] Furthermore, scholars believed that young states, to which Germany and Romania both belonged, tended to expand and that many 'Grosstaten', which included the Netherlands and its colonies, were resigned to their position. Some of these *'old states'* tended to shrink, *'like old people'*. Furthermore, states practised reproduction, such as new states that emerged from the British overseas empire. This too, they argued, was of all times, like Carthage once breaking away from Tyre.[4]

For Karl Haushofer, the takeaway from 1914-1918 was that Germany had not understood its geopolitical lessons, and needed to be re-educated. Within the newly emerging ideas, there were also specific lessons for Germany as a central power in Europe, a traditional *'transit country'* as Prof Z.R. Dittrich put it, with many neighbours. Its location in Central Europe (in itself a controversial concept, did Germany belong to the West or to the East?) brought *'geopolitical'* consequences. One had to relate to many neighbouring countries. After 1918, many more were added, so people sometimes spoke of a *'devil's belt'* being formed around Germany, where the language border and the territorial border did not coincide.⁵ According to many geopoliticologists, *'emerged'* was actually not the right word in this regard. Wilsonian self-determination, which emerged after November 1918, would have been used to create a ring of states around Germany. Even a historian like the Dutchman Jan Romein pointed to the French influence in this regard and people spoke of a *cordon sanitaire around* Germany. In the struggle for hegemony in Europe, Paris tried in this way to stay ahead of Berlin and spoke of the *'French circle'*, the *'French bloc'* and the *'pseudo-French Empire'*.⁶ Within this complex fact, the young Germany had to develop into a 'Kernraum' from which power from this *'geometric Ort'* had to spread. Kjellén pointed to the importance of a Berlin-Baghdad railway line, which immediately gave some insight into the scale of thought.

Kjellén's vision was prompted by Germany's lack of colonies. Since Germany had only come into existence in 1871, it had no position overseas and had far fewer colonies than small powers like Belgium and the Netherlands. Germany had come *'too late'* in the division of space on earth7 and a *'Volk ohne Raum',* as Hans Grimm wrote in his popular 1926 book.⁸ Prof Albrecht Penck, affiliated with the *Institut für Meereskunde* in Berlin, had calculated that Germany had to make do with 1/1000th of the earth's surface, with the result that Germans lived in a *'narrow and small country'*.⁹ Nazi Germany therefore turned to the Eurasian continent, along the lines defined by the British Sir Halford Mackinder. That distinguished between the *'Heartland'* (the Eurasian landmass) which the Germans often called the *'Kernraum Europa'* or the *'Kontinantalblock'*; versus *'The World Island'*. The Germans spoke of *'Weltinsel'*, referring mainly to North and South America.

Achieving Lebensraum for the *'Kontinentalblock Europa'*, which was to provide Germany with a *'Grosswirtschaftsraum'*, was Hitler's foreign political agenda. This vision was highly deterministic, maintaining the status quo was not an option and would mark the downfall of Nazi Germany. The *'Lebensraum'* policy, which this entailed and which included *'Südost-Europa'* - and thus Romania - had many facets. It was part of the *'Raumpolitik'*, in response to the lack of German colonies. The *'Auslandsdeutschtum'* had an important role in this.

The so-called '*Volksdeutschen*' (in Romania or in areas occupied by Romanians), Romanians with an ethnic German background, played an important role in this. Still under the influence of the Poland conquest, Hitler had already spoken on 6 October 1939 about the '*important task*' of rearranging '*ethnographic relations*', which in practice caused an 'Umsiedlung der Nationalitäten'. This was a programme of deportations and repopulation. It is perhaps worth emphasising here that this was decided for the 'Volksdeutschen', just as they were forced to fight in German military service.

In the occupied parts of Poland, which had been added to the Third Reich as 'Reichsgau', 'Volksdeutschen' were brought in from Romania or areas occupied by the Romanians. By 15 November 1940, nearly 300,000 Poles had already been deported from these regions in 303 trains to make way for the 'Volksdeutschen'. Until October 1942, 81,089, 75,533, 12,581 and 32,366 'Volksdeutschen' were to be moved from the regions of Bessarabia, North Bukovina, South Bukovina, Dobrischka and the Romanian core country, respectively. Their interests were looked after through the 'Volksdeutsche Mittelstelle: VoMi' commanded by SS-Obergruppenführer Werner Lorenz and his right-hand man SS-Oberführer Dr Helmuth Behrens, who, in the field, made officers like SS-Oberfüher Hoffmeyer and SS-Oberführer Siekmeier and their army of 600 men responsible for the retreat of the 'Volksdeutschen'. For the Reichsführer-SS, this was a major spearhead of his policy. He had already been appointed 'Reichskommissar für die Festigung deutschen Volkstums' on 9 October 1939.

Himmler had a romantic idea in mind, drawing comparisons with the '*eastern mission*' of the Saxon peasants in the Middle Ages. Again, there was talk of a 'Wehrbauertum', a kind of soldier farmers who were to defend the 'Deutschtum' in the newly occupied territories. SS Mountain-toops general Arthur Phleps, who in 1944 would be responsible for the retreat westward of the remaining 'Volksdeutschen' (towards Budapest) as a result of the Soviet advance, believed that the Romanian 'Volksdeutschen' were a '*dynamic source of strength*'. Through them, it would be possible to control the 'Südost-raum' and encapsulate the rival 'Magyarentum'. Phleps saw German opportunities here- through this, especially in a *'south-eastern direction'*, referring to the Ukraine, the Bosphorus and the Dardanelles.[10]

Indeed, the plans went a long way beyond the 'Bessarabiendeutschen' and other 'Volksdeutschen' from the Romanian area. It was hoped to soon include the 'Russlandeutschen' in ethnic politics as well. Morover, it was planned to deploy some of the Bessarabian Germans in Russia in order to push it eastwards again. This would involve 3,000 families. However, first *'new land'* had to be *'taken with the sword'*.[11]

On 22 October 1940, Hoffmeyer informed Berlin that the last procession of 'Volksdeutschen' had crossed the Pruth river. The last trains from North Bukovina towards Kraków left on 17 November that year. Hoffmeyer, incidentally, was not a *'supervising'* official in Himmler's service. In Transnistria, he would have been involved in executions of Jews with the 'Sonderkommando R' (Russia), which further hunted Bolshevists in the region and fought against resurgent Catholicism in Ukraine. The latter was mostly the work of 'Volksdeutschen', who - regardless of Himmler's daydreams - still had a will of their own. The 'Sonderkommando' fell under the 'HSSPF Russland-Süd'.[12] The executions of Jews by the 'Sonderkommando R' were allegedly authorised by Berlin in January 1942. Although the reports of many 'Einsatzgrup- penkommandos' still exist, this is not the case with these. It is assumed that these were destroyed at the end of the war.

In a 22.10.1940 speech to the NSDAP's 'Landsgruppe' in Madrid, Himmler was very clear about the future. He spoke of the *'re-unification'* of the German 'Volkstum' by the Nuremberg Race Laws. The war won (against Poland) freed up *'new fields'*. True, Germany had had to absorb 8 million new *'countrymen'* (the joining of Polish territories to Germany), but these were to be kept apart with a clear separation. In practice, this meant shifting Poland to the 'Generalgouvernement' (Polish rump state). All the 'fremde Volkstum' were gathered there, and above all the Jews. These were to be ghettoised again within the 'Generalgouvernement', and these, he stressed, were all Jews from the 'Grossdeutsches Reich'. To repopulate the new areas, 250,000 'Volksdeutschen' had been taken from Bessarabien, Southern Bukovina and Dobreschka. This *'repotting'* ('verpflanzt' says Himmler) would bring *'revolutionary changes'*, according to the Reichsführer-SS. The ground would be enriched and made into fertile fields, and the landscape would be completely rearranged as well. From windy steppe to cultural landscape. As a result, the empire would grow together eastwards: *'Es wird keine Kolonie mehr geben [...] sondern nur Wirtschaftsgebiete'.*[13]

Indeed, on their advance into the Soviet Union, the German troops encountered members of the 'Russlanddeutsche' community, some of whom had been deported to the east by Stalin. The various Nazi authorities started interfering with them directly, so that they too became a plaything of international politics. In the end, it was the 'Sonderkommando R' that had the most influence. It was difficult to achieve real *'politics'* because the 'Volksdeutschen' lived over a wide area and partly lived within the Romanian sphere of influence, or in the army's 'Korpsrückwärts' area.[14]

Meanwhile, the 'Volksdeutsche' community in Romania became more tightly bound to Germany. The foreman of the 'Volksdeutschen' was Andreas Schmidt, under the name of Volksgruppenführer, who had already advanced to this position at the age of barely 30 and without any significant training. This he did not do on his own. In Berlin, he had been in contact with the head of the SS-Hauptamt Gottlob Berger, who happened to be his father-in-law. The latter had subsequently catapulted Schmidt into Romanian politics. Berger argued that the 'Volksdeutschen' had to operate in line with the Reichsführer-SS Heinrich Himmler. He quickly climbed up the ranks of SS loyalists; the Reichsführer-SS attended his wedding in March 1943 and considered him one of the most reliable forces in the Romanian political playing field.

Schmidt was only regarded by part of the 'Volksdeutschen' as their representative, but there was no real counterforce.[15]

Morover, there was the military factor. Due to the 'Blitzkrieg', Hitler had the military instrument to back up his politics. All campaigns up to the Russian campaign were completed within six weeks, an unprecedented achievement. Coalitions were formed where necessary, but Hitler was so convinced of the German victory that he was not keen on this. As the war worsened for Germany, the Romanians were called upon more.

The economic foundations for the 'Blitzkrieg' had been laid in the German planned economy, and especially the 'Vierjahresplan'. This prepared Nazi Germany economically for war and focused on the synthetic manufacture of raw materials that Germany lacked. Bucharest was very important to Berlin in light of oil supplies; through the Ploesti fields and a series of oil companies. The Romanian oil position internationally at that time was completely different from today. In the 1930s, Romanian oil production reached the same quantity as that of, say, Persia (Iran).[16] From the late 1930s, German influence on the Romanian fuel industry increased rapidly. Together with the Soviet Union, Romania was Nazi Germany's main oil supplier. The attack on the Soviet Union only increased Romania's importance. Part of the military elite had therefore warned of a possible conflict with the Soviet Union even before 1933. A good relationship with Moscow was actually necessary for Germany. Back then, a general like Hans von Seeckt warned for an ideologisation of relations with the Soviet Union, apart from the danger of a two-front war.[17] However, this good advice was ignored. Still, the German position in Romania was strengthened. Many foreign interests in the Romanian oil industry were bought out by Germany.[18]

Furthermore, the 'Bauerntum' knew its position in the whole and was highly ideologically charged. Autarchy was pursued in that area. Romania played a not insignificant role in this as a supplier of food. In his book *Das Agrarpolitische Weltbild,* Karl Haushofer's son Heinz Haushofer discussed this at length. At its core, the German problem lay in the fact that Germany could only provide 83% of its own food production.[19]

Infrastructure-wise, there were also all sorts of desires. We already saw the Berlin-Baghdad railway, and indeed Hitler dreamed of superfast and extra-wide trains in which the 'Herrenmensch' could be transported through the 'Kontinetalblock'. In addition, the further opening up of the Danube as a water transport route, especially for raw materials, played an extremely important role. In addition, the Black Sea was included in the German geopolitical concept and through a series of Sonderbeauftragten, Berlin tried to increase German interest in these strategic sectors. Via the Danube, the transport went inland from the 'Kernraum'; via the Black Sea, this mainly supplied the front to the east.

Ideologically, there were similarities between both Marshal Antonescu's regime and Berlin, as well as the position of the Iron Guard and Nazi Germany. Roughly sketched, one could say that the Iron Guard was better suited to National Socialism, and thus the Reichsführer-SS and its agencies sought close affiliation with the Guard and protected it when they were squeezed by Marshal Antonescu's takeover of power. Antonescu followed a somewhat more pragmatic nationalist line - although he was a staunch anti-Semite - which allowed him to count on support from the NSDAP and party structures. Within the German camp, tensions regularly arose due to this division.

Collectively, the regime, the gardists, the party and SS stood against the Soviet influence that had become increasingly palpable in the region since the 1930s and the establishment of the Soviet state after the civil war. In the summer of 1940, this intensified via *'Red Week'* (Soviet invasion of Bessarabia and northern Bukovina). The Soviet Union and the ideology of communism clearly operated 'überstaatlich' and fanned out globally. From Moscow, the course was fourfold; the Mediterranean programme, aimed at the Crimea, Black Sea and Dardanelles, the Atlantic programme, aimed at the West, with the Polish-Russian war as the provisional climax, the Asian programme, advancing towards the Pacific, and the Indian programme, in which the Soviets penetrated southwards via the Transcaucasus.[20] In two speeches, Marshal Antonescu's right-hand man and namesake Mihai Antonescu showed his true colours regarding Romanian ambitions. On 17 June, i.e. even before Operation *'Barbarossa'*, he announced that it was time for Romania to move its border eastwards. In doing so, he spoke of the River Bug. Romania had to stake a claim to its 'historical space' and one had to go to extremes in the *'struggle against the Slavic people'*.[21]

German geopoliticians looked with a certain admiration at the 'Bewegungslust' of the Slavic peoples and Moscow. It was all right with the 'Wandertrieb', which *at the point of the bayonet brought communism westwards*.[22] In this sense, they spoke of *'nomadic Raublust'*.[23] Here lay a great challenge for Germany. In short, from the ideas of Kjellén, Mackinder and Haushofer, one came to the conclusion that the final battle for the 'Kontinentalblock' would ultimately be Germany versus Russia (Soviet Union). Here, most thinkers assumed that Russia had the best papers. On the other hand, Germany was *'forced'* by geopolitical circumstances to go on the offensive. Haushofer stated: *'Weiter raum wirkt Leben erhaltent'*.[24] This involved the specific factors mentioned above: the 'Auslandsdeutschtum', the raw materials policy, the agrarian worldview, food production and military developments. During the coalition war with Romania against the Soviet Union, there was initially enthusiastic support for the operation through Marshal Antonescu. In fact, Bucharest more or less forced itself into this operation. Hitler recoiled a little from the familiar problems of coalition conflict, with overlapping command structures and subsequent (territorial) claims lurking. In the process, the coalition partners did not trust each other, with sentiments between Budapest and Bucharest being particularly strong.

Finally, the *'Jewish question'* had its geopolitical component. Important geopoliticologists may not have been so anti-Semitic, but things like the stabbed-in-the-back myth (in which the blame for the German defeat was sought outside their own ranks, usually referring to communists, Jews and socialists) was widely entrenched. Even someone like the Weimar politician Friedrich Ebert believed in this myth. As a result, self-reflection and self-cleansing from the bloody lessons of 1914-1918 were not the case at all. Within militant 'Volkstum thinking', and the increasingly muddled international relations were also increasingly viewed in these terms, equating Judaism with Bolshevism and declaring the old Tsarist family that had previously ruled Russia 'Aryan'. In this way, they strengthened the claim to a *'European Russia'* that had been *'stolen'* by Jews and panslavists.

These elements had repercussions in Romania, where anti-Semitism had ancient Christian Orthodox roots but had increased enormously as a result of Greater Romanian thinking in the 20th century. Among the Iron Guard, this took on mystical forms. In the late 1920s and early 1930s, Codreanu travelled on horseback from village to village, dressed in green with a white cross on his chest to make speeches everywhere at churches, which were directed against the Jews and in favour of Greater Romania. His contention was that he did not bring *'election promises'*, that *'he didn't like that'*, those were the words of politicians he looked down on. Codreanu was what the Germans called a 'Tatmensch'; acting was the main focus: loyalty and belief in self, which had to be defined newer and bigger. He spoke in Erich Obst's terms of the *'birth of a new world'* and *'new people'*. Young people followed his example and groups on horseback moved through the country - singing national songs - from place to place, while the population welcomed them with burning candelabras by the roadside. *'We look like crusaders fighting godless Jewry in the name of the cross to liberate Romania,'* he spoke on one of his treks through Bessarabia. His antipathy towards communism was as great as against Judaism. *'When I say communist, I mean Jew,'* was a phrase of his.[25] Romania, too, fought for its place under the sun, to the Allies, and its participation in World War I in 1916 should therefore be seen in that light. Romanian irredentism produced a more than strained relationship with its neighbours. In fact, the Romanians had no friends in the region. Through politics and military operations, they tried to strengthen their own position. Although participation on the side of the 'Entente' seemed opportune in 1916, a swift German military response quickly settled Romanian ambitions. Only the eventual collapse of the three monarchies, Russia, Austria-Hungary and Germany in 1917 and 1918 brought an unexpected twist. The realisation of Greater Romania was later nullified by Molotov's revolver diplomacy, in which - during the *'Red weeks'* in June 1940 - he suddenly lost Romania, Bessarabia and North Bukovina again. The role of the Jews in Bessarabia was magnified in the process; like Nazi Germany, Romania pursued its own 'Volkstum' policy, reinforced by the humus of the mys- tical-nationalist worldview of Corneliu Zelea Cod- reanu's Iron Guard. This created the prerequisite for mass murder, which began with bloody pogroms in the town of Jassy, the same town in which the Romanians and Germans in 1944 suffered their heavy defeat against the Red Army.

Europe and the world were under the spell of *'world-moving forces'*, fuelled by *'unbearable tensions'* as the geopoliticians described it.[26] The 'Raum- schicksal' could be broken.[27] The result was a deterministic course characterised by a dangerous cultural pessimism. Struggle was the father of all things.[28] The individual, (the 'völksiche') was opposed to the 'Fremd- körper' and the *'Germanic man'* (Aryan) was opposed to the *'Slavic man'*. The 'Kernraum' stood against the 'Weltinsel' and in the 'Kernraum', Germany stood against Russia. The German stood against the Jew, nationalism stood against internationalism or the 'überstateliche', the 'Volksdeutsche' stood against the host country. In *Weltpolitik von Heute*, Haushofer called this, in concurrence with Kjellén, *'state biological precepts'*. The German 'Volksgemeinschaft' was divided among 18 countries and this was seen as a problem. The 'Volks- deutschen' outside Germany were mostly suppressed by the 'Hauptvolk' of the country in which they lived.[29] It was established that one was 'hineingeborn' in one's ethnicity and country assimilation was thus not an option. This produced the iron schism that gripped the world. War was the result.

The Soviet Union was the ultimate goal for Hitler. Geopolitically, there were special opportunities here. Erich Obst called this Russia's 'raumschicksal', which was unique in that motherland (nuclear Russia) and colonies were merging through westward and eastward expansions. By comparison, the British empire had crumbled, *'vielteilig'*, as Obst put it, while in Russia the *'civilisation mission'* emerged via the Eurasian route. Within Russia, a mountain range like the Urals was not a border and neither was a wa- ter road like the Volga. Here were continental colonies, *'einzigartig auf der Welt'*.[30] The Romanians went along with this to the extent that they still had historical claims eastward. Few Romanians protested at the capture of Odessa and the entry into Transnistria, but interest did not extend much further east. The campaign against the Soviet Union was equally unconstrained and Romania was dragged into the all-or-nothing scenario.

For Nazi Germany, the plans of conquest to the east revolved around concepts such as 'Heim ins Reich', 'Lebensraum' and the often in a general sense formulated 'Ostraum'. Behind these notions was an expansive ideology with the aim of destroying existing social structures in the eastern areas (of Germany) to be conquered. These plans were formulated in the so-called 'Generalplan Ost', whose main compiler was the agricultural expert Konrad Meyer. The 'Generalplan Ost' sounded less guilty than it was. Not for nothing had Meyer been appointed by the Reichsführer-SS Heinrich Himmler as *'Leiter des Stabhauptamtes für Planung und Boden'* of the *'Reichskommissariat für die Festigung Deutschen Volkstums'*. The name of this last body already brings us closer to the core of what was at stake. The 'Generalplan Ost' was a programme aimed at a very large-scale 'Umsiedlung' and 'Aussiedlung' of people in Eastern Europe, above all the Soviet Union. In the process, the Slavic peoples and the Jews were rücksichtslos sacrificed for the space to be made for German 'Siedlers', who were to be settled, in the east, in 'Hauptdörfer', 'Wehrdörfer' and 'Wehrbauernhöfe'.

In this 'Umvolkung-Strategie', about 50% of Poles were stripped of their homes and tens of millions of Russians had to *'disappear'*. Polish border areas were annexed by Germany (the 'Altreich') and east-west zones were built, creating 'Verbindunsgbrücken' between the 'Altreich' and the newly conquered territories, where the Germans were going to settle. The new zones - Konrad Meyer christened them 'Grenzkreise' - were created roughly along the line Kaunas - Bialystok - Lublin - Zamosc and Lemberg. To this end, some 64% of the population of Ukraine had to be deported and 75% of Belarussians.

This made the conflict between Nazi Germany and the Soviet Union more than a traditional (border) conflict or classical war, but thus became an ideological war. Marshal Antonescu's regime supported these operations militarily for traditionally irredentist reasons (Bessarabia, Northern Bukovina and Transnistria), but equally for ideological ones. 'Raumpolitik' was no stranger to Bucharest in this either, although it lacked the global mission that the German conquest programme had, Romania's relied more on that of a regional (great) power with nearly 20 million inhabitants. The murders of Soviet Jews, largely carried out on the ground by the 'Einsatzgruppen', created the basis for the brutal 'Umsiedlungspolitik' that was planned. Romania went along with this to the extent that they used the conquered territories of the Soviet Union as *'shear zones'* for the Jews they wanted to get rid of, above all those living in the newly conquered areas (Northern Bukovina and Bessarabia). This deportation to their areas of interest was not convenient for the Germans, and a shifting back and forth between the two spheres of influence ensued, with all the human dramas that this entailed.

Thus, Romania rendered its services as a brother in arms to the German ideal until the 'Kernraum Europa' under German hegonomy. This produced a dubble *'achievement'*. No country supplied more troops to Nazi Germany than Romania.

From King Carol II to Marshal Antonescu

Initially, nothing suggested that Romania, under the leadership of the military dictator Ion Antonescu, would develop into one of Nazi Germany's staunchest allies. Indeed, after the *Treaty of Versailles*, in which the new areas of influence had been outlined in Europe, Romania had profiled itself from the newly created situation. It was thus among the winners of World War I, although its own military action had been far from successful. Nevertheless, Bucharest had been able to benefit territorially from the outcomes of the war and the collapse of the central powers - the weakening of Russia (Soviet Union) by the Russian Revolution. The Romanians' attitude had been opportunistic during the First World War. Romanians sought their way to *Romania Mare*, the *'Greater Romania'* that had been dreamt of for decades. The Great War seemed to offer opportunities. Timing was everything. In the summer of 1916, the right moment seemed to have arrived. The German troops had been completely swallowed up by the perils of Verdun and the rigid front, while the Austro-Hungarian troops were facing the *Brussilov Offensive* - named after the general Alexej A. Brussilov - which came with 600,000 troops and 1,770 artillery pieces against the Austro-Hungarian army. From the positions around Rowno, Dubno and Tarnopol, the 8th, 11th, 7th and 9th Russian armies arrived for an offensive from the Pripjat area to the Black Sea. A huge front moved in and the operations were well prepared. In a very short time, the 4th Austro

Hungarian Army was more or less wiped out.[31] The war gods seemed to be on the side of the 'Entente' and negotiations between Romania, France, Britain, Russia and Italy were in full swing.

Bucharest had drawn up a neat list of areas it was interested in. One wanted a free hand in Bukovina, the Banate and large parts of Transylvania, even extending to the Debrecen-Szeged line, i.e. in the middle of *'Hungarian'* territory. This was ambitious, but the 'Entente' did not want to let it escape momentum. World War I had become a war of attrition after the failed 'Schlieffen Plan' of 1914, and any support was more than welcome. Bucharest could supply troops as well as withdraw economic support to the central powers. The 'Entente' therefore agreed to the Romanians' shopping list, but on condition that hostilities against the central yachts would be opened almost immediately (in ten days). As a result, Romania declared war on Austria-Hungary on 27 August 1916.[32]

The Romanians were blinded by the treasures that beckoned and made a misjudgement. The idea that they could limit the war to the (relatively weak) Austria-Hungary and keep Germany out of the hostilities was naïve, to say the least. Germany reacted like a viper bitten by a snake and as early as 5 September, German zeppelins appeared over Bucharest to bomb the Romanian capital. It was more or less the same reaction Hitler would have to the Romanian *'betrayal'* of August 1944, when he had the Royal Palace and ministries in Bucharest bombed for defecting to the Allies.[33]

History consists of a grab bag of coincidences that come together in time. At the very moment of Romania's entry into the war, an important change of position in the German military leadership had taken place. German commander-in-chief Von Falkenhayn's playbook at Verdun had literally got stuck in a meat grinder. Even Kaiser Wilhelm II had finally lost patience with his favourite general. Von Falkenhayn had to take the field. The change of power was a *'necessity'*, as Czech historian Karl Tschuppik put it, and the general duo of Paul von Hindenburg and Erich Ludendorff took over his position.[34] Both generals were idiosyncratic and collectively quite a successful military couple. In the August days of 1914, through the battle of Tannenberg and the battle of the Mazurian lakes, they had already stabilised the frontline situation in East Prussia and kept the eastern front and their weak Austro-Hungarian ally afloat with limited resources. Immediately after being installed in the military summit, they made three decisions:

- the massacre at Verdun had to end,
- there would be front reductions on the western front, freeing up

troops and increasing the number of guns per kilometre front (Germany then defended successfully until spring 1918),
- people wanted to deal with Romania's betrayal.³⁵

On 28 August, Romanian general Averescu had invaded Transylvania. The area - called Zevenburgen (Siebenbürgen) by the Germans - had always been controversial land. Even on the ethno-demographic composition of the population - essentially simple statistics - opinions differed. There possibly was a slight demographic predominance of Romanians in the area, but Hungarians could rightly lay much claim to the land as well. Harald Roth, the area's monograph, named Transylvania as a *'cultural crossroads'*. That was far too kind an approach for the deep rift, which ran through the country.³⁶

In 1526, the historic battle of Mohacs had taken place between the Hungarians and the Ottomans. This was deep in the soul of Budapest. In the preliminary stages of this counter-offensive against the Turks, Buda (Budapest) had been recaptured. For Austria, Transylvania was a *'crown country'*, so any encroachment by the Romanians in the region was, by definition, fraught. After all, the Romanians feared the *'magyarisation'* of the country or its marginalisation as a *'Habsburg outpost'*. At the end of the 18th century, there had been uprisings led by Vasile Nicola Ursu, also called Horea, and in 1791, the petition *'supplex libellus valachorum'* had been drawn up, stressing Romanian rights. The revolution of 1848 had brought things further to a head. Its place within the Habsburg monarchy was in question and *'linguistic nationalsime'* reigned supreme. Even in the Banaat, uprisings had occurred at that time. Matters were so sensitive that the spark easily flew. The Banaat was the disputed border region in present-day Romania, Serbia (Vojvodina) and Hungary, sandwiched between the Danube, Tisza, Mures and Carpathian rivers, around the city of Timisoara. On the eve of 1848, Romanian nationalists here, led by Eftimie Murgu, had tried to connect with Transylvania. As Russia was involved in the matter at the time, Vienna saw this as Slavic irredentism that needed to be quelled.³⁷

In 1916, the time finally seemed to have come for Bucharest. Chief of the general staff, Alexandru Averescu, from Bessarabia, seemed to

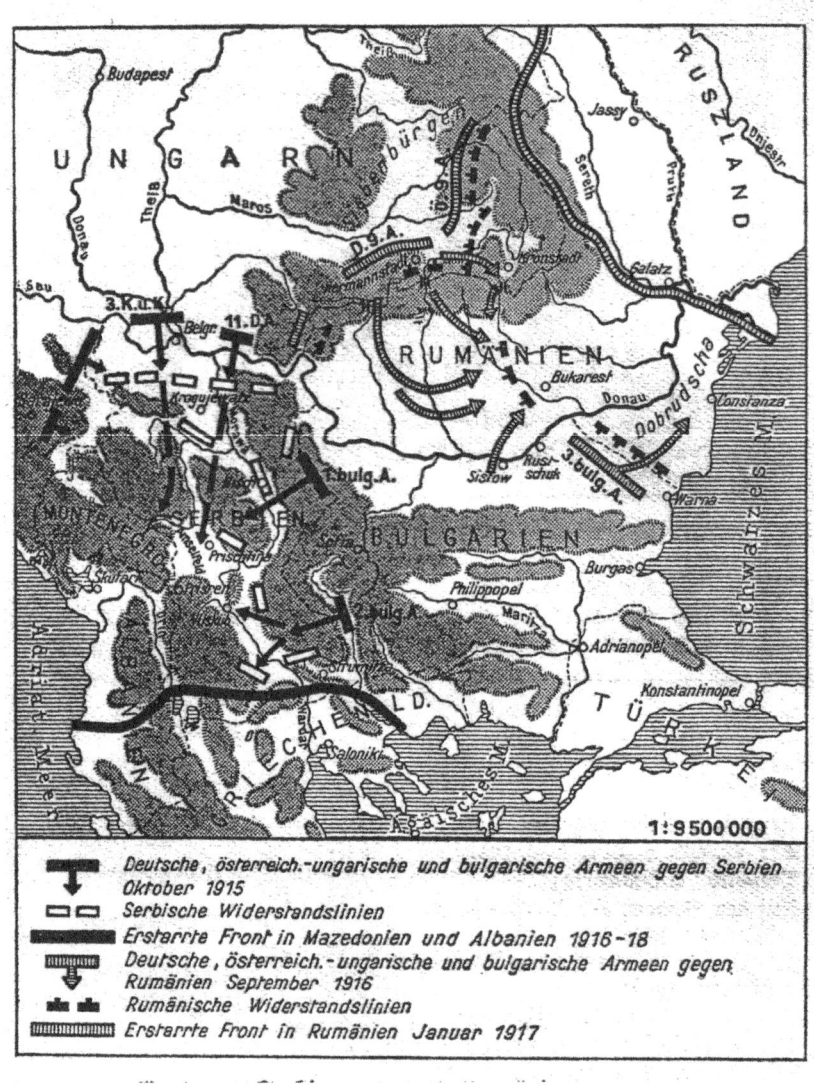

German campaign against Romania during the First World War.

achieve nice results in the beginning of hostilities. Romanians in Transylvania received Romanian troops with enthusiasm while Hungarians fled. The city of Brasov, or Corono (Kronstadt) founded by Saxon settlers in the 13th century, was captured by the Romanians. The Romanian army, 370,000 strong, was in good spirits. The dual monarchy had only managed to hastily scrape together a force of 34,000 men, made up mostly of ethnic Hungarians. Things looked bad, but the new OHL of Von Hindenburg and Ludendorff had driven the playbook. While on the western front the Germans concentrated on the 'innerner Konsolidierung' (which in practice meant the retreat to a more defensible front by means of the 'Alberich-Rückzug' and the expansion of the new *Siegfried-Stellung*), they gave the taunted Von Falkenhayn, who had failed at Verdun, the chance to revenge himself against Romania. At the head of the 9th Army, the Germans rushed to meet the forces of Austria-Hungary. At the same time, on the southern front against Romania - commanded by Marshal August von Mackensen - German, Bulgarian and Ottoman troops were assembled, advancing into Dobroedzja.[38]

'What wonderful victories,' concluded a young German Erwin Rommel - later to become famous as commander of the Afrika Korps - about the campaign against Romanians.[39] Romanian troops in Transylvania were soon in trouble. The Romanian armies were advancing without any notion of cartography. Railways, stations and foraging junctions were completely ignored. Before long, the Romanian attackers' supply situation was catastrophic. They depended heavily on allies for ammunition. What ammunition there was did not get to the front easily. *'The Romanians are bad soldiers,'* Erich Ludendorff mused in these days.[40] *'This is an enemy we can defeat in the field,'* Von Falkenhayn concluded next.[41] Meanwhile, Von Mackensen was advancing towards Bucharest.

There, boats were requisitioned to cross the Danube, and Von Mackensen had a military chapel play cheerful tunes while the crossing took place. On 6 December 1916, Von Mackensen marched into Bucharest as a modern marshal 'Vorwärts' in the best *Blücher tradition*.[42] Blücher was nicknamed *Marschall Vorwärts* for his offensive disposition on the battlefield. To his great surprise, the city's terraces and restaurants were full. *'What a flippant and superficial people,'* he mused with some surprise.[43] The Romanians were on the run and Von Falkenhayn's reputation saved.[44]

How important strategic oil was even then was shown by the fact that simultaneously with the capture of Bucharest, Ploesti and its oil fields also fell into German hands. But before the German entry, the fields, machine houses and drilling rigs had been severely damaged by the British. The oil reservoirs were on fire.[45]

While this fiasco was taking place, the *Brussilov* offensive had ultimately not gone as desired. The Russians had initially gained considerable ground and inflicted hefty losses on the Austro-Hungarian army, but German intervention did not stabilise it, while the Russian attack faltered as it operated further from its own supply lines. There was very little the Russians could do to help the newfound ally Romania, let alone the western 'Entente' powers.[46]

The government of Ion Constanliu Bratianu, who came from a family of great landowners and was also foreign minister, and King Ferdinand emigrated to Moldova and settled in Jassy, the town that in August 1944 would give name to the dramatic and decisive battle on the Romanian front in World War II. On 7 May 1918, the *Treaty of Bucharest* was concluded.

In doing so, Romania had take the losses. South Dobroedzja fell to the Bulgarians, all the Carpathian passes - the strategic passages - were ceded to Austria-Hungary. Romanian granaries and oil were at the disposal of the Central Powers. The oil fields near Ploesti were *'leased'* to Germany for the period of 90 years. Just before the takeover of the oil fields by Germany, British pioneers had rushed to thoroughly destroy the oil installations, thus giving the Germans the least possible advantage. Romania was occupied by von Mackensen's army.[47]

It looked like everything would end in total catastrophe, but the Centrals' success against Romania was only an intermediate step in the Great War. By 1918, the Centrals were in a much weaker position. Meanwhile, the US had joined the side of the 'Entente' and the German Spring Offensives of 1918, with which the general duo Von Hindenburg and Ludendorff wanted to turn the tide, had failed.

The German front faltered similarly in Romania, where the Romanians, supported by the allies, had inflicted some vicious defeats on the Germans. The power shift in Russia meant that the Russians had dropped out of the war; the Romanians were now on their own. They therefore saw no other option to conclude a separate armistice with Germany. This came into force on 9 December 1917 and was further ratified by the Bucharest Treaty signed on 7 May 1918. Salient detail, this treaty was not signed by Romanian King Ferdinand, but the new government that was subsequently installed went along fully with German demands. These included making reparations and granting free passage of Bulgarian and Austro-Hungarian troops, leasing Romanian oil wells for the duration of 100 years and the far-reaching mobilisation of the Romanian army. With the latter, it did allow the Romanians to keep four divisions on standby in Bessarabia to use them to fight Russian influence in the area. Bucharest had already taken a lead on the course of events by entering Bessarabia in February 1918.

Bessarabia, like Transylvania, was a disputed strip of land, located between the Pruth and Dnieper rivers and included the Danube Delta and the coastal strip with the Black Sea. In 1806, it had been conquered by Russia from the Ottomans. Since then, the area had been oriented towards Russia, but now that the Russian tsarist empire had collapsed, four Romanian divisions, which no longer had to align themselves with Germany, could assert their authority in Bessarabia. In the end, the treaty of 7 May 1918 turned out to be nothing more than a scrap of paper because Germany could not win the war. This led to Romania even being able to declare war on Germany, which took place on 10 November 1918. Germany, which was now on its knees, ensured that Greater Romania's ideas could continue. Romanian sights were now set on Transylvania because the Habsburg throne in Vienna and Budapest had fallen. The Romanians saw their chance - during the negotiations in Paris where the map of Europe was redrawn - to reinforce their demands - by taking possession of Transylvania and pulling the country entirely into Romania. Following the conqueror's recipe, Bucharest had the transfer approved by referendum. Yet, what was perhaps even more important was the fact that Bucharest could submit the bill for their war effort to the 'Entente'. The conquest of Bessarabia was approved by the drafters of the *Peace of Versailles*, which meant that only Russia did not recognise the new conquest. The appropriation of Bessarabia was to remain a territorial dispute. No more than 44% of the population was ethnically Romanian, so large 'minorities' existed. In Russia, the *Committee for the Liberation of Bessarabia* was formed by Christian Rakovsky and the situation remained tense in the region. A French report from that time states that *'the population detested the Romanians and the Romanians tried very hard to deserve it'*. The hatred was so great that people preferred the Russian ruble to the Romanian. Politicians acted brutally in an attempt to maintain order.[48]

Romania therefore developed into a legalistic country, which recognised the *Treaty of Versailles*, relying heavily on the 'Entente' powers, especially France. It also supported the League of Nations, which *'guaranteed'* territorial integrity after Versailles. The shortening of the Central powers took place on 4 June 1920 with the *Treaty of Trianon*, in which the Hungarians in particular lost out. Count Albert Apponyi, the Hungarian negotiator sent to the conference, had to conclude that there was nothing to negotiate. The correspondent A.G.M. Abbing felt that the country had been *'shaken to the skin'*.[49] Transylvania and the Banate fell to Romania, the upper lands or Upper Hungary (north of the Danube) and Carpatho-Roethenia were granted to Czechoslovakia. In doing so, the Romanians were at odds with the revisionist attitude of Germany, Austria and Hungary, which had emerged from the Habsburg Empire.[50]

More treaties followed Trianon. The *Treaty of Saint-Germain* with Austria, the *Treaty of Neuily* with Bulgaria, the *Treaty of Sèvres,* which would later be amended with the *Treaty of Lausanne* and with it the territorial disputes with the Turks were settled. Equally, the outcome of all these international conferences and treaties was that Greater Romania was on the map. That Romania would still end up as an ally of revisionist Germany had several causes. The two main ones were the rise of Nazi Germany and the continuing tensions with the Soviet Union over Bessarabia. Romania tried to deal with this through a threefold deal with Yugoslavia and Czechoslovakia, but this did not carry enough weight. This was mainly due to the fact that the Western 'Entente' powers were unwilling to act against the growing German influence in the Balkans and Mid- den Europe after 1933.

After the Reichstag fire in 1933, followed by the *Night of the Long Knives* in 1934, Nazi Germany worked towards the 'Führerstaat'. Revision of Versailles was one of the goals towards the expansion of the 'Grossdeutsche Reich', the pursuit of 'Lebensraum' and Germans outside the homeland 'Heim ins Reich'. A very long series of rapidly succeeding measures propelled Germany back to the forefront, such as the pursuit of autarky, the 'NS-Grossraumwirtschaft', rearmament, construction of numerous organisations such as 'Hitlerjugend', SS and 'RAD', as well as a long series of treaties with which Hitler, as history taught, *flexibly* agreed: *Concordat with Vatican*, treaty with Poland (1934), Britain (1935), Italy (1936), Japan (1936) the *Anti-Comintern Pact* (1936) followed by the *Munich Conference* in 1938. The 'Anschluss' with Austria and the policy towards the Sudeten Germans and Czechoslovakia, made it clear that this was not just about paper influence.

For the Romanians, this became particularly evident through the so-called *'Erste'* and *'Zweiter Wiener Schiedsspruch'*. The *'Erste Wiener Schiedsspruch'* on 2 November 1938 took place under the supervision of Germany and Italy under the coordination of German foreign minister Joachim von Ribbentrop and Italian counterpart Galeazzo Ciano. The aim of the conference was to further roll back the peace treaties of 1919 and the following years. This conference provided the Hungarians in particular with substantial territorial gains vis-à-vis Czechoslovakia.

The *'Zweiter Wiener Schiedsspruch'* on 30 August 1940 was particularly detrimental to Romania. Large parts of Transylvania and other areas were assigned to Hungary. Nazi Germany was already lord and master over large parts of Europe by then and opposition was futile.

These setbacks hit Romania hard and contrasted sharply with the image of the Greater Romania that they sought. However, the consequences of the Vienna agreements were overshadowed by another problem. From the second half of June 1940, the Soviet Union again stepped up pressure to regain the area of Bessarabia, as well as Bukovina. There had been animosity around these issues throughout the period from the Romanian occupation. In this, Moscow took a rather unsubtle approach. On 29 March 1940, the Soviet foreign minister reminded Bucharest that there was no non-agression pact between the two countries and that this was the result of an *'unresolved legal dispute'*. Molotov did not do this directly, but in a speech to the Supreme Soviet. It was clear that this was about Bessarabia. The message was not misunderstood in Bucharest. People tried to get in touch directly with Rome and Berlin to field a counterweight, not knowing that Berlin was tied to the Soviet Union by the *Molotov-Ribbentrop Pact* and that Italy would follow Berlin in this. For Hitler, the knife now cut both ways. One could have done business with the Soviet Union, rolled up Poland, and by *'abandoning'* Romania, the country was actually handed over to them. In turn, Hitler, in April 1940, occupied Denmark and Norway. This set a dangerous precedent, which naturally did not escape Moscow either. Meanwhile, Bucharest was being massaged in the *'right direction'* by Berlin. In May, there was a meeting by Baron Manfred von Killinger, Hitler's special envoy in Bucharest, with the head of Romanian intelligence, Mikhail Murozov. Von Killinger made it clear that Romania had more to gain from Germany than from the West (or the Soviet Union). This was further underlined by Wilhelm Fabricius, who announced on 15 May 1940 *'that the Romanian future lay with Germany'*. He was able to reinforce this by the German invasion of the West. This included French and British sabotage attempts to inhibit Romanian oil supplies to Germany. This was a violation of Romanian neutrality. Earlier French proposals to support Romania with troops, made in March by Maxime Weygand, later commander-in-chief (17 May 1940) of the French army, proved unrealistic. The contingents would have to move into Romania from Syria over Turkish territory. Turkey did not allow this.[51][52]

By 9 June, there were already signs that Moscow was mobilising and large numbers of troops were being drawn together on the border with its Romanian neighbour. Meanwhile, the Soviets were testing how Berlin would react to any Soviet actions. After all, Nazi Germany was the only country that could take serious action against

Stalin. More talks with German ambassador Friedrich-Werner von der Schulenburg took place in Moscow in the second half of June. The Germans indicated that they were not very enthusiastic about the Soviet plans and the direct way Moscow expressed its desire. They eventually gave in, simply because Nazi Germany could not use a new conflict at that time with the Western campaign against France and allies. Besides, the *Molotov-Ribbentrop pact* had been concluded on 23 August, and the secret clause noted that the Soviet Union was interested in Bessarabia and Berlin had declared that they had no claim to the area. This definitively placed Bessarabia within Moscow's sphere of influence.[53]

Now that the way was clear, Moscow directly addressed Bucharest on 26 June 1940 with an ultimatum, to be fulfilled within 24 hours. The Soviets had not even bothered to present the whole thing with any substantive argument. It was power politics pure and simple. At the time of the Russian Civil War and afterwards, there had been different views in Russia regarding Bessarabia. Leon Trotsky and Maxim Litvinov had initially been willing to recognise the Romanian claim. Other Soviet leaders, such as the Bulgarian-born Christian Rakovsky, who held sway in communist Ukraine, thought otherwise. That line eventually continued. In the process, the irredentism of Bulgaria and Hungary towards Romania was supported by the Soviet Union. Military plans had even been developed early on to bring Bessarabia back under Soviet influence by force of arms. Generals like Mikhail Frunze and Klement Voroshilov had developed plans to this end. Ultimately, they shied away from this. Moscow, however, felt strong enough to take on Bucharest. Through a series of endless diplomatic protests, the issue was kept alive. In doing so, it was entirely preceded by endless border provocations.[54]

There was hardly anyone in Bucharest who dared to confront the communist neighbour, and there was little left but to give in to this gun-toting diplomacy by Soviet foreign minister Vyacheslav Mikhailovich Molotov. Moreover, the Romanians felt less strong in Bessarabia. The virus of communism had gained a greater foothold in this region than elsewhere in the country. The reason was that there was a large Slavic community in Bessarabia and a large Jewish minority. Both these groups were more open to Russian influence. In the process, the situation had been stoked by communist agents who had illegally crossed the Dniestr and were trying to gin up revolutionary momentum. Bucharest had tried to eliminate the worst social ills in the region through land reforms, but this had been insufficient to completely shackle communism. Moscow had also sheltered in exile many Bessarabian and Romanian communist (mantle) organisations working to permanently undermine Bucharest's authority. In cities like Odessa, Kharkov and Moscow, these revolutionary bastions were active and working against Bucharest. Some of the agitators had been recruited from World War I prisoner-of-war camps, just as had happened to Hungarian council communist Béla Kun.[55]

People had proceeded confidently, entirely on the basis that the world revolution was about to break out. The revolutionary Romanian-inspired organisations had even set up a provisional government in Odessa shortly after World War I, in anticipation of the expected developments. Three previous direct confrontations had taken place between the communists and the Romanian authorities. The first two were shortly after World War I - the border incident at Hotin in January 1919, where the communists formed a bridgehead and smuggled wapeons into Bessarabia - and in May of that year at the revolt in Tighina (Bendery). The latter revolt in the Dnjestr town was soon put down by the Romanian army. The most serious incident took place in September 1924 during the so-called Tatar-Bunar revolt in southern Bessarabia. This quickly spread to places in the area and the Bessabarian Soviet Republic was even declared. Only after weeks of struggle did the Romanian army regain control. Consultations in Vienna reconciled the issue between Moscow and Bucharest, but in 1925 Stalin again had plans to export the revolution to Romania and Bessarabia. International developments, however, put a stop to this.[56]

Moscow subsequently developed a different strategy. In Transnistria, the so-called Moldovan Soviet Republic was established. This had a twofold purpose: it was a catalyst for revolutionary sentiments of working-class people on the other side of the Dniester River and was the answer to Ukrainian nationalism, which the communists disliked as well. Moscow, incidentally, accused Romania of supporting nationalist elements in the Ukraine that resisted the communists. The leadership of the new initiative was based in the city of Balti and the whole thing was above all an initiative of Rakovsky as well as the communist general and military-philosopher General Frunze. Incidentally, the Soviet republic's ambitions included the entire territory of Bessarabia.[57]

The occupation that followed in 1940 was rough in its approach, entirely in line with Molotov's characteristic brutality. In 48 hours, the country was occupied. Units even pushed across the Pruth river and into the town of Herta (Hertza) and other parts of the Dorohoi district, against agreements. Some 300,000 civilians were simply deported to the gulag because they might pose a threat. The German minorities in the area were able to take advantage of the 'Heim ins Reich' policy and were evacuated. The area newly acquired by the Soviet Union was divided up between the communist authorities in Ukraine and Moldova. That not everything went to Moldova was due to the new communist head of the Ukraine, Nikita Breschnew, who wanted to maximise his own influence (from Kiev).[58]

The *'red week'*, as the Soviet entry for the Romanians went down in history and the retreat from Bessarabia, were humiliating experiences for the proud Romanian people and army, which could nevertheless field 1.2 million troops. Bessarabia was simply inserted into the Soviet Moldovan republic.

With the Pruth river as its western border. The Soviets gave the Romanians only four days to leave the area. Officers, police and priests began hastily organising the retreat. The Romanians had two evacuation plans in the drawer, plan *'Tudor'* (by road) and plan *'Mircea'* (by rail) but in practice it became a chaotic retreat. This had to do with Moscow. It is true that the Romanians were given an extra 1 day (until 3 July 1940) in agreement with the Soviets in Odessa, but this did not take away from the fact that at the same time, on the night of 27-28 June, Soviet forces simply crossed the border. The next day, a number of places were already under Soviet occupation, such as Cernauti, Hotin, Chisinau.

Meanwhile, motorised troops went deep and raced towards the Pruth river. The retreating Romanians thus had to pass Soviet military posts, during which Romanian soldiers were humiliated, threatened and weapons taken away. Disturbing reports were constantly coming into Bucharest. The retreating Romanian troops suffered from increasing desertion. Many soldiers with roots in Bessarabia chose to desert and return to their families. Some five divisions thus lost half of their normal occupancy rate. A total of nearly 50,000 men were involved. In addition, large amounts of equipment were simply left behind in Bessarabia. Due to lack of communication between the Romanian units, many had set off too late. The Soviets closed the border exactly at the appointed time. At that time, some 15,000 Romanian soldiers had not crossed the border. Most did not return home.[59]

Romania was in shock. This had major consequences. In terms of foreign policy, they had no one else to shelter with but Nazi Germany, the revisionist regime. It was to be the beginning of the 'Deutsche Heeresmission' in Romania, in which German troops both protected and started training the Romanians, which started in October 1940. Domestically, the knee-jerk reaction to Moscow had major consequences, especially for King Carol II. As recently as 6 January of that year, Carol II had manfully stated that Bessarabia would be *'defended at all costs'*.[60] The accelerated developments contrasted sharply with the course set by Bucharest, which prescribed a policy of peace and balance, which was supposed to result from protection by the western powers and, after the successful German conquest of Poland in 1939, from neutrality. King Carol II had adopted and shaped this policy with his immediate collaborators prime minister Armand Calinescu and foreign minister Grigore Gafencu. This was now collapsing like a house of cards. It was fatal for the king's reputation, which was already not the best.

Its history was somewhat frivolous. Carol II was the son of King Ferdinand of Romania and Princess Marie von Edinburgh. Carol II did not marry a Royal, as he was supposed to, but the daughter of a general. With some difficulty, this *'mistake'* was reversed a few years later under the guise of an *'unvalid marriage'*. Thereupon, Carol married Helen of Greece after all and the marriage took place in Athens. Despite this, peace had not yet returned. The king had an extramarital affair with Magda Wolff, the daughter of a Jewish pharmacist, better known as Elena Lupescu. This was considered a disgrace in traditional Romania. Evil tongues within the Iron Guard claimed that Lupescu was the illegitimate child of Carol I, Carol II's great-uncle, which further magnified the scandal. Pressure mounted on the king and he stepped down in 1927 in favour of his son Michael, who was still an infant at the time. In 1928, the marriage to Helena was dissolved. The Iron Guard, founded in 1927 by Corneliu Zelea Cordreanu represented the conservative current in Romania. They opposed widespread corruption in the country. The Guards increasingly formed a parallel society in Romania.[61]

Carol defected to Paris and a difficult reign around regents and cabinets took effect in Bucharest. Finally, in 1930, this resulted in a request to the king to return to the country. This he did, without Lupescu, as had been the request, but by August, two months after Carol II's return, she was back in the country and in the monarch's life. His lawful wife left Romania and the new situation was thus a fact.

Carol II took a dim view of constitutions as well. The Greater Romania idea was accompanied by the revival of strongly nationalist groups, often of an anti-Semitic nature. Romania came under the spell of the Iron Guard (Garda de Fier), also called the *Legion of the Archangel Michael*, founded by Corneliu Zelea Codreanu who had been active on the far-right flank and other fascist groups since his student days in Jassy, and had opposed, among other things, the removal of the *numerous clauses* for Jews at university.

The governments that emerged from the fascist groups were characterised by vicious chaos. Political assassinations were the order of the day.

At that time, much humus was laid for the later disastrous developments, including with regard to the Holocaust in Romania. The wishful thinking towards the new Romanian state (Greater Romania) had similarities with the development in the young states in Europe: Germany and Italy. The new state was linked to the concept of the new man, the *'omul nou'* as it was put in Romania. An irrational politics, full of symbolism (cult from or- thodoxy around- the archangel Michael), slogans, irrationalism formed the basis of a cultural revolution, in which the new identity - the pure man in Greater Romania - was contrasted with diversity ideas such as liberalism and democracy. This led to a core reaction of overidentification with individuality, coupled with a drive for action. The Italian writer/poet Gabriele d'Ann- unzio called this the *'constant feeding of one's own exaltation'*.[62]

Speaking to *La Stampa* newspaper, Codreanu revealed that he had been strongly influenced by Mussolini, who in turn had influenced Hitler. It was based on the *'ideal type concept'*, which had dangerous repercussions for those who did not fall under it. It was similar to the vitalism of fascism and the 'Tatmensch' which in Germany had emerged from Prussian cheesy mentality coupled with the emerging racial thinking; which found its expression in 'völkische' thinking and later perverted further into ariosofie and the Nuremberg Racial Laws.

In practice, the Iron Guard developed the idea that the state was a living organism (organicism), and therefore *'homogeneous'*. Democracy and the multi-party system was seen as a threat to national unity. Issues like equal rights and protection of minorities also stood in the way of the country's homogeneity and were thus consistently rejected by the Romanian fascists. With this, Romanian fascist doctrine was identical to such movements elsewhere in Europe. The rise of the legionary movement followed a familiar pattern. The initial phase was messy and underbelly-oriented in terms of ideology, without many institutions. That period played out between 1927 and the early 1930s. After 1933, things accelerated. Romanian students were able to study in Nazi Germany and now came into direct contact with the really excitable German Nazism and exhibited copycat behaviour. The *'national revolution'*, as brought about by the NSDAP, was copied to Romania.

Later that year, Romania was already developing into the third phase, in which the in- frastructure and institutions in Romania itself took off, including youth movements and training encampments. The aim was to establish moral purity, through hard work, struggle and self-sacrifice. This should harden the people and bring about palingenesis, the *'reinvention'* of the Romanian people. In this sense, the legionaries were not actually a political party, but a *'movement'*, a school of thought and action that was vitalistic and would have a great impact on the country's tense political situation and was a major driving force behind anti-Semitism, as minorities were now considered *'enemies'* of national unity. The historian Marius Turda, in line with the historian Constantin Iordachi, characterised this as *'sacred politics'*.[63]

According to many observers, the king had cleverly played off the parties of extremes against each other. The call for a strong man had automatically come along with the chaos and the king was perfectly capable of filling this gap. A firm hand eventually intervened and Codreanu was shot dead and doused with acid, as were other leading members of the Iron Guard who lost their lives. Thus, since 1938, Carol II sat firmly on his throne and political parties were banned.

However, the Bessarabia issue shook the little-loved king's throne; but this was not the only problem. His promiscuous way of life was not appreciated by traditional Romanians, and the fascist element in the country not only dislike his reckoning with the Iron Guard, but also his relationship with his Jewish mistress. Thereby, the abandonment of Bessarabia encouraged Bulgaria and Hungary to irredentism. In practice, Romania lost a third of its territory in a short time and three million Romanians became residents of neighbouring countries as a result. Carol II had failed badly in the eyes of Romanians.[64]

As a dictatorial monarch, Carol II could not hide behind anyone and on 7 September 1940, the king abdicated the throne, again. His 19-year-old son Michael became the new monarch. Together with Madame Lupescu, Carol II emigrated abroad, never to return and to die in Lisbon. This was the momentum for Marshal Ion Antonescu, an incorruptible military man - descended from a military family - who had previously been military attaché in London and minister of defence in 1937-1938. He had a good reputation within the armed forces, which were a driving force behind the Greater Romania idea. Antonescu became *'regent'* instead of the young king becoming head of state, and on 15 September 1940 he had himself proclaimed *'conducator al statului'* -or *'leader of the state'*. With this, Antonescu became a new Mussolini in the making.

Antonescu first availed himself of the forces within the Iron Guard movement and with the members of this group he had many things in common such as the pursuit of a Greater Romania, anti-Semitism and anti-Slavic holding. Together with the guardsmen, led by Horia Sima who had been a member of the legion since 1928, Antonescu ruled the country. On 6 September, Romania had been declared a *'national legionary state'*. For Antonescu, it was skirmishing with the orderless elements of the Guard. The country deteriorated into lawlessness, with looting, murders and pogroms a recurring phenomenon. It was also a vulgar power struggle. Antonescu, as man of the army, wanted to tighten the reins, but the gardists were not about to give up their position just like that. As so often in Romania, the game was played very personally.

In an earlier conflict between King Carol II and Antonescu, the former had used an earlier marriage of Antonescu, to a French woman, who had previously married a Jewish man, to show that Antonescu was not very serious about marital fidelity, by claiming that the divorce had never been pronounced. Antonescu then had to save his honour by coming up with the right papers, which he succeeded in doing, causing the crisis to blow over. Now, with the gardists, the stranded marriage resurfaced and links were suggested between the marshal and Judaism.

Furthermore, Antonescu's name was said to be related to Freemasonry, which stood for *'pure Romanians'* internationalism, humanism and a Jewish mantle organisation.[65] German First World War chief Erich Ludendorff, who continued to play a political role after 1918, characterised Freemasonry as *'the uncircumcised Jews'*. Many period documents of the time, which found eager reception in the 'völkische' and ariosophical circles, shared antipathy to the Masonic world, which was seen as a *'deep state'* that went against the interests of the people.

The Iron Guard had come into possession of the documents of the freemasons, threatening to discredit known Romanians. The head of the security service, Ghica, had found incriminating material during home raids on known freemasons. These they then wanted to expose. This would further inflame the political climate in the country. However, support for the Freemasons came from an unexpected quarter. It was the German diplomat Wilhelm Fabricius who protested vehemently against it and did so publicly. He thought the actions should be stopped.

According to insider circles, Fabricius' action came not so much from ideological motives - he was seen as an admirer of the Führer - but from amorous motives. Fabricius was in thrall to Romanian Lilette Butculescu, who had once been recruited as an agent by court minister Urdareanu. She was of a personality and beauty that impressed men of stature, such as former Romanian foreign minister Grigore Gafencu and French ambassador M. Adrien Thierry, and she now had Fabricius on a leash. Now, the Nazis were no friends of Freemasonry, but one was rather lenient on this diplomat's somewhat curious escapade. *'It is possible to turn a blind eye to this matter,'* reported an internal *'report'* on the matter. Fabricius was *'of the old school'* and did not see it all through. He was brushed aside as naive. A fuss about this freemason case was inconvenient for Berlin, given its good relationship with Antonescu.[66] Antonescu was looking for a way out of the situation as well. As with all recent problems, the solution lay in Berlin. Antonescu could not operate without the support of Hitler.

Now it was the case that the Iron Guard could also count on a certain sympathy in Nazi Germany given that there were ideological similarities. Iron Guards had fought in the Spanish Civil War, where Germany was represented by the Condor legion. The Romanian guards had travelled to the front to support General Franco under the credo of *'the defence of Christianity'* and as a defence against the *'Jewish-Bolshevik threat'*. Iron Guard officers like Ion I. Mota and Vasile Marin had been killed at the front. Their bodies were brought home on a German train, and members of the SA and SS had given them a salute of honour.[67]

Hitler was a realist and realised that, for his far-reaching plans with Eastern Europe and the coming campaign against the Soviet Union, business with the army was better than with the ideologues. Wilhelm Fabricius had already warned Berlin that Sima was *'unstable'*. He had insufficient cover within his own movement. In doing so, he pointed out that there was unrest among the Romanian population due to the anarchist actions of the gardists who were also increasingly taking over the administration of the country. The German embassy in Bucharest warned on 8 January 1941 that the guards were becoming a kind of *'state within the state'*. In this, *'economic efficiency'* was the priority for Germany, with an emphasis on oil. Sima had asked Antonescu for a monopoly position for the Guard regarding the economy, but Antonescu had refused. Berlin had its concerns about this too. In doing so, it irritated the Nazis that there were growing tensions between the increasing sense of self-confidence of the 740,000 'Volksdeutschen' in Romania and the Iron Guard.[68] On the other hand, there was positive talk of the Iron Guard from 'Volksdeutsche' circles. They were more Germany-minded that the circles around Antonescu. Andreas Rührigs, Stabsführer at the 'Deutsche Volksgruppe in Rumänien', wrote a long letter to 'Volksdeutsche Mittel- stelle' SS-Obergruppenführer Lorenz on 1 February, in which he made a case for Sima, portraying the legionnaires as *'disciplined'*. With Antonescu, *'the Jews'* would *'rise again'*. He claimed that Antonescu's right-hand man - his namesake Mihail Antonescu - was a Freemason, or had close ties to them.[69]

Hitler was in doubt. He invited both Antonescu and Horia Sima to the *Berghof*. Sima, who was not fully informed until late, was reluctant to make a joint appearance with Antonescu and declined, although he did send a critical letter about Antonescu. Sima's absence gave Antonescu an edge, especially considering that Hitler, since their first meeting in November 1941, had been very fond of Antonescu.[70] On 14 January 1941, Antonescu visited Hitler to cut things short. This provided the marshal with back cover for his plans.[71] He was helped by the ineptitude of the gardists who exerted an uncontrolled violence on anyone who opposed them. Jews in particular were the victims of this. Now Antonescu was not so much opposed to anti Jewish measures, but he could use the lack of discipline and increasing disorder to carry out purges in favour of the army.

A direct cause was needed that would compel action and it came. On the night of 19 January 1941, German major Helmut Döring, chief of the DHM's 'Transportabteilung', was murdered in Bucharest. The circumstances of the murder have always remained foggy.

A killer was arrested who appeared to have a double passport and identity: Dimitri Sarandos or Dimitros Sarandopoulos. The papers referred to both Turkey and Greece. Investigations revealed that the man was of Greek descent. He was a professional boxer and had come to Romania via Brasov (Kronstadt) on 16 October 1940, shortly before the DHM's arrival. Döring had gone for a drink with a colleague on duty and, after leaving the restaurant, was shot from behind close to the 'Heeresmisison'. He died from a shot to the lower body. Nine hours after the attack, Antonescu struck. Romanian Interior Minister Constantin Petrovicescu was sacked, followed by police chief Alexandre Ghika, head of the Bucharest police, Schickert of the Dt. Nachrichten Buro (DNB) jumped into the breach for Sima. The Königsberg-born Schickert was a former student of the well-known Münchener Prof Karl Alexander von Müller and his dissertation was called *Die Judenfrage in Ungarn*. He was further affiliated with the Hohen Schule der NSDAP. Both Fabricius and von Killinger whistled back at him.

Radu Mironovici and the head of the Siguranta, Constantin Maimuca. These were all confidants of the legionary movement, which reacted as if stung by a wasp. Ghika and Maimuca barricaded themselves in the Siguranta's main quarters and calls for resistance came from across the country. Satanist elements were said to be involved, and an accusing finger was pointed at Eugen Cristescu, the head of the secret service. Döring's murder was allegedly 'carried out by the British secret service'. The murder was condemned by the Iron Guard and people demanded a legionary government.[72]

Both Antonescu and Sima looked directly at how Berlin would react. Antonescu's line ran through Fabricius, Sima's through Neubacher. The simplest solution was for Antonescu to restore order and be able to lead the Iron Guard himself. Then the legionary movement would be preserved and order would return. The DHM was instructed through Franz Halder to remain neutral, to intervene only if it was necessary and if there was a request from Antonescu's side. Meanwhile, the gardists did not wait it out. On the morning of the 21st January, legionnaires marched into Jewish neighbourhoods and homes where people were mistreated and murdered, and homes burned down. Some other places in the country were also unsettled, including Jassy. A total of 120 Jews were killed in the pogrom in Bucharest alone. Petrol bombs and street terror were used in Bucharest to corner and imprison the marshal and his most loyal officers. Antonescu's position had become extremely shaky.[73]

As the gardists coalesced around the son of Foreign Minister Constantin Petrovi- cescu, dismissed by Antonescu on 19 January, units of the army gathered outside Bucharest. The military had remained largely aloof from the fighting until then, but were often threatened and humiliated by the gardists. While gardists, students, gypsies and others committed murder and robbery, an army force, under general and instructor at the Ilie Steflea school of war, unexpectedly entered Bucharest. This assault force had tanks and the gardists were no match. Over 200 of them died and Antonescu was relieved. A German military unit which, as part of the 'Heeresmission' was stationed in the city, also marched through the streets to underline Antonescu's position. An attempt at *mediation*, to which Neubacher reported to Antonescu, was rejected.[74]

The tactics Hitler followed were similar to his actions around the *Night of the Long Knives*, choosing *'das Miltär'* over the party militias of the SA under Ernst Röhm. Berlin thus supported Antonescu, but did turn a blind eye to the fact that the SS continued to support Iron Guard comrades in the background and their leaders were given shelter in Germany. Among them, in addition to the leader Sima, for example, were the gardist Traian Boeru, who was responsible for the murder of the royalist former prime minister Nicolae Iorga. The latter was in turn linked to the murder of gardist leader Codreanu. Iorga's murder took place in Sterjnic on 27 November, the day of the solemn reburial of Codreanu and 12 other legionnaires who had been murdered by royalist forces.[75]

Antonescu could now rule authoritatively in Romania. He upheld and preserved the monarchy, bringing Queen Helena back from Greece to be with her son. In practice, the young monarch's power was mostly symbolic. Yet, by rubbing up against this, Antonescu increased his own tangent. Already under the struggle against the gardists, he had suffered from the lack of organised popular support for his power base and in this way he managed to increase it. Additionally, he strove for a national government above which he could stand as a kind of father of the fatherland. His foreign policy was very practical and simple to summarise. Antonescu pursued restoration of Greater Romania. To restore order, he was even willing to come to terms with the Jewish community. He reassured the president of the Jewish communes in Romania, Wilhelm Filderman, that he meant no harm and that nothing would happen to the Jews as long as they did not turn against Romania. *'Let Dr Filderman know that Antonescu keeps his word,'* the marshal informed him.[76]

The course of fate for the Jews was also provided towards Germany. On 22 November 1940, Romania joined the threefold pact between Germany, Italy and Japan, which was mainly a military aid. This was a military extension of the previously concluded 'Anti Kominternpact', which was against the Soviet Union and communism. This definitively pulled Romania into the camp of the Axis powers; although Nazi Germany and the Soviet Union were still complying with the non-aggression pact at the time. Concretely, this meant that a 'Deutsche Heeresmission' was coming to Romania, which would help the Romanians modernise their armed forces and defend their country in times of war. An earlier request had been made by King Carol II, but Hitler had refused it. Now with Antonescu in the saddle, Hitler saw his chance. On 19 September 1940, Hitler ordered the start of the 'Heeresmission'. In practice, this was clearly directed against the Soviet Union. The 'Deutsche Heeresmission' (DHM) was commanded by General Erick Oskar Hansen, reinforced by a 'Luftwaffemission' under General Wilhelm Speidel, 'Wirtschaftsstab' under Oberst Karl Spalck and a 'Marinemission' under Admiral Friedrich Wilhelm Fleischer.[77]

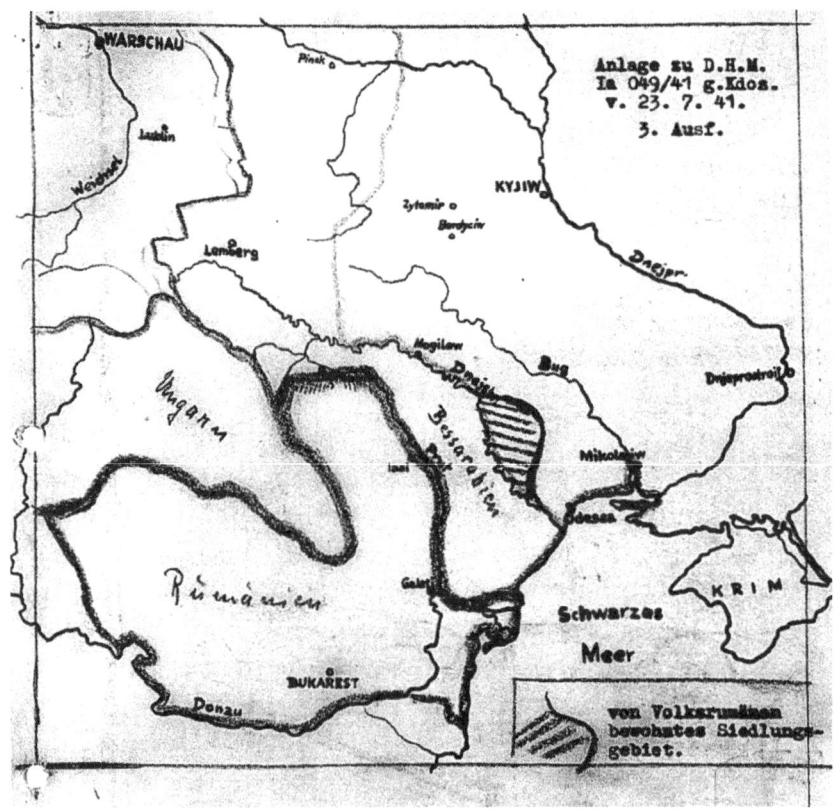

The controversial map of Romania in the region.

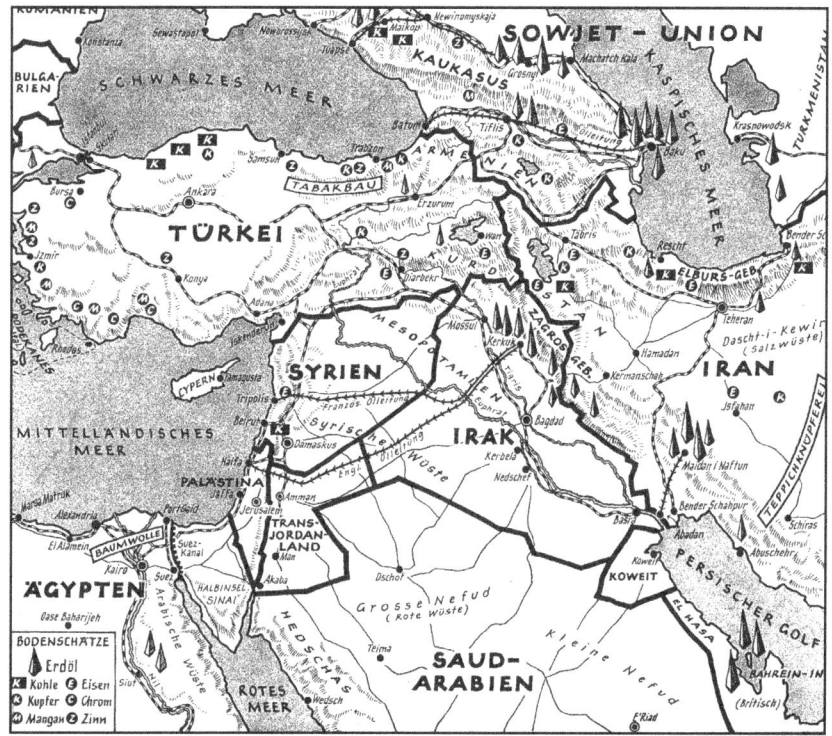

Oil was very important within the German geopolitics. Besides the Romanian oil, the oil of the Caucasus and the Middle East.

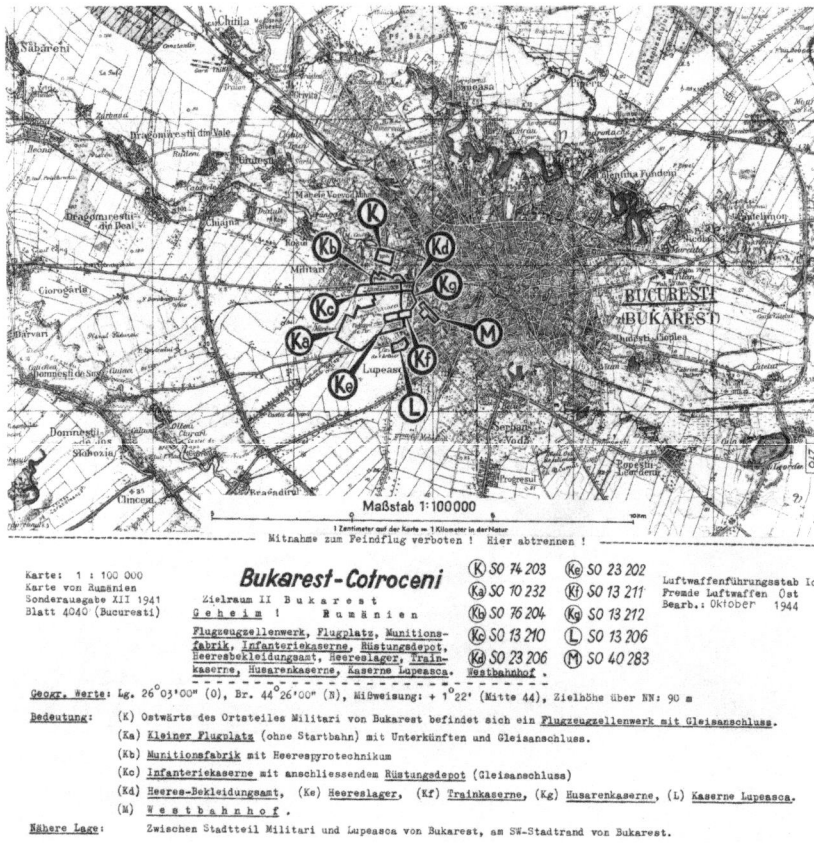

Strategic goals in Romania - surrounding Buckarest.

The oil of Ploesti

Romania was an important country for Germany. Interest focused above all on its geographical position as a large and population-rich area in south-eastern Europe, where Berlin had many interests as part of the 'Grosswirtschaftsraum' Europe. In addition, Romania was a major food production and there was the oil around Ploesti.

With its 20 million inhabitants, Romania was one of the region's most populous countries. Within the 1940 borders, 72% of the population were ethnic Romanians, 8% were Hungarians, 5.5% Russians and Ruthenians and 4% (Volksdeutschen) Germans. (Volksdeutschen). Of working population, 78% were employed in agriculture, which entailed a large livestock population of 2.6 million horses, 4.1 million cattle and 12.8 million sheep. Economically, therefore, the country was little industrialised.[78] According to a 1938 German census, the country had 3767 factories in 1938, of which 974 were in the food industry. This was not exceptional for the region. In a way, Romania was not doing too badly. For instance, for every 777 Romanians there was a motorised vehicle in the country. Hungary did better (1: 438) and Greece (1: 496), but Yugoslavia and Bulgaria were again far behind Romania with 1: 1034 and 1: 1484. In comparison with Germany, south-eastern Europe's lag behind Nazi Germany became very clear: 1: 41. The railway network was 11,216 km in length, compared with Yugoslavia 9,471, Hungary 7,823 and Germany 54,556 km.

The country was agriculturally autarkic and also exported. The population was growing and 51.9% of the population was under forty in 1940.[79]

With the shifting balance of power in Europe, Germany became an increasingly important trading country for Romania, with trade treaties following. Trade even doubled between 1938 and 1939. The year 1938 brought a record harvest for Romanian agriculture, while there was an international recession at the same time. Romania now sought contact with England and France to be able to sell part of the harvest. Germany reacted like a wasp stung. Berlin openly threatened to freeze trade contacts, which would be very unfavourable to Romania (as well as Berlin). Thus the bond was forged closer although the cause was often a power-political reality.[80]

Germany's main interest was in the oil industry. They, like Japan, had a huge shortage of oil and the fields therefore had great strategic significance for Nazi Germany. Hitler was obsessed with it. During Operation *'Barbarossa'*, the vulnerability of the Romanian fields was constantly taken into account. Oil partly determined German strategy, or in the words of German 'Blitzkrieg' expert Heinz Guderian; *'Oil was written with capital letters for Hitler'*. Until the end of the war, oil would keep a great influence on German military decisions. We saw this in the German operations in the Caucasus, where Germans got as far as 20 km before Grozny and the oil fields. The Caucasus supplied 86.5% of the Soviet Union's oil.[81] Similarly, the final battle in Hungary- operation 'Frühlingserwachen' -in March 1945, centred on protecting the oil fields south of Lake Balaton near Nagykanizsa in south-western Hungary. In the process, the Hungarian capital Budapest was sacrificed as a 'Festung' with an occupation of 70,000 German and Hungarian soldiers under the IXth SS-Bergle- gerkorps to defend strategic interests. On 13 February 1945, the last resistance collapsed and only about a hundred soldiers managed to reach the German lines again.[82] Later, Hitler would insist on maintaining the oil installations in Austria at Zisterdorff and Mauthausen. Hitler was 80% dependent on oil from Hungary and Austria after the loss of Ploesti. The Hungarian fields produced some 810,162 and 655,772 tonnes of crude oil in 1944 and 1945, respectively.[83]

With the rise of Nazi Germany, German-Romanian economic involvement grew stronger over the years. Whereas in the mid-1930s Germany was still Romania's 17th largest trading partner, by the late 1930s it had moved up to fourth. This only increased during the war, with the main focus on oil exports to Germany and German-occupied territories in Europe. In tonnages, this involved:

1939: 988,000 tonnes
1940: 1,050.300 tonnes
1941: 2,717,000 tonnes
1942: 2,047.800 tonnes
1944: 987,100 tonnes[84]

There is some diversity in the numbers regarding Romania's deliveries. In part, these can be explained by supplies to areas outside the German Reich, such as the protectorate, as well as the distinction made between crude oil, petrol and the like. Jonathan Morales, for instance, calculated that more than half of Romanian oil exports in 1941 went to Germany, amounting to 3.6 million tonnes a year.[85] *Das Ölproblem* referred to products of 5,648.538 tonnes of crude oil for the year 1942 and 5,315.382 tonnes in 1943. Given that half of this oil went to Germany, this is close to Hillgruber's figures. Supplies to Italy during this period were about 403,610 tonnes, Bulgaria 24,157 tonnes, Slovakia 35,647 tonnes, Finland 4,484 tonnes and France 14,936 tonnes. An OKW report from 1940 spoke of Romanian oil supplies to Germany of 848,459 tonnes in 1939 and supplies of 436,584 tonnes to the *Protektorat*, totalling 30.8% of Romanian oil exports (against 22.2% 704,342 tonnes and 294,898 tonnes) in 1938.[86]

German-Romanian cooperation on oil had not come about without a struggle. A trade treaty had been signed between Berlin and Bucharest in October 1939, but in practice the Romanians did not adhere to the agreements regarding oil supplies. This was due to the powerful position of the Allied powers regarding the possession ratio of oil fields. Since September 1939, Germany had been at war with the French and the British, and King Carol II and the Tatarescu government did nothing to improve relations with Berlin. The situations were dramatic. A *'stormy'* meeting took place at Hermann Göring's country house *Karinhall*, where the leaders of the Nazi war economy, the 'Vierjahresplannen', met. Something had to be done, that much was clear. In December, Hermann Neubacher, a prominent Nazi who was the mayor of Vienna at the time, was directed to Berlin for a meeting with German foreign minister Joachim von Ribbentrop.

Here, it was decided that Neubacher would be appointed 'Sonderbeauftragter' for the oil issue. To make this happen, he was given temporary leave from his position in Vienna. Hitler believed that an Oriental understood the Romanians better.

Neubacher's choice was smart and strategic. The mayor of Vienna had an edge. This had to do with the fact that the former mayor of Vienna, Karl Lueger, had publicly spoken out in favour of Romania in the Transylvania issue in the past. This had not been forgotten in Bucharest, and the Romanian capital even had a street named after him. Neubacher used this positive legacy to break through the Latin sentiments between France and Romania. In this, he was helped by rising tensions in the region. Romania sensed the irredentism of surrounding nations and felt increasingly threatened. This gave Neubacher the opportunity to strike an oil-for-arms deal, which he short-circuited with the 'Wi-Rü-Amt' ('Wirtschafts und Rüstungsamt') and General Georg Thomas. Germany mainly supplied Pak and Flak, but could draw from the large quantities of weapons captured from Poland as well, which had been overrun by Nazi Germany in September 1939. In March 1940, Neubacher was able to announce the result of his mission; the 'Öl-Waffen-Pakt' with Romania. With the 'Deutsche Heeresmission' that followed the Soviet intervention towards Bessarabia, the German grip on the country was further strengthened.[87]

With the German arrival in Romania, it was hoped to further rationalise the Romanian oil industry. Until 1940, the lion's share of oil production was in the hands of foreign-funded majors: 35% was Dutch-British ownership, 25% Romanian, 22% Belgian-French, 10% American. The remaining 8% was divided among other countries, including Germany. The main companies were: *'Astra Romana'*, *'Unirea'*, *'Dacia Romano'*, *'Danube Oil'*, *'Concordia'*, *'Columbia'*, *'Foraj Lemoine'*, *'Romano-Americana'* and a number of other companies, which together formed a group of nineteen companies.

As the German grip on the country improved due to the 'Heeresmisison', Berlin was able to draw production to itself. Only 4.5% of Romania's oil production came from smaller drilling companies, but that did not take away from the fact that it was still distributed among 150 companies, with companies such as *'Buna Speranta'*,

'*Craiova*', '*Duplex*', '*Petrolina*', '*Sospiro*' and '*Voints*'. There were also 60 refineries in the country. There was overcapacity here and some of the firms were not in operation. So there was still an important battle to be fought here.⁸⁸

Logically, these strategic stocks had all the attention of the German security authorities. For instance, before the pact with Antonescu, there was already a German 'Abwehrcentrale' in Romania which was specifically focused on oil. This was the *'Ölschutz Organisation Rumänien'* of the *'OKW/Amt Ausland Abwehr'*. It was headed by the lawyer, major Dr Hans Wagner, who was attached to *'Ausland Abwehr Sektion III/F'*. The umbrella organisation under which the *'Ölschutz Organisation'* fell was the *'Kriegorganisation Rumänien'*, designated as *KOR*. This *KOR* did even more than protect oil. One was in the outpost Romania of German military intelligence and reported about everything that came out through diplomacy, espionage and 'Vertrauens Leute' (V-Leute). The organisation worked in secret and, in post-war documentation, first surfaced in a telegram addressed to German former minister Wilhelm Fabricius, warning of Russian troop concentrations on the Polish border. Dr Wagner's organisation continued to watch over the oil until the Antonescu regime was settled in Romania and the political situation in the country stabilised for Germany. Romania came within Germany's sphere of influence during 1940. The *KOR* merged into the *'Abwehrstelle Rumänien'*.⁸⁹

Moreover, the Sonderbeauftragter Hermann Neubacher reported all kinds of secret sabotage missions around the oil fields. For example, even before Operation *'Barbarossa'*, the Germans had found that many hundreds of crates were being loaded into two Danube boats. One reported Bucharest about these suspicious activities. Bucharest did nothing, but Neubacher had the boats trapped with German barges. Bucharest was then urged to search the boats. In doing so, they threatened to stop arms deliveries. This prompted the Romanians to move and more than a hundred British marines, explosives, heavy equipment and even an artillery piece were found in the boats. The Romanians expelled the British.⁹⁰ In addition, Italian confederates caused headaches. During the period of fighting for Greece, the Italians asked the Germans for permission to have oil transports for Italy carried out by Italian shipping companies from now on. Neubacher could hardly refuse this. Not long afterwards, it was discovered that oil was being sold in the Aegean Sea and pumped over into British tankers.[91] Due to the same miraculous things, it could happen that Africa Corps General Erwin Rommel trampled over a British base in North Africa and found oil barrels labelled *'Deutsche Wehrmachtsmission Rumänien'*. Furthermore, it was uncovered that deliveries for the 'Heeresmission' in Finland were running through miraculous routes but not arriving in Helsinki. Investigations revealed that the scams extended as far as Switzerland. Neubacher solved such cases with the necessary tact; a *'pedantic attitude'* was out of place here. One gently informed the Romanians that the illicit business was known and then it stopped with a gentle hand.[92]

The British services were well aware of German engineering around the fields. This came to Neubacher's attention via a Dutch engineer working at *'Astra Romana'* in Ploesti. The latter told him that people and ears were in short supply to answer questions from a wide variety of Romanian ministries on the progress of production, repairs and transport. It was clear that some of this data went straight to the Allies. In addition, train transports of oil were hampered by the British secret service. The wheels of the wagons were smeared with a flammable substance, so that when they were driven over time, a fire started.[93]

It was hoped to scale up production from Romanian fields. Berlin was optimistic in this and spoke of doubling, but this did not materialise in practice. New drilling rigs planned for 1943 were delayed and production fell short of plans. This put Nazi Germany in a paradoxical situation. One needed oil to transport oil, but scarcity was only increasing. As early as the autumn of 1941, General Georg Thomas, responsible for the economic part of the 'Generalplan-Ost' (the German plans with the Soviet Union) had warned that Germany would soon have fuel reserves for only two months.[94] That Thomas was not exaggerating became clear during *'Fall Blau'*, the German summer offensive of 1942. In the Kalmückensteppe, towards Stalingrad and the Volga, the 6th Army halted for almost a week due to the simple fact that there was no fuel.[95]

With the approach of the front, the fields near Ploesti came under pressure. They were targets of large-scale air raids on several occasions, as will become clear. As always, Berlin sought a way out via special emissaries who could overrule anyone with powers of attorney, in order to bypass bureaucratic obstacles and achieve production output. To this end, on 31 May 1944, Hitler had appointed Edmund Geilenberg, who wanted to *'boost'* German (oil) industry through decentralisation of German industry (thereby making it less vulnerable to air attacks) and the shift to underground production. Although this Geilenberg programme employed 350,000 troops at one point, it did not take away from the fact that the problems concerning shortages remained structural in nature, to which the tilting victory odds contributed as well.

Until the very end, one German body after another - the army, the party, the economists and the SS - bent over Ploesti's oil fields. Their importance became clear, given that everyone liked to have this influential department under their command, leading to fierce competition between them. Even within the SS, this led to great tensions, forcing the Reichsführer-SS Heinrich Himmler to intervene. Even international public opinion was played on to keep the oil fields safe. For example, the International Red Cross was invited to Ploesti to investigate the consequences of the Allied army's *'terror bombing'*. Here, of course, they mainly pointed to civilian targets; the gymnasium, for example, which had been hit in its place.[96] In the military field, securing the oil fields of Ploesti had quite a few consequences. This concerned not only the fields of Ploesti itself, but also pipelines, such as the one from Ploesti to Constantza. The pipelines ran along the bridges of the Danube towards Fetesti and were guarded by security forces. Fire crews were stationed at various positions along the oil routes. These were enormous undertakings. The pipeline built under German supervision between Ploesti-Valcea and to Sibiu and Cluj (Klausenburg), was no less than 400 km long. At the start of the German 'Heeresmission' in 1940, Romania had 2770 km of oil pipeline, of which 2015 km were owned by the companies and 755 km by the Romanian state. Some important sections were Baicoi-Constantza (320 km), Baicoi-Giurgiu (180 km), Baicoi-Bucharest (875km).[97]

As Standortälteste in Ploesti, the commander of Flak regiment 180, Oberstleutnant Von Grapow, wielded the sceptre. Other officers involved in anti-aircraft were: Major Hoffmann (Flak Abt.191) and Major Tepper (Flak Abt. 125). To ground troops in 1941, there was also the lehr-Pz. Jg. Abt. R.1 of Oberstleutnant Scholz was stationed there, as well as territorial units such as the 'Landsch. Rgt. 108' (Stab) z.b.V., Ldsch. Btl. 235, 514 and 563 (Standort 06.03.1941) in addition there were special security forces, 'Sicherungs- kräften', partly Romanians, led by Major Von Gregory. Through a network of Standortältesten, who were the eyes and ears of the 'Heeresmission', the Germans tried to get a grip on the security situation in the whole of Romenia.[98]

On 6 March 1941, the air defences around Ploesti - in view of the upcoming battle against the Soviet Union - were once again reinforced, both in terms of anti-aircraft guns and by means of fighters. The 'Jagd- geschwader 52' was the main air force unit in the area. Moreover, measures were taken against enemy airborne operations.[99] The defensive measures around Ploesti would only increase during the course of the war. With the loss of the oil fields in August 1944, the already weak German resource position deteriorated.

Besides oil and agriculture, the Romanian economy was not very important to Nazi Germany. Extra attention was paid to the metal industry which was important for arms production. On the eve of World War II, Romania was unable to meet its own ammunition needs. Ammunition production for rifle cartridges was 15 million a month. Artillery ammunition was produced in 13 factories, such as the *Malaxa* concern in Tohanul-Vechiu, and amounted to 120,000 pieces per month. These were of 7.5cm, 10.5cm and 15cm calibre. Cannons were produced at the *Astra* factories in Brasov. Gunpowder came from *Pulberia* and *Rupul*, two state-owned companies in Bucharest. There were also three small aircraft factories, *J.A.R. Aeronaut*, *J.C.A.R.* and *Set*, all based in Bucharest, which could produce about 50 aircraft a month in wartime and with extra effort. These included the type *JAR 80*, which reached 3,000 metres altitude, could accelerate and had a speed of 540 km per hour. Tanks were produced at the *Malaxa* factory in Budapest. These were licence-built tanks from

France's *Renault*. What Romania did make plenty of, but which ultimately turned out not to be needed, were gas masks with a production of 50,000 per month.[100]

The Romanian Holocaust

'I am not concerned that we will be seen as barbarians by history'
Mihai Antonescu 8 July 1941

The Holocaust in Romania is an isolated story. Unlike many other countries in the part of Europe dominated by Nazi Germany, Romania implemented its own Jewish policy, with characteristics of what Goldhagen called *'extermination anti-Semitism'*.[101] An anti-Semitism which aimed to exterminate Judaism. Anyone reading time documents from those days realises that Judaism was seen, even by Marshal Antonescu, as a 'Fremdkörper' within Romanian society and as such was seen as a threat to the Greater Romania envisioned by the nationalists. In addition to the more traditional anti-Semitism that had existed in the region, hyper-nationalism driven forces - from which the Iron Guard also emerged - added an extra dimension. The rise of communism, of which the Jews were seen as an exponent, pushed things further, as well as the uncertain geopolitical situation and power shifts following the various peace treaties in 1919.

It soon became clear that under Antonescu there would be no room for the Jews in the new Greater Romania. Tensions had risen seriously in June 1940 when the Soviet Union harshly reclaimed Bessarabia from Romania. This public humiliation led to a wave of nationalism and pogromism in the country.[102] While many ethnic Romanians had crossed the Pruth, headed westwards and on the run from the Red Army, the Jews (who often spoke Russian) had mostly stayed. Historian Petru Negura researched the writers' guild in the region, giving us an insight into the difficult Romanian-Jewish relations. According to Negura, most Romanian-oriented authors had fled, and of those who remained behind, many made a remarkably quick turn in their work and oeuvre choices. While some had long expressed themselves as autonomist (for an independent Bessarabia), the communist message was now being proclaimed. Most of these authors were Jewish, and the top of the writers' union created by Moscow was entirely Jewish. Regional writers who had stayed behind in Bessarabia ran the risk of being persecuted for their *'bourgeois decadence'*. According to Negura, the Jewish intelligentsia in Bessarabia had an edge. This was due to Soviets' distrust of ethnic Romanians in the region. The NKVD and the 'Agitprop' targeted them. Many Jews who had suffered under Romanian rule had hopes of gaining security and legitimacy under the Soviet regime. Thus a miraculous *'pact'* emerged, stemming from a long history of difficult integration (lasting segregation) and historical anti-Semitism.

The history of Bessarabia was rewritten at breakneck speed. The Romanian period was dismissed as *'occupation'*, the new Soviet period as *'liberation'*. Furthermore, communist historians argued that a *'centuries-old link'* already existed between the occupied territory and Russia. In the time of the Ottomans, the Moldovans were said to have asked the Russians for help. Panslavism was brought to bear on the matter. Earlier, they tried to introduce the Cyrillic script, which failed. It was an alternative attempt at *'nation building'* where regionalism was more appropriate. Historian Marina Furima spoke of the region's history as that of an *'identity crisis'*.[103] In any case, these were examples of *'forceful inclusion'*, as Igor Cascu described it. Since, apart from the writers, most intellectuals had fled Bessarabia, the Soviet authorities relied heavily on the Jewish intelligentsia. In addition, 5,000 cadre communists had been recruited from Ukraine and Russia. Under communism, Jewish culture flourished and there was even a Yiddish writers' collective. The revival was short-lived, because after 1945 - when, in addition to Bessarabia, the whole of Romania had fallen within the Soviet sphere of influence - the special status of the Jews was no longer necessary and they suffered the same fate as other population groups.[104]

The first significant incident occurred at Dorohoi on 1 June 1940. It had been preceded by a border incident with the Red Army in which there had been deaths. At the funeral, things went south and a dozen Jewish-Romanian soldiers were killed by other soldiers. Afterwards, the angry mob marched through Dorohoi. According to official figures, the incident left 51 dead and only ended when General Constantin Sanatescu of the 8th Army Corps intervened. *'I am surprised that this is happening by units we thought were elite troops,'* remarked the latter gloomily. On 30 June, things went wrong in Galati. Here, a group of Jews allegedly disrupted the marching order of a Romanian unit. The soldiers shot indiscriminately at the group of Jews. As in Dorohoi, there was no order from on high in Galati. It was the frustrations of local units and officers. Again, a senior officer - General Aurelian Son, commander of the 11th Army Corps - put an end to the disturbances and killings.[105]

In January 1941, during Iron Guard riots, a pogrom followed in the Moldovan city of Jassy. It began on 21 January and several synagogues were burned to the ground. Some 2,000 Jews were rounded up and detained and mistreated in various places. The worst abuses took place in an abattoir where 15 Jews were tortured to death and hung from meat hooks. The Romanian fascists spoke of *'kosher slaughtered meat'*. Others were taken away to the Jilava forest and 68 of them executed. A total of 125 Jews lost their lives.[106]

The Second World War set things in motion. On 19 June 1941 there was a meeting of Marshal Antonescu and his key advisors. It was known that Operation *'Barbarossa'* would soon start and Antonescu despaired of the loyalty of the Jewish community. He gave orders for their activities to be closely monitored and further mapped out. Moreover, it was decided to take important Jews hostage so that they could be used as means of coercion in the event of riots and threats of execution could be made.[107] Mihai Antonescu let slip on 3 July 1941 that a historic opportunity had arisen for Romania to purify the country once and for all.[108]

When hostilities began against the Soviet Union on 22 June 1941, it was the starting signal for a huge anti-Semitic smear campaign in Romania. Posters had been put up all over the country blaming Jewry for the war. A pogrom-like atmosphere ensued. Jews were rounded up in towns like Targu Jiu, Craiova, Cavacal, Turnu, Severin and other places. The situation spiked further on 24 June due to Soviet air raids on the country. Jews were accused of provoking these bombings and informing the pilots where to bomb.[109]

These were nonsensical claims, as the bombing of 26 June also showed, since *Saint Spyridon Hospital* was bombed and there were 38 Jewish casualties. However, the propaganda did its work. It focused on the headquarters of the Romanian 14th Division, which had been bombed, and a telephone exchange. In riot-hit Jassy, where the division was stationed, tensions rose enormously. On 27 June, *Pruth*, Jassy's evening newspaper, published an appeal by the commander of the Romanian 14th I.D., General Gheorghe Stavrescu, in which he stated that the enemies *'had to be caught'*, and that anyone *'working in the service of the enemy would be dismembered'*.[110] Romanian soldiers and members of the Iron Guard went on a Jew-hunt. The Jews of Jassy were seen as 'the greatest threat'.[111]

A dangerous mixture of paranoia and hyper-nationalism led to excess. Eventually, three Jews were arrested by the military authority for allegedly sending *'signals'* to the Soviet air force. The suspects, Jewish residents of Jassy, Losub Cojocaru, Leon Schachter and Wolf Herscu were arraigned to the Romanian military leadership in the district.

Interrogation revealed no evidence for the wild accusations. Nevertheless, the Romanian general Stavrescu did have all telescopes and binoculars of the Jewish population confiscated. Several executions for *'spying'* followed in the days that followed.[112] The three civilians were removed under escort from the forbidden military zone and taken back to the city. On the way back, however, the military escort chose a different (detour) route and tried to shoot the trio. Cojocaru died instantly, Herscu was shot unconscious and Schachter managed to escape through the cornfields.[113]

However, the measures in Jassy were not just spontaneous actions on suspected Jewish involvement in the air raids. After short-circuiting with the Germans, it was Marshal Antonescu himself who had personally ordered the anti-Jewish actions in Jassy on 27 June 1941. To this end, there had been telephone contract with Colonel Constantin Lupu, who was ordered to evacuate the Jews from Jassy and execute anyone who resisted. When that did not go smoothly enough to Antonescu's liking, Lupu was replaced on 2 July 1941.

Meanwhile, actions had begun with the aim of making Moldova Jew-free. The order came through Mihai Antonescu. To this end, the

Jews were driven up to the railway station. Everything happened in chaos because not all Romanian authorities had been informed; rumours played a role. The Jews were said to be communist traitors. On the way to the station, the road became littered with corpses. On the platform, the Jews were first forced to lie down on the ground, with other passengers walking over them. Then, with too many people, they were herded into carefully locked carriages and the trains started moving. Some without purpose and others towards the south, for example to Calarasi. Those trains were nicknamed *'death trains'* - *'trenurile mortii'* in Romanian.[114] Of the 5,000 Jews driven into those wagons, only 1011 survived. Many died of hunger and thirst. Other trains travelled the same route endlessly up and down, simply waiting until the lion's share of the Jews had died.

They were indescribable scenes. Probably 14,850 Jews lost their lives in the Jassy pogrom.[115] Because of Jassy, a frontier had shifted.

The ancient problem of anti-Semitism and po-gromism had been carried out on an unprecedented scale. Simon Geissbühler of the *Yad Vashem Holocaust memorial institute* called this a *'definitive paradigm change, both qualitatively and quantitatively'*.[116]

The invasion of Bessarabia and northern Bucharest was directly accompanied by (war) abuses against Jews. The regions were seen by Bucharest as an integral part of Romania. With regard to Bessarabia, there was serious concern. According to Bucharest, an anti-religious policy had been conducted under communism, *'led by the Jews'*. As a result, the people of Bessarabia would no longer feel *'Romanian'*, and they would have *'lost discipline'*. The aim was to reverse this 'Bolshevisation'. Marshal Antonescu called for the best officials to be sent to Bessa- rabia (and Bukovina) with this assignment. Bessarabia would have to *'rehabilitate'* itself. Part of the administrative apparatus was provided by the Bessarabian elite who had left Bessarabia in haste during the Soviet occupation in 1940. These all still had a score to settle with whomever they held responsible for the earlier debacle. Incidentally, it was a misunderstanding to think that the local Bessarabian population had jubilantly supported the Soviet occupation. If there was any enthusiasm, it had been tempered after a year of boundless repression by the Soviet security forces. That said, the NKVD, the

Soviet secret service, was now replaced by the Romanian variant, the *'Sigurantja'*.[117] Most of these crimes were committed by the Romanian army and police. German troops and the 'Einsatzgruppe D' made bloody contributions, as did volkmilities made up of Romanians, Ukrainians and 'Volksdeutsche' militias. The 'Einsatzgruppe D' was under the command of Otto Ohlendorf, an economist by trade, who had studied the theory of National Socialist economics before their bloody handiwork, along the lines of 'nationalökonom' Jens Peter Jessen. The 'Einsatzgruppe D' consisted of five commandos who executed tens of thousands of people. These included Jews, communists (commissars), *'Asian inferiors'* and *'unnecessary mouths'* (who had to be fed). In the 'Einsatzgruppen' trial, Ohlendorf testified extensively. In it, he claimed that he had given orders to carry out the killing squads with military precision so that there would be *'humane executions'*. Ohlendorf ran along the lines of the 'Generalplan Ost', in which Eastern Europe was to be transformed into the new 'Grossraum' in which Germany could exist at the expense of other peoples. He explained during the trial how he struggled intellectually with the question of the existence of Germany and peoples in general. Clues were sought from the past regarding the *'rise and fall'* of peoples. The end goal was the 'Aurtarkie policy'. This is why Ohlendorf was prepared to kill. This happened in Bessarabia and later in Ukraine and Crimea, where he constantly collaborated with local militias, including Tatar units in Crimea.[118]

Besides Ohlendorf's unit, the 'Sonderkommando R' (Russland) also operated in the area under the command of SS Brigadeführer Horst Hoffmeyer. This operated in collaboration, with 'Volksdeutsche Selbstschutz' units. Some 50,000 Jews probably lost their lives due to the operation of this unit. The main centres of massacres were at Mostovoi, Balaiciuc, Cihrin, Zaharovca, Rastadt and Vasilinovo.[119]

Overall, practically all crimes in the northern part of Bukovina and the northern part of Bessarabia had been carried out by the Romanians. Most killings took place through mass executions, which took place after the Red Army withdrew. There was not much paperwork or orders involved. The *Geissbühler* described it as; *'One felt they had the right to kill ideologically and politically'*. In this, the war created the right conditions.[120]

One of the first excesses took place in Stanca Rasnoveanu. The population of the town of Targu Sculeni was evacuated as a result of the fighting. This involved separating the Christian residents from the Jews. While the Christians were escorted towards the villages of Carlig and Copou, the Jews were put on separate transport towards Stanca Rasnoveanu. Here, the Romanians, led by formerly Bessarabian-Romanian militia, commanded by Captain Stihi and Lieutenant Mihailescu, took revenge for the *'Jewish insults'*. They had had to suffer these when the Soviets reclaimed Bessarabia from Romania on the eve of World War II. Forty Jews had to dig a mass grave into which the bodies were dumped after execution. In September 1945, the grave was opened and 311 corpses emerged, including seven babies, many children and 91 women. The commandant on whose orders all this had taken place was Colonel Emil Maties of the 6th Romanian Mountain Regiment. He later apologised for having *'committed too few crimes'* in the campaign in Bessarabia.[121]

Not long after the start of Operation *'Barbarossa'* - the attack on the Soviet Union in June 1941 - the deportation of Jews and Gypsies from Romania to Transnistria began, the area between the Dniester and Bug rivers, which had been obtained in the advance against Moscow. By Bucharest, Gheorghe Alexianu had been appointed governor who was based in the city of Odessa, painstakingly conquered by the Romanians. Odessa was a city of 600,000 at the time of the Soviet invasion. About 200,000 of them were Jews, many of whom had fled after the German invasion of the Soviet Union. The area of Transnistria was then divided into 13 districts, which were in turn divided into regions. It was in this area that the massacres were said to have taken place, with a centre of gravity in the southern region. Historian Svetlana Suveica spoke of Transnistria as Romania's *'ethnic rubbish dump'*.[122]

Just as Nazi Germany was deporting the Jews to occupied Poland, the Romanians were kicking the Jews off to occupied Transnistria. This went in waves. The first Jews who arrived in the region and were *'taken in'* ghettos - the Romanians spoke of colonies - were the Jews from Bessarabia and North Bukovina. These deportations started in September 1941. The Jews from southern Bukovina were to follow in 1942. In 1941-1942, this would have added up to around 195,000 Jews, on top of the number of Jews who first lived in Transnistria. It is unclear exactly how many Jews lived in Bessarabia and Bukovina before the deportations began. Censuses from 1930 indicated 206,958 Jews in Bessarabia and 69,151 Jews in northern Bukovina, a total of 277,949 people. With the deportation of 195,000 people by the Antonescu regime in 1941-1942, the bulk of this community was affected by the deportations to Transnistria. As in Nazi Germany and with the deportations to Poland, it was unclear exactly what the end goal of the policy was. Of course, the authorities also benefited from not disclosing the plans. The Antonescu regime made it clear that they wanted to deport the Jews further *'eastwards'*, i.e. east of the Bug River, which would bring the Jews into the Ukraine, into the territory controlled by the Germans. In the meantime, ghetto's were set up where people took incoming Jews in the meantime. Labour battalions made up of Jews were also established. Meanwhile, the massacre of the Jews still present in Transnistria had already begun and partly taken place. Jan Ancel quantified the remaining Jews of Transnistria with around 35,000 Jews in northern Transnistria, some in central Transnistria, 4,000 Jews near Mogilev, the bulk (100,000 men) in the south, around Odessa, and 70,000 men in other positions in the south. The majority of which was murdered in the winter of 1941-1942.[123]

The 195,000 newly arriving torpedoed Jews from Bessarabia and Bukovina, were accommodated in ghettos, many of which were *'built'* on, or consisted of, burnt down housing estates that the Red Army had destroyed on the retreat. Living conditions were very poor. In addition, the deportees had been victims of pogroms in their home areas, so most were already mentally broken. The Bessarabian Jews were in particularly bad shape. They had been under Soviet rule for another period and persecution there too had been severe. The social structures of the community had been destroyed by Moscow and they were exiled to the gulag. Thus, in the practice of Jewish organisations in the ghettos of Transnistria, it was the Bukovina Jews who were largely the *'official'* functions, insofar as those functions existed at all in the chaos of the Romanian *'administration'*. Thereby, the Bukovina Jews were more German-Russian oriented, in terms of language as well, while the Bessarabian Jews mostly spoke only Russian and/or Ukrainian. Suicide was the order of the day and there was a typhoid outbreak. In practice, the ghettos functioned only to a limited extent and thousands of Jews literally roamed the fields, constantly being hunted and looted by militia and military. Sometimes they were driven back across the Dniestr and then into Bessarabia, where they came from. On the western bank of the river, temporary camps and encampments thus re-emerged.[124]

The chaos was symbolised by a group of Jews arriving in the Mogilev ghetto on 25 July 1941. The group had taken 25,000 Jews to Transnistria, but on arrival, only 21,000 of them were still alive, the rest had been murdered during the journey. This first and deadliest phase of the Holocaust in Romania ended around 15 November 1941, when the final number of Jews deported to Transnistria stuck at around 119,000 people. The rest were stuck in temporary camps on the Dniestr or had been killed or succumbed during deportation. Jews who had fled to the mountainous area east of the Bug river fell victim to the German and Ukrainian militias operating in the area. Those who returned reported back, so the people of Transnistria realised they were trapped like rats.[125]

The persecution of Jews was not uniform. Antonescu was more reluctant to persecute the Jews in 'Old Romania'[126] . In this core Romanian country, they were an indispensable part of the economy and Antonescu feared chaos if he intervened too harshly there.

As a result of this policy, 30,000 of the Jewish commune, in and around the Czernowitz ghetto which comprised some 50,000 people, were finally deported. The rest were given permission to stay as 'specialists'.[127] The paradox was that Romania had been working on a Romanisation of the economy since the 1920s, all from the idea of a great Romania and independence from foreign countries. Since Romanians at that time thought only from the point of view of Romanian citizenship - and not ethnicity - Jewish citizens belonged there too. These were to a not-insignificant extent money lenders to the economy, so their share in the Romanian economy had only increased since that period. Hans Schuster figures- in his book *Die Judenfrage in Rumänien*- that the share of Jewish capital in trading companies was 78.1%, 81.5% in insurance, 74.4% in transport and 68.2% in the chemical industry. It was also above 25% in other strategic sectors, such as oil production and coal mining. That it was still relatively *'low'* here was due to the fact that foreign investment in these areas had been substantial. With the Romanianisation policy, the various (right-conservative) cabinets in Romania wanted to reduce foreign influence, which automatically increased the Jewish share.[128] The economic necessity to save part of Romanian Jewry.

The Holocaust in the Romanian territories was not separate from the Holocaust carried out by Germany. At key stages, Bucharest closed course briefly with Berlin. By 12 June 1941, Antonescu had been informed of the German *Richtlinien zum Behandlung der Ostjuden*. In August there was contact with Reichsführer-SS Heinrich Himmler, and on 23 and 24 September consultations took place between German Foreign Minister Von Ribbentrop and Mihai Antonescu on cooperation on the Jewish issue.

All this led to the terrible result that more than 200,000 Jews lost their lives in Romania, supplemented by victims of 'Einsatzgruppen' in Transnistria.[129] Of course, there were also deaths in the parts of Rumania taken over by neighbouring countries, so the final number depends on which borders one uses. What is clear is that in Romania the Holocaust came about almost without German intervention (though consent) with terrible consequences. There was no country in Europe where the Germans had to do less than Romania. On the other hand, from October 1942, the Holocaust slowly died out. Life in the ghettos for the survivors slowly improved. As if they already suspected the impending doom, they became more restrained. There was never a Romanian train carrying Jews to Auschwitz, as one historian rightly mentioned. Yet, that does not alter the fact that mass murder had indeed taken place, even if it was *'a forgotten Holocaust'*, as Romanian Chief Rabbi Alexandru Safran characterised it.[130]

Within this *'forgotten'* Holocaust, even less was known about the fate of the Gypsies in the region. They too became victims of the racial hygiene that gripped the Third Reich. As early as March 1936, there was a 'Reichszigeunergesetz' in which the rights of the gypsies were restricted. After that, concentration, followed by thinking about the future. The *Artzeblatt* of 1938 already gave a glimpse of the not very bright future by speaking in terms of an *'endgültige Lösung'*. Initially, there was still talk of sterilisation of the 30,000 Gypsies who were on German territory. However, from the *Wann- see Conference*, in January 1942, the Gypsies were to be deported towards the extermination and concentration camps, with dire consequences.[131]

Operation 'Barbarossa'

On 12 June 1941, just before the German invasion of the Soviet Union, a consultation between Hitler and Romanian Marshal Antonescu took place in Munich. The Romanian was a man after Hitler's heart. He was brisk, strongly anti-communist and anti-Semitic and, on top of that, loyal to Germany. The reasons for conversation were the future German expansion plans towards the east. Antonescu was told what he had suspected for some time; Nazi Germany would invade the Soviet Union via a surprise attack, Operation *'Barbarossa'*.

In late April, Antonescu had had another extensive meeting with his military attaché in Berlin. The conversation had revolved entirely around rising tensions in Europe. There were many indications that Nazi Germany was getting ready to leap eastwards. Antonescu asked the attaché point-blank and he confirmed that there were already plenty of rumours, but of course he could not give a definitive answer either. Now that the was out of the sleeve, Antonescu was full of fire. Hitler told the marshal that no military efforts were expected from Romania, but that the main thing was ensuring smooth cooperation in German troop movements through Romanian territory. For Antonescu, however, this was not enough. He immediately let Hitler know that Romania would not remain on the sidelines, but would join the battle against the Soviet Union. For Romania, this would be a *'holy war'*. Hitler could therefore count on his Romanian ally, however, he had mixed feelings. He was reluctant to give the allies of central Europe too much space. Hitler knew history and was somewhat fearful of coalition wars with, especially World War I still in mind. Cooperation between different armies often resulted in getting in each other's way. Hitler wanted a unified leadership. That this leadership was in German hands, and only there, was not a subject up for debate. Romanian participation was tolerated and exploited for propaganda, but Bucharest would have to comply. For Antonescu, besides ideological motives, this was an opportunity to conduct border revisionist politics. In April 1941, for example, a claim had already been made to the Banat area, which had been brought within the sphere of Berlin's influence by the German invasion of Yugoslavia on 6 April.

On this, Bucharest was competing with Budapest. Here, too, the problem of coalition warfare became clear. There were legion border incidents between Hungary and Romania.[132]

With the Romanians on its side, Berlin had gained an ally. In itself, this was a German success, because after 1914-1918, Romania initially seemed to fall mainly within the sphere of influence of the 'Entente'. However, it had been the Soviet Union's irredentist policy that drove Romania into German hands. There were several territorial disputes with Moscow and in June 1940 Stalin played *'hardball'* with the Romanians. Without much ado, Bucharest was informed on 23 June that Bukovina and Bessarabia belonged to the Soviet Union, and a few days later the *'request'* had already turned into an ultimatum. The Romanians understood that there was no one who could help them except Nazi Germany. Romanian King Carol II hastily appealed to Hitler, but even he could no longer reverse Moscow's advanced moves.

The loss of these two major border areas caused huge political unrest in Romania. People took to the streets en masse. People's national pride was clearly hurt. When in August 1940 the second 'Wiener Schiedsspruch' came on top of this and millions of inhabitants were forfeited to neighbouring countries, especially to Hungary, the floodgates were wide open. The Romanian government and the king were pushed aside by Marshal Antonescu, who used the disturbances as a strongman to turn the chaos around. The Gigurtu government was sent home and Carol II thanked for the throne. Antonescu was officially the strongman in Bucharest from 4 September 1940.[133]

Romania being drawn within the Axis camp affected German military plans. On 28 August 1940, Romania's name had still been dropped in the *Marcks* plan (attack on Soviet Union) suggesting that, no matter which regime was in power, Romania should be used as a base for attack. So now that Antonescu was there, that all became easier. The arrival of German army troops in Romania on 15 September (prepared by General Kurt von Tippelskirch), foreshadowed what was to come. After the first meeting between Antonescu and Hitler on 22 November, relations were further strengthened. That there was growing political and military confidence was evidenced by the fact that on 27 December of that year, Bucharest was officially informed about the German attack plans regarding Greece. At this, General Hansen tentatively broached the subject of Soviet Union as well. Not that Germany was already in the picture, but the mutual antipathy towards Moscow was clear.

This was reaffirmed by Romania's accession to the Three-Power Pact, which included Italy and Japan. In February 1941, when the German general staff consulted the new plans regarding the upcoming conflict with the Soviet Union, the Romanian contribution was again taken into account. For the time being, this was mainly territorial, in the sense that Hitler wanted to make use of Romania as a base of operations. German concerns about the quality of the Romanian army and the problem of coalition wars hung over the cooperation like a thundercloud. During a meeting in February 1941 on the *Obersalzberg*, during which Hitler spoke to his top military officers, he vented his heart about the quality - or rather lack thereof - of the Romanian army. The Romanians, Hitler argued, lacked '*defensive strength*' and were therefore of very limited use in conflicts. The Romanians could best take shelter behind natural obstacles and confine themselves to the defensive. There was some veiled criticism of Romanian defence policy too, which was very much focused on expanding the army rather than improving it. Quantity took precedence over quality.[134] In addition, Hitler made prophetic statements at the meeting on the *Obersalzberg*. He stated that the fate of the German army should never be made dependent on the fortitude of the Romanians. However, this was exactly what would later happen at Stalingrad.

On 9 June 1941, the plans for the attack on the Soviet Union were again reviewed on the German side. It was decided still not to inform the Romanians. However, it was clear that they would operate in

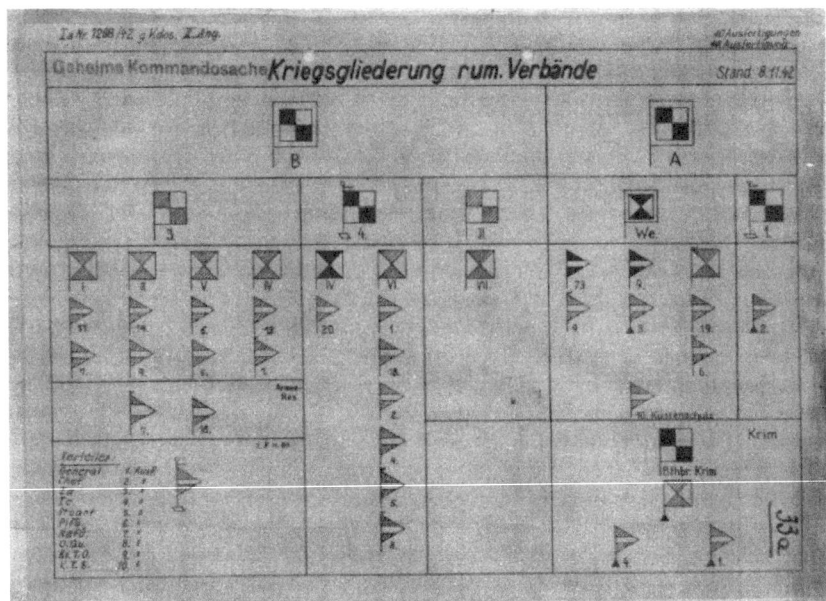

Tactical setup of the Romanion troops.

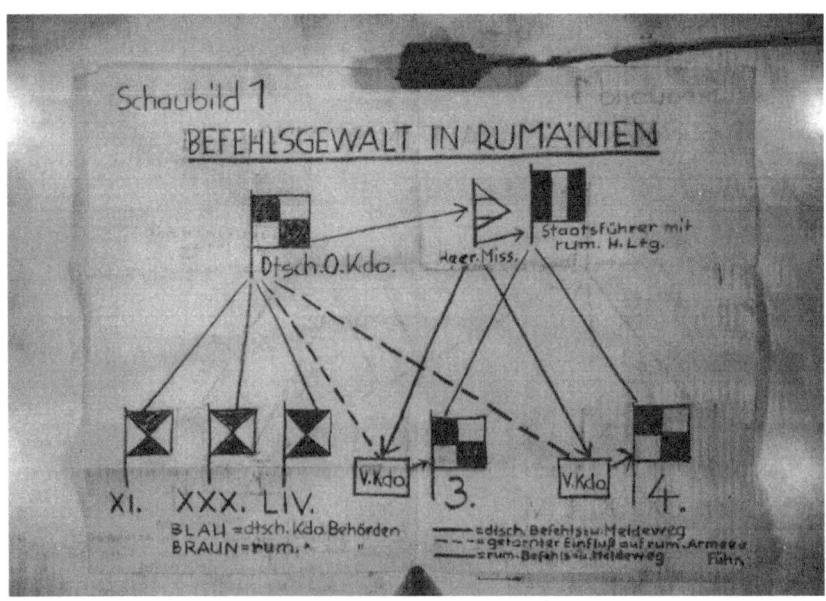

Chain of command of the Romanian army.

Abschrift.

Adolf Hitler

Berlin den
zur Zeit Führerhauptquartier
den 29. Juni 1941.

-46-

Euer Exzellenz !

Schon die ersten 7 Tage des Feldzuges gegen Sowjetrussland haben zu grossen Anfangserfolgen besonders nördlich der Pripjetsümpfe geführt. Die in den Grenzräumen aufgeschlossenen feindlichen Armeen mussten an der gesamten Angriffsfront den Kampf annehmen. Sie wurden vor allem durch unsere Panzerkeile durchbrochen und sind schon jetzt nicht mehr in der Lage, einen geordneten Rückzug durchzuführen. Im Raum zwischen den Pripjetsümpfen und der Ostsee reifen Vernichtungsschlachten grössten Ausmasses heran, die die Grundlagen für eine weiträumige Verfolgung schaffen werden.

Für die Operationen im Südraum bitte ich, Ihnen, General Antonescu, zunächst meinen aufrichtigen Dank für die von der rumänischen Armee sowohl am Pruth wie in der Nordbukowina gezeigte tapfere Haltung und Aktivität aussprechen zu dürfen. Sie hat in diesem ersten Abschnitt des Feldzuges zur Fesselung der gegenüberstehenden Feindkräfte Wertvolles beigetragen.

Seiner Exzellenz
dem rumänischen Staatsführer
General Antonescu,
Bukarest.

- 2 -

A thank you note from Hitler to Marshal Antonescu.

Abschrift

-47-

1. Juli 1941

Exzellenz!

Mit grösster Bewunderung habe ich die siegreichen Operationen der deutschen Armeen an der gesamten Front vom Baltikum bis Lemberg verfolgt.

Die auf der Erde und in der Luft erzielten glänzenden Erfolge lassen einen Endsieg in kürzester Zeit voraussehen. Die sowjetrussischen Armeen können bereits als zerschlagen angesehen werden.

Im Verlaufe dieser 7 Tage gelang es den deutschen und rumänischen Armeen, die sowjetrussischen Kräfte an der rumänischen Front zu binden und die Luftherrschaft zu erringen. Gleichzeitig wurde die Offensive vorbereitet, die die feindlichen Kräfte am Südflügel vernichten wird.

Um eine einheitliche Führung zu gewährleisten, wurden der 11. deutschen Armee folgende rumänische Kräfte unterstellt:

6 Divisionen, 3 Geb.-Brigaden, 3 Kav.-Brigaden, die Pz.-Division und als Ergänzung schwere Artillerie, Pak - und Brückenbaueinheiten usw.

Entsprechend den Richtlinien Euer Exzellenz, wird diese Armee die Haupttätigkeit entwickeln und in der allgemeinen Richtung Vinnica angreifen, um in Südgalizien den feindlichen Kräften in den Rücken zu fallen.

Der Angriff der 11. deutschen Armee wird von rechts durch die 4. rum. Armee gesichert und zwar durch 6 Divisionen und 1 Kav.-Brigade, die zu diesem Zweck in der allgemeinen Richtung Husi, Chisinau, Dubosani angreifen wird, um mit fast sämtlichen Kräften den linken Flügel zu fesseln.

Eine in der Dobrogea angesetzte Aktion wird die Donau in der Gegend Tulcea mit 2 Divisionen überschreiten und nach Norden angreifen.

Zur Sicherung des Erdölgebietes wurden alle Maßnahmen getroffen. Nach meinem Dafürhalten besteht in dieser Gegend keine Gefahr mehr, da die sowjetrussische Luftwaffe auch an dieser Front vom ersten Augenblick an beherrscht wird.

f. E. dem Führer

Hitler thanks the Romanians for their effort and talks about the security of the oilfields at Ploesti.

Units that were deployed at the siege of Odessa.

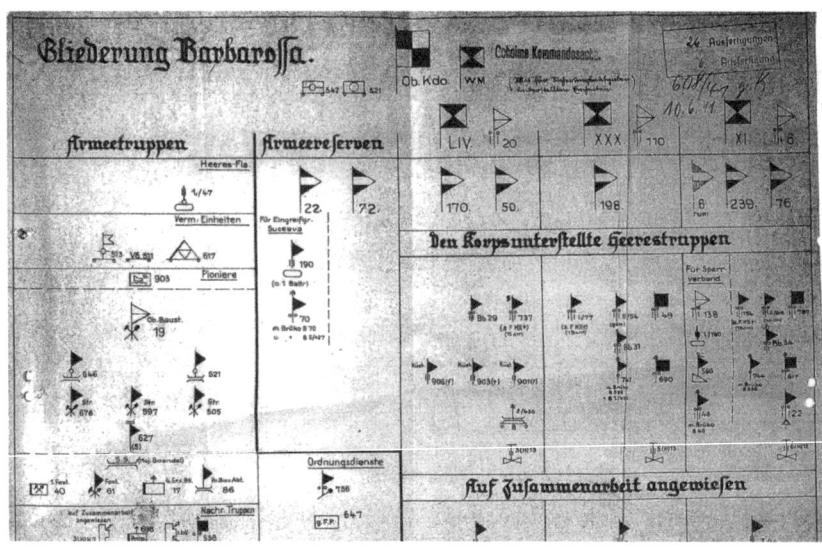

The devision of the troops after operation 'Barbarossa'

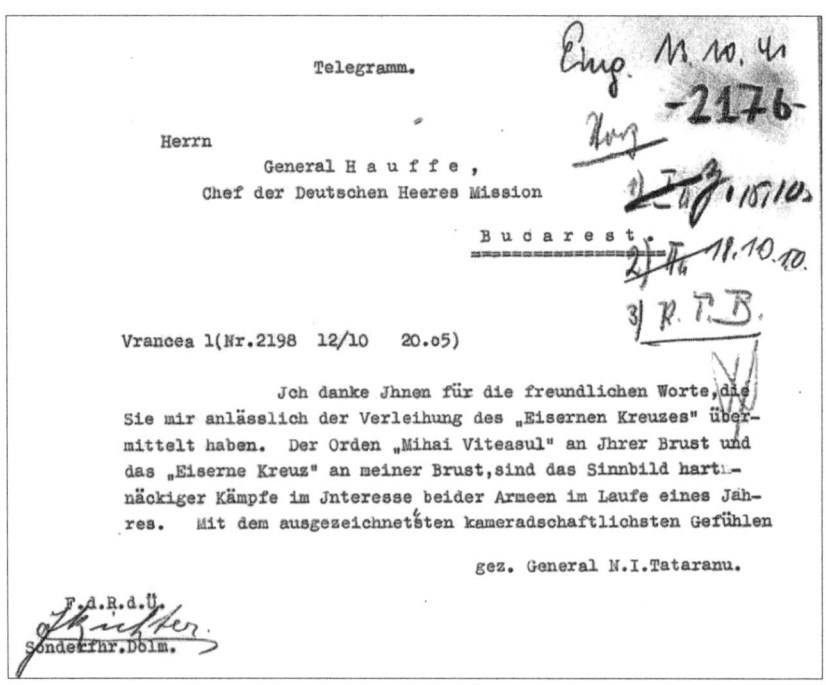

The Romanian general M.I. Tararanu thanks the German general Hauffe for his award.

Anlage 3 zu OKW/ WFSt/ Abt.L IV/Qu
Nr. 44560/41 g.K.Chefs. 11.Ausf.

Richtlinien für das Verhalten der Truppe in Russland.

I.

1.) Der Bolschewismus ist der Todfeind des nationalsozialistischen deutschen Volkes. Dieser zersetzenden Weltanschauung und ihren Trägern gilt Deutschlands Kampf.

2.) Dieser Kampf verlangt rücksichtsloses und energisches Durchgreifen gegen bolschewistische Hetzer, Freischärler, Saboteure, Juden und restlose Beseitigung jedes aktiven oder passiven Widerstandes.

II.

3.) Gegenüber allen Angehörigen der Roten Armee - auch den Gefangenen - ist äusserste Zurückhaltung und schärfste Achtsamkeit geboten, da mit heimtückischer Kampfesweise zu rechnen ist. Besonders die asiatischen Soldaten der Roten Armee sind undurchsichtig, unberechenbar, hinterhältig und gefühllos.

4.) Bei der Gefangennahme von Truppeneinheiten sind die Führer sofort von den Mannschaften abzusondern.

III.

5.) Der deutsche Soldat sieht sich in der Union der Sozialistischen Sowjetrepubliken (U.d.SS.R.) nicht einer einheitlichen Bevölkerung gegenüber. Die U.d.S.S.R. ist ein Staatengebilde, das eine Vielzahl von slawischen, kaukasischen und asiatischen Völkern in sich vereinigt und das zusammengehalten wird durch die Gewalt der bolschewistischen Machthaber. Das Judentum ist in der U.d.S.S.R. stark vertreten.

Communism was declared mortal enemy.

6.) Ein grosser Teil der russischen Bevölkerung, besonders die durch das bolschewistische System **verarmte Landbevölkerung** steht dem Bolschewismus innerlich ablehnend gegenüber. Im nichtbolschewistischen russischen Menschen ist das **Nationalbewusstsein** mit tiefem **religiösen Gefühl** verbunden. Freude und Dankbarkeit über die Befreiung vom Bolschewismus werden ihren Ausdruck häufig in kirchlicher Form finden. **Dankgottesdienste und Prozessionen sind nicht zu verhindern oder zu stören.**

7.) In **Gesprächen mit der Bevölkerung** und im Verhalten gegenüber Frauen ist grösste Vorsicht geboten. Viele Russen **verstehen** deutsch, ohne es selbst sprechen zu können.

Der **feindliche Nachrichtendienst** wird gerade im besetzten Gebiet besonders am Werk sein, um Nachrichten über militärisch wichtige Einrichtungen und Massnahmen zu erhalten. Jede Leichtfertigkeit, Wichtigtuerei und Vertrauensseeligkeit kann deshalb schwerste Folgen haben.

IV.

8.) **Wirtschaftsgüter aller Art und militärische Beute**, insbesondere Lebens- und Futtermittel, Betriebsstoff und Bekleidungsgegenstände sind zu schonen und sicherzustellen. Jede Vergeudung und Verschwendung schädigt die Truppe. **Plünderungen** werden nach den Militärstrafgesetzen mit den schwersten Strafen geahndet.

9.) **Vorsicht beim Genuss von erbeuteten Lebensmitteln !** Wasser darf nur in gekochtem Zustand genossen werden (Typhus, Cholera). Jede Berührung mit der Bevölkerung birgt gesundheitliche Gefahren. Schutz der eigenen Gesundheit ist soldatische Pflicht.

10.) **Für Reichskreditkassenscheine und -münzen** sowie für **deutsche Scheidemünzen** im Wert von 1 und 2 Pfennig sowie 1, 2, 5 und 10 Reichspfennig oder Rentenpfennig **besteht Annahmezwang. Anderes deutsches Geld darf nicht verausgabt werden.**

OKW/WFSt.

Militär-Kabinett
des Staatsführers
Büro 2

Tighina, den 16. Okt. 1941

An den

    Grossen Generalstab

Wir bitten, den nachstehenden Fernspruch Herrn General Hauffe, Chef der Deutschen Heeresmission zu übermitteln.

                  I. A.

              Chef des Militär-Kabinetts
              Oberst
                  gez. Davidescu.

"Ich danke Ihnen wärmstens für die herrlichen Worte, die Sie an mich anlässlich der einjährigen Zusammenarbeit zwischen der Deutschen Heeresmission, die Sie führen, und der Rumänischen Wehrmacht richteten.

Die glänzende Mitwirkung der Deutschen Heeresmission anlässlich der Kriegsvorbereitungen unserer Wehrmacht und während der Operationen dieses Feldzuges bestätigen Ihre Verdienste und bleiben mit der Befreiung unserer Provinzen verbunden.

Gleichzeitig danke ich Ihnen persönlich wie der Mission aufs lebhafteste und wünsche Ihnen, wie bisher, weiteren Erfolg zum Wohle der beiden Länder und der beiden befreundeten und verbündeten Armeen."

                        Marschall
                        gez. Antonescu

A thank you note from Antonescu to Hauffe.

Telegramm

An
   Herrn General H a u f f e
   Chef der Deutschen Heeresmission

<u>B u k a r e s t</u>

Vrancia Nr. 2125   12.10. & 13. 10.

   Heute am 12. Oktober 1941 jährt sich der Tag des Beginns unserer gemeinsamen Arbeit. Ich gestatte mir, Ihnen Herr General die Gefühle wärmster Zuneigung, die ich all denen entgegenbringe, die in der ganzen Zeit unserem Herzen so nahe standen, zum Ausdruck zu bringen. Ihr wohlwollendes Empfinden bei allen Gelegenheiten unserer so fruchtbaren Zusammenarbeit war mir von grösstem Nutzen. Ich werde immer unter den ersten sein, die Ihre grossen Verdienste um den Sieg unserer Waffen würdigen.

                                    gez. General Tataranu
                                    Subchef des Grossen Genst.
                                    u. Chef des Genst. der 4. Armee.

F.d.R.:

Memorial of the German-Romanian collaboration by general Tataranu.

Abschrift.

DRINGEND!   Funkspruch.

KTB -218-

Absendende Stelle: A.O.K.11
Empfangende Stelle: Marschall Antonescu
Aufgenommen: 12.10. 0215 Müller

Herr Marschall !

Ich melde Eurer Exzellenz den Abschluß der Schlacht bei Melitopol, in der die 3. rum. Armee Schulter an Schulter mit den deutschen Kameraden den Sieg errungen hat.

gez. v. Manstein

F.d.R.d.A.
[signature]
Feldw.

German general Von Manstein expresses his appreciation for the effort of the Romanian 3rd army at Melitopol.

Ich habe alle Massnahmen getroffen, um den Öltransport mit aller Intensität durchführen zu lassen. Alle verfügbaren Kesselwagen stehen zu diesem Zweck zur Verfügung.

Ich möchte an dieser Stelle Euer Exzellenz bekanntgeben, dass zwischen mir und Generaloberst Ritter von Schobert das beste Einvernehmen besteht und dass allen operativen Anforderungen der Heeresgruppe Rundstedt entsprochen wird.

Mit dem Glauben an den Endsieg und an die für immer unzerstörbare Freundschaft, die Rumänien an das Grosse Reich bindet, bitte ich Euer Exzellenz, den Ausdruck meiner vollkommenen Ergebenheit entgegenzunehmen.

ss. General Antonescu

F.d.R.d.Ü.:
Godelnäge
Sonderf.

Part of the document in which Antonescu esnures the continuation of oil.

cooperation with the German 11th Army under the command of the army group ('Heeresgruppe') south ('Süd') led by Gerd von Rundstedt. On the 12th, as we have already seen, Hitler decided to play open cards with the then overenthusiastic Antonescu.

How enthusiastic he was proved shortly afterwards when the attack on the Soviet Union began on 22 June. Antonescu, via radio stations, proclaimed the *'holy war'*, and then himself travelled east by special command train to be with the troops in person. His namesake, 37-year-old professor of international law Mihai Antonescu, was installed as a temporary supervisor. In the haste, Bucharest had completely forgotten to alert Grigore Gafencu, its own ambassador to Moscow. The latter was taken completely by surprise by the war. In fact, he had to hear it from a German diplomat. The degree of confusion was was also shown by the fact that Moscow too did not seem to know exactly with whom they were at war. Although the Soviet ambassador in Bucharest had often warned of the omnipresent presence of German troops in the country moving eastwards, these warnings had been ignored by Stalin. The German embassy in Moscow was immediately surrounded by the Red Army on the 22nd, but the Romanian one was still unmolested. By the 4th, it was finally clear what was going on and the Russians realised that on the border river Pruth, Romanian units were involved in the fighting as well. Gafencu was summoned to Molotov, the Russian foreign minister, who, with a white and tired face, calmly shook hands with him and asked if the countries were at war. Gafencu swore to Molotov that he had known nothing about it, but did emphasise diplomatically that Soviet policy towards Bukovina and Bessarabia in June 1940 did not deserve a beauty prize.

The Romanians themselves were soon reminded that they were now at war. Firstly, the 3rd Romanian Army on the Pruth River was indeed in action against the Red Army and managed to gain some ground by surprise, but was also soon faced with well-organised resistance. On the 26 June, the first Soviet planes appeared over Bucharest and the government quarter was bombed from the air. It was small-scale and more symbolic, resulting in four deaths and 12 wounded. Nevertheless, the war was a fact and no one could ignore that anymore.[135] The Soviets had brought in reinforcements along the Romanian border before the war. By 10 June, according to the 'Deutsche Heeresmission', these movements had been completed in Romania. The Romanian front had already been equipped with 168 pieces of German anti-tank artillery for reinforcement on 30 April of that year, as the convergence of Soviet forces could be understood offensively. The Romanian bunkers on the border were equipped with MG positions and anti-tank guns, painted in camouflage colours. The strategic oil area around Ploesti, which was of great strategic importance to Germany, was protected by German units, namely the 72nd I.D., which had taken over the positions of the 22nd I.D.

The 4th Romanian I.D., located near Bucharest, was to assist there in case of emergency.[136] In any case, the communist strategy had a strong offensive element and, in the event of an outbreak of hostilities, tried to move the war into enemy territory as quickly as possible.[137]

'I would never be forgiven if we took a wait-and-see attitude,' Antonescu mused to his men whom he was continually visiting at the front. The Romanians were going to get their share of victory, but the conflict in the east proved no easy operation from the start. The Soviet forces were initiating and were constantly trying to throw the units of the 3rd Romanian Army back on the west bank of the Pruth. The 4th Army initially remained in reserve. Besides the Romanian units, the 11th Army of the Germans was active as well. Von Rundstedt's objective was the *Stalin Line* (a long series of bunker fortifications), Spanish horsemen and minefields to break through, in order to advance into the depths of the Soviet Union. The great rivers were milestones on the way in this regard, the Pruth, the Dniester, the Dnieper, and later they would advance as far as the Volga, the Kuban and so onto the Crimea. Furthermore, the *Black Sea coastal line* was important here. The Germans saw the Romanians struggling. As early as 23 June, a German liaison officer had noted with certain cynicism that the Romanian army could not match the Red Army in all respects. Hitler subsequently decided on the 29th of that month to urge Antonescu once again and point out that the overall command on the southern front lay in German hands.[138] Antonescu must certainly

have been hurt in his pride, but as a military man he was realistic enough to know that Hitler was right.

Despite the initial difficulties, things eventually got off to a flying start. This had everything to do with German breakthroughs elsewhere. On 5 July, the *Stalin Line* was broken and the push through to Berditschew and Shitomir followed. The latter city fell four days later, but the German 6th Army, which would fall so mercilessly at Stalingrad later, pushed on to Kiev, the capital of Ukraine. As the successes loomed, the 4th Romanian Army also moved into action. Commanded by General Nicolae Ciuperca, the army tried to break out from its bridgehead on the Pruth. Meanwhile, the Soviet front was shifting and an advance followed. Bessarabia was evacuated by the Red Army and on 18 July the river Dniestr was reached. This was a symbolic moment. Marshal Antonescu thereupon decided to leave the troops and devote himself again to state affairs in Bucharest.

On paper, much had been achieved for Romania. In barely a month, the disputed territories with the Soviet Union fell back into the hands of the Axis powers and were entrusted to Romania with some restriction. Public opinion was raving about the results and Antonescu could count on acclaim. Yet there was a downside. You can start a war relatively easily, but how do you end a war? For many Romanians, the matter was now settled and a further fight against the Soviet Union no longer served Romanian interests. However, Operation *'Barbarossa'* was simply not like that. The German armies encircled Kiev in a gigantic encirclement battle, one penetrated the Crimea and down the middle went towards Smolensk, more north to Leningrad. This war had only just begun. The Germans were initially optimistic. Halder, for example, revealed in his diary on 3 July that the war would be over in a fortnight. However, reality would prove much more unruly. For Romania, this became clear when the 4th Army was told to take the port city of Odessa. Yet the city's Soviet garrison doggedly defended itself and the 4th Army's losses under Ciuperca's command only continued. Terrain gains were few and far between, so the Germans became increasingly involved. The pressure became so great that the leadership of the army was replaced by Romanian defence minister Losif Lacobici and new chief of staff Nicolae Tataranu.[139]

This brought only limited progress. Although the Romanian army was at the gates of Odessa, it was not moving forward. This came to a head as the Soviets themselves decided to give up the Black Sea port. This was the result of requisitioning elsewhere on the front. Kiev had fallen on 26 September with over 600,000 Russians going into captivity, and Crimea was threatened by the Germans (and the 3rd Romanian Army) with the capture of the 'Tatarengrab' at the Crimea's entrance isthmus. So the focus for Stalin simply became Sebastopol and no longer Odessa.

The way the Soviets left Odessa was masterly. By way of deception, they opened a surprise attack on the Romanian besiegers from the suburb of Dalnik on 2 October 1941. These were hit completely *'off guard'* and suffered heavy losses. While chaotic fighting was going on, the bulk of the garrison embarked and escaped. On 15 October, all strategic objects in the city blown up. Only the next day did the Romanians shuffle into the city. There was no more resistance. The Red Army had left and Odessa could be declared as conquered, though it was a meager victory. The 4th Romanian Army had 110,000 killed and wounded, including more than 4,000 officers. Had the army not been continuously reinforced, it would have ceased to exist.[140]

With Odessa, an important city did fall into German-Romanian hands. The city had about 600,000 inhabitants and, after Leningrad, it was considered the Soviet Union's main port. Odessa was an important city in the region because the few industries located in the area were concentrated in this city as well as in the smaller towns of Perwomajek and Woshnjessensk.[141]

The Romanian occupation of Odessa had other remarkable major consequences. First of all, the city made a ghostly impression. The tire storage facility was on fire and clouds of black smoke hung over the city. The port area was littered with disarmed Soviet weapons, including 15 howitzers. Many cars and trucks had been pushed right off the quay into the sea. The Romanians became more suspicious when they found many young men in civilian clothes, of conscript age. They were arrested - this involved some 7,000 *'prisoners of war'*. What worried Bucharest was the fact that there were endless catacombs under the city, totalling some 200 km in length and 160 exits. It was hardly surveyable. Some 300,000 Jews lived in the city before the war and even now the number of Jews in the city was large. Relations were reasonable shortly after the occupation, but the atmosphere soon changed. Indeed, the city remained restless, with gunshots, fires and small explosions. Moreover, it was rumoured that the Russian secret service, the NKVD, had supplied the large government buildings on English Street in the city with explosives. The Romanian General Staff was keen to make use of the stately premises, which had first housed communists. Earlier, investigations were conducted and, after warnings, premises were again temporarily evacuated. It seemed to be a false alarm. On 22 August, a warning came from two arrested communists who claimed that the NKVD was going to blow up the premises. This was not believed and no action was taken, but at 5.50pm that same day, bombs went off anyway. The premises were in use at the time, causing several German naval officers to lose their lives, as well as the commander of the Romanian 10th I.D. General Glogoianu and his complete staff. The Romanians immediately started salvage operations, but many casualties could not be saved, among them officers. The total number of casualties was said to be around 80.

The anger in Bucharest was enormous. Immediately, it was urged to strike back hard. But at whom? The Jews had to pay the price, especially after a telephone connection was found in one of them with the NKVD, which had apparently been able to commit this attack remotely and from the catacombs. The revenge was terrible and disproportionate. In the process, they hit the *'wrong people'*. Nevertheless, the order from Bucharest was clear: *'Execute all the Jews from Bessarabia, who are in Odessa'*. Another point of the order in the telegram with the order stated: *'Destroy this order after reading it'*. The order was signed by Colonel Davidescu. About 19,000 Jews were gathered in the port area and executed. Their bodies were doused with petrol and set on fire. This was Odessa's introduction to the new regime. [142]

This eruption of violence was not isolated. Romania had an anti-Semitic tradition and Antonescu, Romania's strongman, was blinded by the idea of a pure Romanian race. He made it clear on several occasions that he wanted to expel the Jews from the annexed territories as well. In total, around 250,000 Jews died at the hands of Romanians during World War II. Those Jews who survived the executions in Odessa were deported, most to the infamous Bogdanovka camp.[143]

Now that a large area had fallen into the hands of Nazi Germany and its allies, the Romanians became involved in the occupation of the area. To this end, above all, the 4th Romanian Army was deployed. This army consisted of the VIth and IInd Army Corps based in Nikolajew and Tiraspol, respectively. The 4th army itself was based in Odessa.

Liaison with the German authorities was provided by the D.V.K., the 'Deutsches verbindungskommando'. Each Romanian unit included a liaison officer. For the 4th Army, this was Hauptmann I.G. Hofmann, with his interpreter Gefreiter Bemischek.[144]

German-Romanian cooperation was by no means always easy. It was clear from surviving documents that the Germans had to constantly push to get the Romanian occupation forces into the right positions. They fell under the command of the German 11th Army, the five infanterial divisions (1st, 2nd, 4th, 10th and 18th) and two cavalry brigades (1st and 9th). These were to be stationed in Odessa, Nikolajew, Kriwoj Rog, Tiraspol, Balta, Beresowka and Tulcin in the area between the Bug and Dnieper riverbeds. Frequent incidents of looting soon occurred, as the 'Deutsche Heeresmission in Rumänien' reported to Romanian general Palangeanu on 23 October 1941.[145]

The Germans were worried about disorder. The area the Romanians controlled was not insignificant. It was a fertile black earth region. Only the narrow strip from Tiraspol to the north along the Dnieper was Romanian-Moldovan in ethnicity. The rest of the area (80%) was Ukrainian. The towns, apart from Rog, were Russian-Jewish. Kriwoj Rog had a not insignificant iron industry and lignite was mined. The countryside was rich in livestock, especially dairy cows, and was similar to the fertile Kuban area. The Romanians, German authorities feared, would not be able to properly administer and control the area. The Ukranians were seen by the Nazis as *'more intelligent and talented'*, and they did not trust Bucharest with *'the Jewish problem'*. Furthermore, they feared the use of partisan groups. As early as mid-August, the Germans had noticed that Russian paratroopers were being regularly dropped in the Romanian-occupied hinterland. These were partisans in civilian clothes.[146]

The German concern was not unjustified. The German 'Einsatzgruppen', which were active behind the advancing armies in the 'Korück' (Korpsrückwärts), also reported them, as on 11.07.1941, 17.07.1941 and 31.07.1941. The first report involved large-scale looting of the town of Faleski, which was badly damaged by the war. In Chotin it came to *'aimless measures against Jews'* and again large-scale looting. Ukrainians were mistreated by the Romanians too. On 17.07 the looting concentrated on Belzy. Fires had sprung up all over the city, lit by the Romanians for no purpose. Of the 60,000 citizens of whom 32,000 were Jewish, many had fled. Looting was going on everywhere.

To counter this, the gendarmerie was brought in from Jassy. When it was believed that Romanian troops had been shot at in the chaos, the Romanian troops wanted to shoot 400 Jewish hostages, mostly greybeards. The commander of the German 170th I.D., General Walter Wittke, managed to prevent this at the last minute. The Romanians then settled for the fusillade of 15 Jews, while 70 were held in permanent hostage.[147]

The cruelty with which the Romanians could act alarmed even the Germans. To the 'Korück 553', the 'SD' reported that the Jews were to be approached *'rabidly and with the utmost suspicion'*, but also believed that the Romanians were acting harshly against the Jews in a way that was *'unsympathetic'* to the Germans.[148] In Belzy, 45 executions took place around 15 July 1941.[149] The 'SD's *Ereignisse Rapport'* of 31.07.941 again reported looting as well as chaos among the supply and removal troops and lack of supplies, especially fuel, as a result.[150]

German criticism of the Romanians did lack self-reflection. At the same moment that German agencies were complaining about Romanian atrocities, several 'Einsatzgruppen' and commandos were active on the Eastern Front and the killing of Jews and Communists was in full swing. On 10 October 1941, the memorandum had gone out (the so-called *Reichenau-Befehl*) on the *'Verhalten der Truppe im Ostraum'* which spoke of ridding Germany of the *'Asian-Jewish danger'* and the need to destroy the Bolshevik fallacy and the Soviet state.[151] In addition to the massacres of Jews and communists, within the 'Heeresgruppe Süd', as well as on other German fronts, the problem of huge numbers of prisoners of war was added. After the German conquest of Kiev, many hundreds of thousands of Russians had fallen into German hands. This led to catastrophic conditions in the prison camps, where there was starvation.[152]

In addition to all the problems with Romanian discipline, it was not easy to streamline agreements between Romanians and Germans either. We already briefly mentioned the D.V.K. and the 'Deutsche Heeresmission' in Romania. In addition to these, there was the direct military command, OKW, OKH, 'Heeresgruppe Süd', 11th Army, the political 'Reichskommissariat Ukraine', based in Rowno, and the military administration (Korück). All had wants from the Romanians, which of course did not favour a unified instruction of the Romanians. Militarily, at least in late 1941, it was urged that a provided infantry regiment, from the 18th Romanian division, be deployed in the Dnieper estuary area. In January 1942, calls were made for the release of the German 113th division commanded by General Günzel from the Odessa area. The division would be transferred to the 6th Army and become involved in the defence battles around Kharkov during General Tymoshenko's Russian spring offensive in May 1942.[153]

The OKH intervened regularly on the problems of the coalition war. In January 1942, a letter went out, drafted by - the later made famous by the attack on Hitler - Claus Schenk Graf von Stauffenberg, to various armies, army corps, the Korück and W.B. Ostland and Ukraine urging camaraderie and cooperation between the Germans, the *'verbündete Staaten'* and *'fremdländischen Freiwilligenverbänden'*. It urged the prevention of conflict, as the allies were fellow fighters for the '*Schicksalsgemeinschaft Europa*' and an ally in the fight against Bolshevism.[154]

Moreover, a huge project was the construction of the Russian railway network on European lines. Within the area of the 'Heeresgruppe Süd' alone, up to the period 08.10.1941, this involved 5034 km of railway, of which 270 km of single track and 1149 km of double track. These were the longest stretches of track on the Eastern Front at that time, because within the 'Heeresgruppe Nord' it was 4594 km and at the 'Heeresgruppe Mitte' to 4414 km (16,148 km in total). Work continued throughout the year, and by 31.12.1941, 7,702 km had finally been converted within the area of 'Heeresgruppe Süd'. Some of this work was carried out by Romanian construction troops. By 31.10.1941, they had retracked 1,500 km, reaching 2003 km by the end of the year. With this, the Romanians had converted almost a third of the railway lines on the Southern Front, which was a considerable contribution proportionally. As far as can be ascertained, the Romanian construction units also continued their work in 1942, and the Odessa-Karoline Bugas line, a short line of 46 km, was in any case added.[155] In his 'Tagesbefehl Nr. 45', Hitler referred to the work of construction troops and engineers, when he referred to the 2,000 bridges over 12 metres long, 405 railway bridges and the 15,000 km of railway that had been converted. Also mentioned by name were the Romanian units, in addition to the Slovaks, Hungarians and Italians.[156]

Besides their work as occupying forces, Romanian troops were actually still at the front after the 1941 border battles. This was with the German 11th Army, commanded by Von Manstein since 17 September 1941. His troops advanced both towards the city of Rostov and towards the Crimea, where from the isthmus of Perekop they had to take the Tatarenwal ('Tatarengrab': an old line of defence, mainly directed against cavalry, consisting of a deep trench in the earth, with bunker works attached) and could advance towards Simferopol and Sebastopol. The latter city in particular had great significance both historically and strategically, as a port on the Black Sea and as an icon of the Crimean War from 1853-1856. It was General Hansen's LIVth Corps that was the first available for a rush to Crimea. The Germans received Romanian assistance in the process. Von Manstein had reservations about his allies. He felt that the Romanian army was rather aristocratic, as it had a huge class difference. Ordinary soldiers were simply foot soldiers. Additionally, the Romanian troops' equipment was not very good, something Von Manstein, incidentally, blamed on Germany. Why hadn't the Romanians been provided with better weapons? Thereby, Von Manstein believed, the Romanians suffered from something that other small Mid-European countries suffered from as well: a historical fear of the great Russia. Von Manstein did feel that the Romanians had lost interest in the campaign after the conquest of Bessarabia, but the war was still not decided.

The storming of Crimea

The battle for Crimea was far from easy. The terrain did not lend itself to motorised warfare and was mainly for an infantery and artillery battle. On 24 September 1941, the Germans attacked at Perekop and two days later the 'Tatarengrab' was taken. While the rest of Von Manstein's army moved eastwards from the Dnieper,[157] the other troops were now moving into Crimea. But the Germans had to operate cautiously, as the Red Army was numerically stronger. Units of three Russian armies had already been observed at the front, while Von Manstein was actually operating with only a handful of divisions. The 3rd Romanian Army was already fulfilling security tasks on the flank of the German forces, on the coast of the Sea of Asov. On 1 November, the German 72nd I.D. took the city of Simferopol, and slowly the port city of Sebastopol came under more and more pressure. Yet it would take until 17 December 1941 before a real attack could be launched. A state of emergency had already been proclaimed in the city on 29 October.[158] Romanian units carried out purges in the Jailage Mountains, with the 1st Romanian Mountain Brigade taking 300 prisoners of war on 15 November.[159] At the 'Zwischenmeldung' of 16 November, the 'Heeresgruppe Süd' honourably commended the 11th Army, and with it the XXXXIInd Army Corps and the Romanian units, for the results achieved so far. It was on the day the industrial city and port hub of Kerch was captured. The army command was able to report more than 60,000 prisoners, bringing the number of Soviet prisoners since 21 September to over 100,000 men.[160] The Romanian deployment, incidentally, was not limited to purges and flank cover. In certain situations, the Romanians could be found directly on the front line, although these were usually limited operations. In late November, for example, the 1st Romanian 'Gebirgsjäger-Regiment' cooperated with the 72nd I.D. in the so-called-'Denkmalshöhe', Kapellenberg (Kamary-Radikowa-Bulaklawa) where Hill 118 had to be captured. From the regimental headquarters in Warnutka, 2 battalions (the 1st and 4th), a machine gun battalion (the 14th) and a mountain artillery division were deployed.[161] This closed a frontal gap between the German 50th and 72nd I.D. Furthermore, in 'Tagesbefehl' No 109 of 25 November, orders were issued that the 1st Romanian Mountain Brigade should clear the area along the coast of partisans and secure traffic along the Alsu-Bajdary line. The 24th 'Gebirgsjäger' battalion was deployed for this purpose. The 2nd 'Gebirgsjägerabteilung' defended the Yalta-Alupka coastline. The 3rd motorised regiment, reinforced by an anti-aircraft battery, guarded the Foros - Yalta - Aluschta and Aluschta - Simferopol roads.[162] The Romanians received relatively strong support from the local population in their guard duties. In the Romanian Mountain Corps area, civilian soldiers even volunteered to fight partisans. This was partly due to the position of the Crimean Tatars, who had been systematically oppressed by Stalin. The Germans gave them more religious freedom, and the Crimean Tatars subsequently turned against the communists en masse.[163]

The Soviets had no intention of idly waiting in Sebastopol to see what the German plans were. Von Manstein could count on growing resistance. At Rostov, resistance flared up again, forcing costly units from Sebastopol to the other front. In the process, the Soviets carried out two landings, at Kerch, east of Sebastopol, and at Feodosia, west of Crimea. The operations took place on 26 and 29 December 1941. So while the German army group 'Mitte' was fighting near Moscow, the situation in the south was very tense too. Near Feodosia, on 18 January, the 170th German I.D. managed to drive the Soviets back into the sea with difficulty. On Kerch, things were tense as well. The German 46th I.D. of General Hans von Sponeck got into such trouble that he ordered a retreat. Von Manstein reinforced the front just in time and another attack, on 13 March 1942, was repulsed with difficulty. The front did falter. The arrival of the German 22nd Pz.D. to the area brought the difference. A new Soviet attack followed on 26 March, but was repulsed and on 9 April things turned in German favour. Soviet 44th and 51st Army were increasingly compromised. Through operation 'Trappenjagd', 26 larger Soviet units were now trapped in a small area. The German offensive had begun on 8 May and was very effectively supported by the 'Luftwaffe', and above all the 'Stuka' (dive-bombers) under the command of Wolfram Freiherr Von Richthofen, which wreaked havoc on the packed troops. Some 170,000 Soviet soldiers were taken captive.[164]

As a result of this success, on 20 May 1942, the attack on Sebastopol was redesigned. The huge forts, supported in part by the heaviest calibre artillery, were eliminated one by one by the German-Romanian attackers. The Romanians were positioned in the centre of the attack and took a mainly defensive stance. Von Manstein struck from the flanks, where the German units were positioned. More than 100 artillery batteries shelled the city stormily. *'The earth was made of steel,'* Von Manstein noted looking back.

By June 26, the suburbs were in German hands. The Soviets were desperate. When the German troops entered the sect cellars, they blew up their own ammunition. The result was a terrible explosion with thousands dead; the lion's share in the cellars were Russian soldiers. The Russian navy began evacuating the survivors. It was the final phase of the battle. On 4 July 1942, the siege ended.[165]

In terms of time, this brings us to the German summer field march of 1942. Weakened by the winter 1941-1942, this left the Germans unable to advance across the entire front.[166] Therefore, the attack plans were concentrated on the 'Heeresgruppe Süd' front. The direction of attack was towards the Volga, and at the Caucasus, a division of the army group into A and B ('Heeresgruppe Don') would form, with A moving into the Caucasus and B continuing the attack eastwards, eventually culminating in the battle at Stalingrad. This plan of attack, 'Fall blau', began with a setback given that the Soviets started a battle in May 1942 by surprise in the vicinity of Kharkov. This offensive by the well-known Soviet general Tymoshenko did not bring the desired result and ended in a Russian massacre. Thereafter, the attack was taken up by the 'Heeresgruppe Süd' in an easterly direction, which went forward energetically, and it should be noted that the rapid advance to the east was something of a battle in the air. The Soviets could no longer be so easily surrounded and eliminated, as in the previous summer.

The Romanians of the 3rd and 4th armies, moved eastward with them. According to Romanian figures, the Romanians had 267,727 men at the front (Russian figures indicated a significantly larger number of soldiers: 355,877 troops). The historian Gosztony quoted from a report by General Petre Dumitrescu, which gave an account of the state of the divisions. Many of them came from the Odessa front and had been reinvigorated in Romania. In reality, however, the divisions were weaker than they should have been. For instance, the regiments had only two battalions instead of three. In addition, the anti-tank capabilities of the units was serious. There were hardly any anti-tank guns and the mines promised by the Germans came late and in too small numbers. What was reasonable was the Romanian artillery, but this lacked supply and disposal troops to properly resupply the units, which came far from the stations. Lastly, their clothing was insufficient to withstand the harsh Russian weather conditions properly.[167]

Nevertheless, the Romanians did achieve some successes in August. They advanced along the Azov coastline. Further north, at Kalatsch, a major showdown was taking place at that time with the Soviet army, which formed a forward post of Stalingrad. Here, the German 6th Army carried out one of the last classic encirclement battles of the Wehrmacht in World War II. As that battle raged on, there was dissatisfaction with the speed of operation at the 'Heeresgruppe A' (which would turn into the Caucasus). In the OKW's diary in those days, we find a repeatedly complaining Hitler. General Warlimont noted dryly that the inactivity had to do with the poor ratio between the stated objectives and the available military potential. The general staff tacitly swallowed Hitler's criticism, knowing that Hitler had caused the overload of the front himself with his two big targets (Volga and Caucasus). As expected from a sinking ship, there were hardly any units left. Hitler indicated that the 3rd Romanian Mountain Division, which was still in the Crimea, should be brought in by land. He did not want to wait any longer until the Kerch Strait was in German hands so that sea transport could take place. One bright spot was the fact that some Romanian units were still gaining ground, such as at Baksanok, where the Romanian mountain troops opereated in cooperation with the German 23rd Pz.D.[168]

Historian Stephen Walsh stresses that the Romanians operated relatively solitarily and purged the Azov coastline, capturing the ports of Temryuk and Anapa on 31 August 1942. General Petre Dumitrescu, who, according to the OKW diary, personally led the attack, was awarded the 'Ritterkreuz' for this.[169] German troops, including those of the air force, hardly played a role in this.[170] After this success, the Soviets were pushed back to behind the Kuban. The successes in the Taman region were immediately followed by Operation 'Blücher-II', in which units of the 3rd Romanian Mountain Corps and the German 46th I.D. were still transferred by the German Navy into the Strait of Kerstj. To avoid any further delay (even the 3rd Romanian Mountain Division was now going by boat after all), OKH officer Oberst Freiherr Treusch von Buttlar-Brandenfels and naval officer Kapitän zur See Junge were directed to the sector to facilitate a quick crossing.[171] According to a statement by Befehlshaber Krim general Franz Mattenklott, which he made in American captivity, the Germans had gathered 80 ships from the Constanta and Odessa region for this purpose. The landing took place in the vicinity of Kuchugury.[172] The sea had been rough the previous days, which had also caused delays, but this, for Füher headquarters, should no longer delay the landing on the other side. In 'Führerweisung' 43 of July 1942, the crossing of the Kersh Strait (Operation Blücher) had already been scheduled for early August 1942. However, sustained fighting in the Crimea had prevented this. Now this omission was rectified via Blücher-II.[173]

There was a certain optimism among the Germans, which extended to their Romanian allies. There is an interesting report from July 1942 in which the German intelligence services shed light on the Romanian forces. Here, the focus was on the Romanian units of the first hour, the so-called '1. Welle'. By now, there were 36 larger Romanian units at the front, but this report thus covered the first four Romanian corps, the VIth and VIIth Corps, the 'Gebirgskorps' and the 'Kavali Corps', consisting of 7 infantry divisions (1., 2.,4.,10.,18.,19. and 20th I.D.), the three cavalry divisions (5th, 6th and 8th) and the 2 mountain divisions (1st and 4th Geb.D.) who had been there since the Soviet invasion and had fought in Ukraine, Crimea on Don and on the Black Sea coast. Despite hefty losses, these '1. Welle' units had been constantly replenished and their armament had been reinforced with captured weaponry from the front.[174]

Moreover, there was due respect for the officers. For example, General Dragalina, the commander of the VI Romanian Army Corps was seen as a capable man, with a broad general development. *'Tall, powerful and good-looking appearance'*, the report described the man. *'Personally very brave'*, and *'does not spare himself'*. Dragalina not only led from headquarters but could often be found at the front, where he convinced his soldiers of the necessity of battle. He fully supported German cooperation and, if necessary, did not shy away from harsh measures either. The only criticism of Dragalina was that he was clearly *'of the French school'*, by which was meant his training time according to French insights, which would make the corps commander *'reserved and too much focused on certainty'*. This sometimes caused delays in the operation of the VI Army Corps. Dragalina himself had taught at Romanian martial schools for several years. Additionally, the Germans were appreciative of his staff officers, Obert Rascu, a former commander of I.R. 26 of the 2nd Romanian I.D. and Ia Major Frunza. Rascu was seen as a quiet somewhat calm man and very diligent. He was both sharp and circumspect and possessed a very pro-German friendliness. Like his chief Dragalina, he lacked a bit of *'schwung'*. Ia Frunza was *'big, powerful and capable'* and could not be shaken. He was somewhat insubstantial, not necessarily German-friendly, and like his chief, schooled along French lines.[175]

Further, the commander of the VIIth Corps, General of Infantry Mitranescu, was praised too. He was an *'energetic and soldierly'* person, of medium height, of good appearance, calm and self-confident. He worked continuously to further train and discipline his troops and carried out orders without objections. He was seen as *'clear'* and militarily gifted. The troops revered and trusted him, insofar as that became evident within the rather rigid and position-conscious rules of the Romanian military apparatus. His staff officers Mihai Camarascu and Ia Major Paul Anastasiu were appreciated as well, although Camarascu was a bit of a stiff fellow, with poor manners and incapable of any military camaraderie. He did have solid professional knowledge and was cooperative. The Germans took the fact that he was not generally liked at face value. At 40, Anastasiu, ten years younger than Camarascu, was modest as well as diligent and, above all, reliable. His health left much to be desired, but he did not spare himself. All in all, the VII Corps had performed well on the Kerch peninsula and thus commanded respect.[176]

Cavalry general Mihail Racovita was an extraordinary figure. Vain, quick-tempered and feared by his subordinates. He did not shy away from dismissing a divisional commander from his post for passing on incorrect reports. His tactical knowledge was good and his command clear. His stubbornness was evident on 07.10.1941, when he ignored an order from the 3rd Romanian Army and allowed his troops to advance unabated, resulting in a considerable number of Soviet prisoners of war. What was important to the German allies was the fact that he spoke fluent German, having been trained at German military academies and having served with a cavalry regiment in Saarbrücken. His staff officer Ioan Eftimiu and Ia Major Georgescu were appreciated too. Eftimiu had been at his post since December 1941, was calm and pensive, and led with a steady hand. He was conscientious and tireless. Georgescu had served with Racovita's cavalry corps only since June 1942, but had already earned his stripes as a teacher at the Bucharest Military Academy. He knew the craft.[177]

The Germans were somewhat more critical of the commander of the Romanian Mountain Corps, General Avramescu, who was seen as a 'weaker' figure. He was hesitant and pushed through his plans and directions with insufficient toughness. His orders were therefore implemented hesitantly. Avramescu's influence on his divisions was thus limited. Personally, he was brave and could often be found in the front lines. However, he lacked a firm hand towards his divisional commanders and also tended to give too much weight tactically to his own losses. This lack of *'schwung'* was particularly evident during the fighting for Sebastopol. His chief of staff, Stefan Constantinescu, could hardly counterbalance this. The latter was described by German intelligence services as a *'sickly man'*, who was hardly in touch with his commander Avramescu, nor with other staff officers. He had served with the corps since July and was seen as *'silent'* and a 'Alleingänger'. The Ia Major Alexander Constantinescu (namesake but not related) was seen as self-confident and diligent. He had completely and thoroughly mastered German methods and carried out orders without hesitation. Through Alexander Constantinescu, therefore, came a *'fine cooperation'*. He was a *'positive presence'* on the staff. All in all, the report concluded that during the fighting for Sebastopol, the corps had both developed well and learnt a lot.

The army had also been scrutinised at the divisional commander level. General Ioan Mihaescu of the Romanian 1st I.D. was described as small in stature, friendly, energetic and tough. He, unlike most Romanian officers, had *'schwung'*. He was the division's new commander since the unit's setback at Losowaja. At the Kessel battle for Varkov, the unit had performed well. Ion Georgescu of the 2nd Romanian I.D. was a former artillery officer of the Vth Romanian Army Corps. He was small in stature too, looked little soldierly, but was calm and humourous and relatively indifferent to danger. As a result, he was much appreciated by the units, and people generally had confidence in him. Gheorghe Cealac was the commander of the 4th Romanian division, decisive, enterprising, but suffered from a stomach ailment in the process. Octavian Georgescu was cut out for the soldier's life. He was hard on himself and appreciated by his troops. However, he did give the impression of listening too much to subordinates, so his leadership was sometimes a bit hesitant. Radu Baldescu was commander of the Romanian 18th I.D. He was a man of open character, quiet and brave, but not a *'draufgänger'*. He had a paternal relationship with his soldiers. Carol Schmidt was the commandant of the 19th Romanian I.D., a quiet and self-confident officer, with a fatherly air. Tactically, he was very strong and difficult to influence. Advice he usually disregarded. He spoke fluent German. Nicolae Tataranu was a commander of the Romanian 20th I.D. and very aware of the Romanian army's internal shortcomings. He was therefore constantly working to raise the level of training. He was strict towards failing soldiers. Despite having served as many as seven years according to French military principles, he had fully internalised German military thinking. He tended to overestimate the enemy, so he acted somewhat cautiously.

The commander of the Romanian 5th Kav.D, Kasile Mainescu, was disciplinary and an energetic go-getter. The commander of the Romanian 6th Kav.D., N. Christu Cantuniar, was not in the picture of intelligence and the commander of the 8th Romanian Kav.D., Corneliu Carp was seen as *'holding back'* and lacking in initiative. He had been commander of the captured city of Odessa in the winter of 1941-1942. He relied very much on his staff officers, with chief of staff Major Plesoianu not highly rated but the division's Ia, Rittmeister Goermann, being described as diligent and intelligent. In the mountain divisions, Constantin Vasiliu-Rasca now commanded the 1st Geb.D. He had the full confidence of his troops and worked on the staff with Chief of Staff Jorgu Enculescu and Ia Alexandre Evolce- anu. The 4th Geb.D. was commanded by Gheorghe Manoliu, trained in French tactics, consistent in his command but lacking in initiative. He admired the German army and worked well with his chief of staff Octavian Catana and Ia Constantin Dinulescu. The unit had fought just fine before Sebastopol and later also fought well against partisans.[178]

Later lightings of the Romanian army had been trained more and more by the DHM and in this sense were closer to the German troops in terms of culture. This included, for example, the 3rd I.D. (General I. Boiteanu), the 8th I.D. (General D. Carlaont) and the 21st I.D. (General R. Niculescu-Cociu). They had received their training in winter 41-42 and spring 1942 from German 'Lehrpersonal'. The big problem there, however, was that the armament was incomplete. Thus there were shortages in light machine guns (85%), heavy machine guns (67%), in the various types of mortars from 60 mm to 81.4 mm and 120 mm between 83 and 90% and - perhaps more seriously - in antitank artillery (Pak) 87% and anti-aircraft (Flak) 66%. Moreover, there were three Sicherungsdivisionen active in the hinterland, '1. Festungs Division' and the 'Garde I.D.' Large parts of the Pak and Flak were missing here. These units were not suitable for front service, with the exception of the 'Festungs Divisionen de Garde'. The 'Sicherungsdivisionen' were under the command of the colonels, A. Nasta, N. Vladescu and D. Dumitrescu-Polichron. The 'Festungs Division' was commanded by General G. R. Gheorghiu and was stationed near Odessa. The guard under the command of General Sova Nicolae, who carried the EK1 and EK2, was made up of men from all over the country and had behaved in an exemplary manner during the campaign against the Soviet Union, although it had also suffered heavy losses. The Germans promised new arms deliveries to replenish the units around 1 October 1942, but this would remain a constant problem.[179]

With the victory for the Germans of the battle of Kalatsch, the march to Stalingrad a fact. *'The Lebensraum has expanded enormously,'* headlined the German press.[180] Groupings were proposed for the upcoming operations. Here it was suggested on 3 September that the 3rd and 4th Romanian Army should become part of the German 'Heeresgruppe B', later (21.11.1942) 'Heeresgruppe Don'. This was important because this brought the Romanian troops to the front at Stalingrad and meant they no longer went into the Caucasus. This was scheduled to be here by the end of September.[181]

Turning point Stalingrad

On 1 October, the first German units reached the outskirts of Stalingrad. The city would soon act as a magnet. As a strategic transfer point in the Wolgaknie and a symbol of prestige, the city bound larger and larger armies to itself. The 6th German Army under General Paulus was slowly consumed in the street battles. The long flanks, where the Romanians were deployed, had become long and vulnerable. On 2 October, another fierce Soviet counterattack was repulsed, which was deployed towards Orlowka. The Soviets lost 65 tanks in the process. The Germans celebrated it as a great success, but in reality it turned out to be completely different. Consequently, this feigned suspicion was nothing but a sign on the wall. 9/10ths of the city was captured, but in the last strongholds on the Volga, the Soviets held on doggedly. The strength of the German units dwindled rapidly. Typical was the tank strength of the 24th Pz. D., which on 3 October still had only 29 tanks and was unable to deploy more than 100 tanks due to lack of spare parts.[182] By 22 October, this number had shrunk to 13 tanks.[183]

The defence success of 2 October was also discussed at length in the 'Deutsche Heeresmission' in Romania and shared with the Romanian General Staff via a memorandum (no.4) and addressed to General Steflea. The conclusion was that troops who overcame their fear of tanks could simply withstand such an attack. Although the Soviet tanks, mostly British and American-made, had broken through the German positions of the 3rd and 60th motorised German infantry divisions, these units had then repulsed the subsequent Soviet infantry. In the hinterland, the lone Soviet tanks were then destroyed one by one. The message to Steflea eventually increased the number of Soviet tanks destroyed to 110.[184]

Memorandum No. 4 seemed mainly intended to reassure its own concerns. Anyone looking at the documentation that has survived on the battle around Stalingrad can hardly claim that the Soviet offensive, which was soon to follow, was a real surprise. Operations were constantly under way to test the alertness of German troops and allies on the flanks. On 18 November, the Soviet offensive finally broke loose. First, the 3rd Romanian Army west of Stalingrad was hit by the Soviet South-West Front On the 20th followed the offensive in the area south of Stalingrad by the Stalingrad Front. Here, the 4th Romanian Army was attacked.

The situation immediately became very threatening. Operation Uranus was a carefully prepared Soviet offensive of more than a million men. The long flanks were difficult to defend and many units fell back in panic. Memorandum No 4 turned out to be a paper tiger now that the hour of truth had arrived. The Germans had started very late to build up a reception reserve in the hinterland of their confederates. In practice, this was the XXXXVIIIth Pz. Corps, which had been reluctantly and very late relinquished by Tank General Hoth for this purpose. This corps was barely bigger than a division and, with support from Romanian tanks (1st pz. Div.), tried to do what it could. On the northern flank, however, it could not prevent three Soviet armies from turning south-west via Chernyshevskaya and Osinovsky, while other ones rushed towards Kalatsch, where they made contact with units of the Stalingrad front and the 51st Army, which had turned north from Abganerovo after breaking through the Romanian lines of the 4th Army. Meanwhile, in Stalingrad, attacks by the Soviet 66th Army tied Paul's forces. On the 22nd, the encirclement ring at Kalatsch was closed. In Stalingrad, about 250,000 men were trapped and the fronts on the flanks had completely collapsed.[185]

On the first day of the attack, the Romanian 3rd Army, the Romanian 13th I.D. lost 115 officers and 3648 men, the 14th Division 98 officers and 2163 men. The 1st Kav.D. had to retreat to Kletskaya. Army commander Dumitrescu urged the support of mobile German units. Only the XXXXVIII Corps was available and this clashed directly with the 5th Soviet Tank Army when it intervened. Any operative movement possibility fell away with this. Part of the Romanian 3rd Army became encircled by the impetuous Soviet advance in the so-called Raspopinskaya Kessel. Between 20 and 25 November, several divisions fought for their lives. Soviet supremacy was 6:1 to 9:1, depending on which sector it was, and the Romanians had no chance. The easternmost part of the 3rd Army, in the area of Kletskaja and Serafimovich was in the worst shape. Three Romanian divisions were fighting for their lives here, under the command of Romanian general Mihai Lascar, who was also commander of the 6th Romanian division. Lascar was a broad and tall man, and bearer of both the 'Ritterkreuz' and the oak leaf. Historian Gosztony cited an account by the German liaison officer who spoke of the heroism with which the Romanians fought in their hopeless situation. When they ran out of ammunition, they went at the Russians with bayonets. A lieutenant of the 5th Romanian I.D. took out a Russian tank with an axe.[186]

The local Romanian commander wanted to expand with the Lascar group. He chose south-western direction (i.e. away from Stalingrad), but did not get permission. The 1st Romanian Pz. D., which had to rely on itself due to the loss of the radio installation and no longer had any contact with the XXXXVIIIth Pz. corps, tried to dislodge the Lascar group. Even so, the attack went completely wrong and the division was virtually destroyed.[187] The men in the Raspopinskaya Kessel did not have much to expect from the Germans either. The Germans were still hesitant about the situation. They still hoped to stabilise the front, but reversal was inevitable. Thereupon, the 3rd Romanian Army decided to turn directly to Antonescu, who in turn took responsibility and put pressure on Hitler, who agreed on 23 November. Even before consent, Lascar's units broke through. One tried to use the night of 22-23 November for this purpose. The breakout largely failed. Many units were destroyed. Generals Lascar and Mazarini were taken prisoner of war. A small group under General Sion's command of some 3,400 men managed to reach the German 22nd Pz. D. They had lost practically all their equipment along the way. Together with the armoured grenadiers of the 22nd division, Sion's men retreated to Tschernischewskaja, killing Sion, rifle in hand.[188] The German general staff tried to halt the retreat somehow, *'by force of arms if necessary'*, the order went out. It was hoped to build a new front behind the Tschur river. From behind the Italian front German units were cleared, the so-called 'Gruppe Hollidt', but the Romanian divisions hardly had to be counted on any longer. The 6th I.D. commanded by General Gheorghe Sanatescu largely capitulated and large parts of the 14th division also fell into POWs. The Germans threatened military tribunals and took away Romanian officers on paper troops that already effectively no longer existed. None of this could prevent a gap in the front of some 50 km.

On 20 November, the debacle south of Stalingrad began. The Stalingrad front bordered the Kalmuckensteppe here. Here, too, the Soviet attack focused above all on the Romanians and, as a result, the 4th Romanian Army received the full brunt. Administratively, this army fell under the 4th German Pz. Army. Immediately, the Romanian army's lines tore apart. The 20th Division was so out of sorts that it would end up with the trapped troops at Stalingrad. Again, the picture was two-fold. There was panic and Romanians rushed to the rear; other units bravely held out. For example, Gosztony reported on the 2nd artillery regiment of the 20th Romanian I.D. holding out to the last shell against Soviet T-34 tanks. This front lacked strategic reserve and motorised troops as well.[189]

When German commander Erich von Manstein arrived in Rostov on 26 November 1942 to put his affairs in order, he was told that both Romanian armies had been largely wiped out. Of the 22 divisions that Bucharest had at the front, four were still fully deployable, nine had been destroyed and nine others on the run. Consequently, Von Manstein did not get much further than an initial shelter behind the Tschur, deploying the 'Gruppe Hollidt' and the 'Gruppe Hoth'.[190] The gunpowder vapour had not yet cleared or the argument began over whose fault the debacle was. The Romanians were not in good standing with many German staff officers. There was much mutual irritation. An interesting telex of 6 December 1942 shed light on this. In it, the 'Heeresgruppe B' complained about soldiers of the 3rd Romanian Army (9th and 14th infantry divisions). These units operated in the area around Nowo Petrowka and Nowo Aidar and looted everything from the land (vegetables and cattle) and whatever else there was to eat. There was no communication with the German authorities about this and the Russians were asked nothing at all. 'The army group again asks the

Romanians to remove themselves from the 'Heeresgruppe B' area,' was the call from the German side.[191]

The German general Dorr did take the Romanians to task. He thought it *'unridiculous'* to blame the Romanians for the unfolding debacle, even though the breakthroughs had taken place there. The Romanians, he argued, had been a *'loyal ally'*, yet their divisions were too weak. Moreover, they had insufficient anti-tank artillery, which was also too light (3.7 cm guns). In addition, the divisions were spread over a long front and each division had to guard 20 km of front line, which was very big. The Soviets chose well where to attack. They preferred the Romanians and stayed away from the German divisions. The cause for this was perhaps most clearly illustrated in the memoirs of Frido von Senger und Etterlin, the commander of the 17th Pz. D. On a lone reconnaissance mission, a lone car approached across the endless snowfields. Von Senger und Etterlin stopped and out of the car stepped a Romanian division commander, a tall lean figure. *'The greeting was formal and stiff. The gentlemen spoke French to each other. From the Romanian general's attitude, a reserved and tired attitude about the alliance as a result of the defeat of his army was evident'*.[192]

The 14th Pz. D. made a relief attack towards the 1st Romanian cavalry division that was under siege. But this could no longer buoy things up. Things were not much better at Constantinescu's 4th Romanian Army in the Kalmuckensteppe. The German 29th I. D. (mot.) was deployed here in support, but this too was a drop in the ocean.[193] The only *'real'* reserve, the XXXXVIIIth Pz. Corps under General Ferdinand Heim (the Heim Corps), could only throw a dozen tanks into the fray, as well as some 40 Skoda tanks of the 1st Romanian Armoured Division, with which, however, as we saw, the connection was broken. The radio installation had been overrun by the Soviets. Heim's units could barely save themselves. The 22nd Pz. D. managed to fight its way westwards with difficulty and then had to turn around to take on the 15th Romanian I. D., who had stayed behind, to help. In doing so, the 22nd again ran into trouble. Hitler then used the unfortunate Heim as a scapegoat and he disappeared into prison for a period of time, only to return to military duty later in the war.[194]

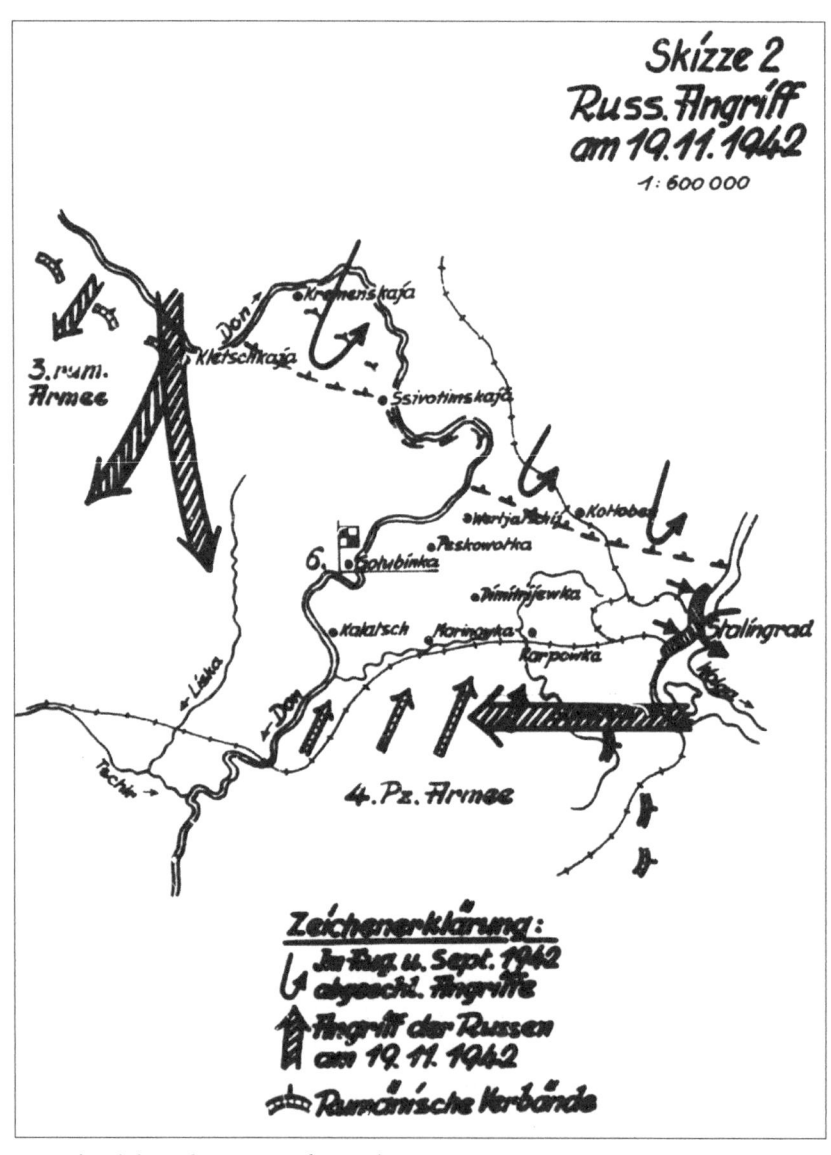

Soviet breakthrough 19 November 1942.

Soviet breakthrough 25 November 1942

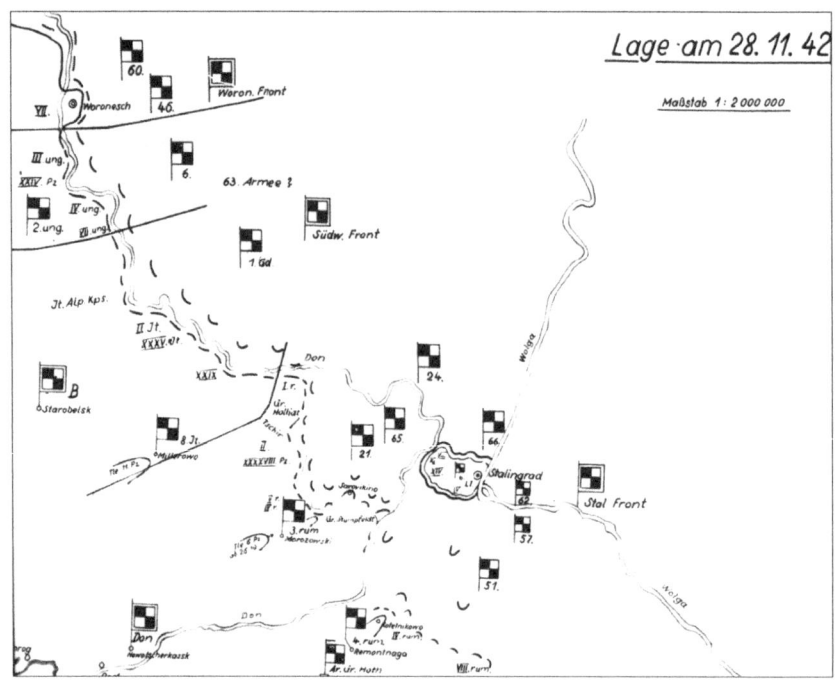

Situation at the front 28 November 1942.

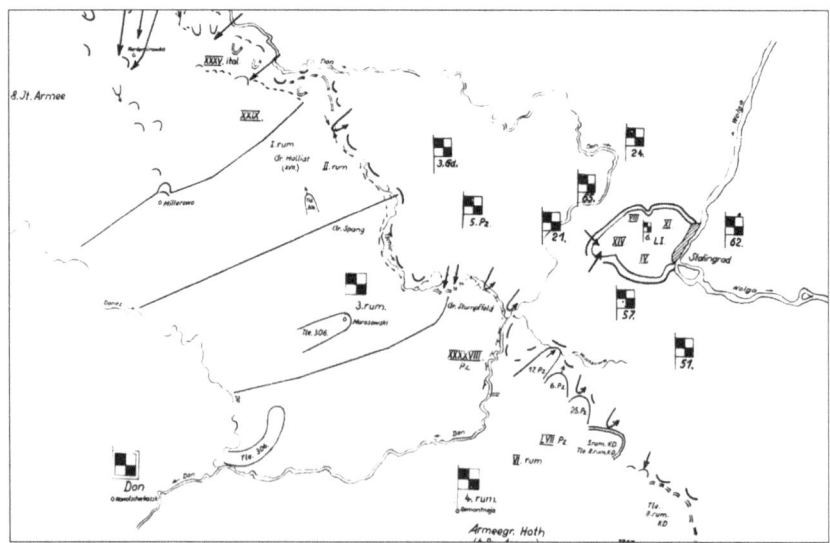

The encirclement of troops from the 6st army in Stalingrad.

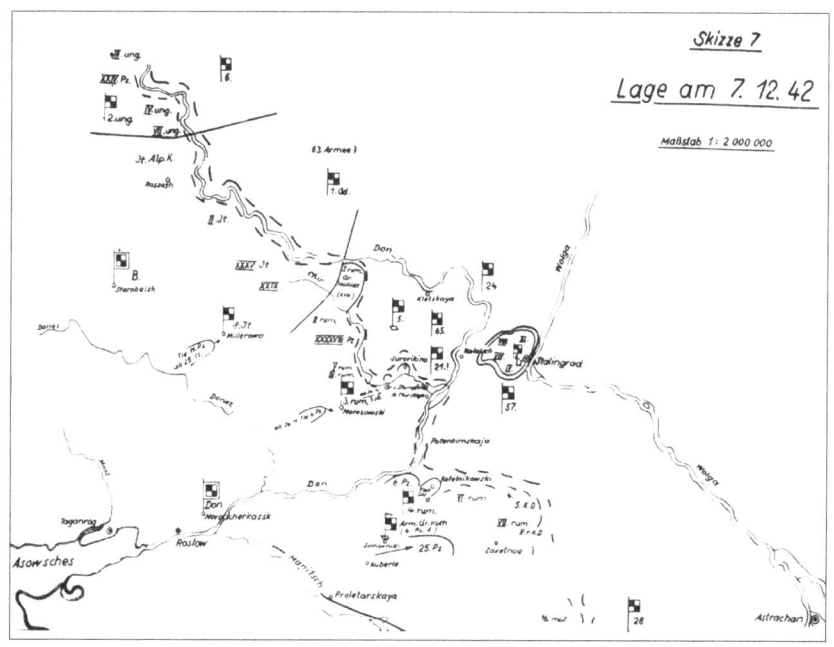

Map of the situation 7 December 1942.

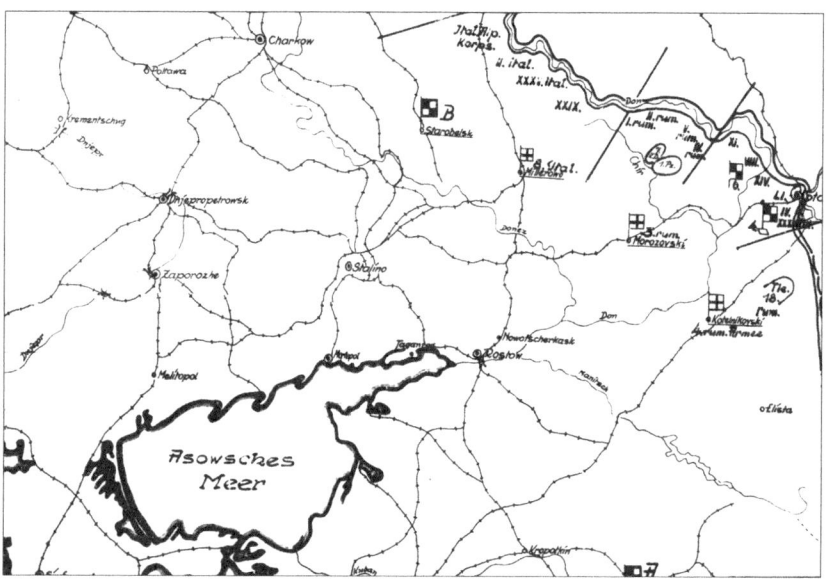

Situation at the Stalingrad front.

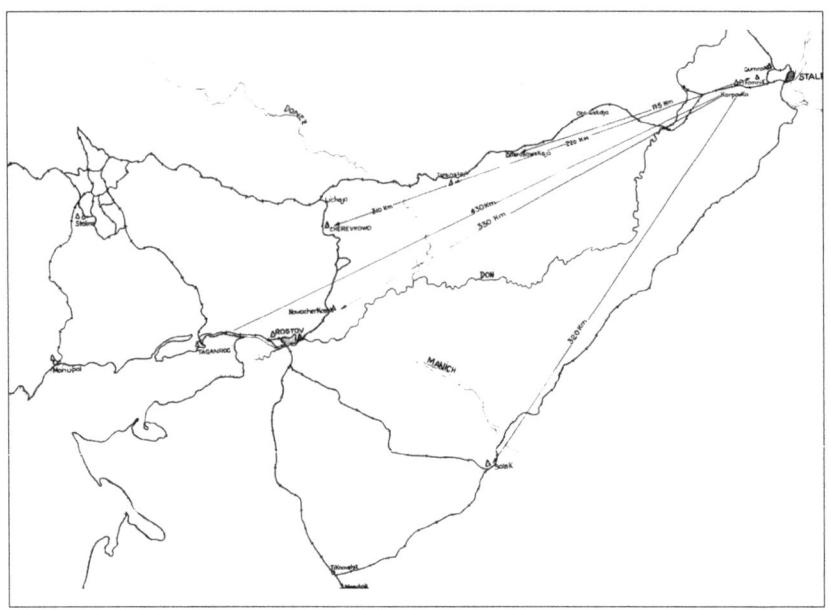

Air routes on the encircled Stalingrad.

The only right decision had been to withdraw the 6th Army from Stalingrad while it still could. The weakened XIVth. Pz.Corps could have been used as a crowbar for this purpose. However, Hitler chose a different solution, Stalingrad was declared a 'Festung' and help would have to come from outside. To reorganise, the Don army group was formed, with the 3rd Roumanian Army, the 6th Army, the 4th Pz.Army, the 4th Romanian Army and parts of the 11th Army. Reorganisations were very important. It had been calculated that the losses of 'Heeresgruppe A' in the Caucasus had now reached 85,000 men, nearly 12,000 of whom were killed. General Antonescu offered fresh troops, but given their poor state of training and equipment, this did not carry much weight.[195] While Paulus asked in vain for freedom of action at Stalingrad, an attempt began on 12 December to fight Stalingrad free from the Kotelnikovo area via operation *'Wintergewitter'*, in which the VIth and VIIth Romanian army corps also took part.

The attack of Hoth's armoured divisions made some progress, but they advanced hesitantly. The waterways running perpendicular to the direction of advance slowed the advance even more. In addition, the Soviets quickly brought in armoured troops to reinforce the southern flank of the Stalingrad front. With the occupation of Stalingrad, they hoped for a miracle, *'Der Manstein kommt'*, they whispered, referring to the German general Erich von Manstein, but the breakthrough failed to materialise. Hoth's armoured units operated in isolation and with little infantry support. On 21 December, the Pz.Rgt. 11 of the 6th Pz. D., the 'Gruppe Hünersdorff', reported from Wassiljewka that ammunition was almost used up. The Russians were within 15 metres of Hünersdorff's headquarters. Supplies of fuel were also extremely tight. The relief of Stalingrad had to be abandoned.[196]

Meanwhile, the Italians were attacked on the flanks of the front (16.12.1944) and maintained pressure on the 4th Romanian Army, which more or less went up in smoke. On this, the southern Donbow was cleared and the retreat of the 'Heeresgruppe A' from the Caucasus began. All this resulted in dramatic scenes, such as the encirclement of German units near Milerovo. In mid-January 1943, Hungarians became involved in dra- matic developments, with the breakthrough by the 2nd Hungarian Army at Storoschewoje. While Stalingrad was lost in February 1943, the Soviet army advanced as far as Kharkov and the gates of Rostov. The Nazi summer offensive had ended in a huge fiasco in the winter of 1943; to the detriment of the Romanians who had been sucked into this.[197]

Still during the battle, the Germans tried to calm the Romanians because the tension was, of course, palpable in Bucharest too. On 28 December 1942 - after a preliminary meeting with Hitler on the 21st - General Arthur Hauffe had had an audience with Antonescu. Hitler had tried to reassure Antonescu before that. The German setbacks at Stalingrad would not be so much military as logistical. Thereby, Hauffe assured, Berlin had not attacked Stalingrad for political or prestigious reasons, but to *flank cover* the 'Heeresgruppe A' in the Caucasus. Lack of supplies eventually killed the Germans. New railway lines were still functioning at only 60 per cent of capacity As a result of partisan activities, especially around the city of Kiev, they had trained German supplies. '*The Romanians did not starve anywhere except Stalingrad,*' Hitler informed Antonescu. '*And nowhere were they hungrier than the Germans*'.[198]

Von Manstein tried to regain control of the situation at the Don army group. Above all, wild flight had to be stopped. Interesting correspondence has been preserved between Von Manstein and several Romanian commanders, such as General Steflea, from the general headquarters and with the commander of the 3rd army, Dumitrescu. These dealt primarily with the Romanian question of why the Romanians had not retreated earlier from the overstretched flanks. Von Manstein therefore argued that the Romanians should have done so much earlier, because just before or during the battle the Romanians on the retreat would simply have become easy prey for the armoured Soviet units. There was no alternative for the Romanians but to fight as they had done, Von Man- stein concluded with military logic. As consolation, he informed the Romanians that the Germans (4th Pz.leger) were still fighting, while the Romanians were fleeing like blind men.[199]

This correspondence showed that the 4th Army, consisting of the VIth and VIIth infantry corps (divisions 2, 18, 1 and 4) and the Popescu cavalry corps (5th and 6th cavalry divisions), had been completely written off militarily. On 31.12.1942, it was also decided to put the Romanian troops under the command of the German II Army Corps. Von Manstein further informed the Romanians that all individually falling back men and units would be received at the German bridgehead near Rostov, to be reassembled from there. The Romanians were used there as a 'Sicherheitsbesatzung'.[200]

The Romanians were in pretty serious shape. A document dated 2 January 1943 showed that the 1st Romanian Armoured Division, as part of the 'Armeegruppe Hollidt' (XVIIth Army Corps), consisted of only 2,500 men, 666 of whom were combat troops. These still had the disposal of 3 PzKpfw IV tanks and a handful of artillery, the bulk of which had been ceded to the 5th and 7th Cavalry Divisions.[201] A report compiled after the battle further illustrated the material losses. The Romanian troops had left 189,000 rifles on the battlefield, 6813 light machine guns, 2184 heavy machine guns, hundreds of artillery pieces and 114 tanks had been lost, 106 of them with the Romanian 3rd Army.[202]

Romanian units not directly harmed by the fighting at Stalingrad were in abominable shape as well. The Ia of the German 9th I.D. stationed on the Caucasus front, wrote to the Vde Corps about the situation at the Romanian 3rd Geb.D. The German 9th I.D. was separate from the Romanian unit, nor was it involved or responsible for provisioning the unit. Nevertheless, the division was so worried that it was reported anyway.

Thus, the number of officers and non-commissioned officers would be at a questionably low level. NCOs had long been in short supply and officers went on leave remarkably often. Most of the Romanian army's company commanders held the rank of 'Gefreiter' and this was the reason why the Romanian troops often did not perform well. The major losses suffered by the division had been replaced by combing the unit's troop units. This in itself was not bad, but because of this, 20% of the front troops consisted of poorly trained soldiers. Combat strength declined as a result. The situation of horses within the division was disasterous too. The 3rd Geb.D. had arrived at the front with 7,000 horses in September 1942. By February 1943, 3,000 of these had already died. On the orders of the German Vth

Army Corps, of the remaining 4,000 horses, 2,000 were taken from the division to be reinforced at Taman. The remaining 2,000 horses could not be taken care of either, so that at the time the 9th I.D. was reported, some 10 horses still died daily. As a result, the 3rd Romanian Geb.D. could no longer maintain its provisions on its own. In the process, the division had become immobile. The hope was now focused on an early spring so the horses could graze.

In defence of the Romanians, it needs to be said that they were divided and allocated areas whose soil had already been *'exhausted'* by German units. This left the Romanians struggling to live off the land. As a result, Romanian units were poor in ammunition and supplies and artillery and could barely move. A 19 March 1943 report to the XXXXIV Army Corps stated that all 22 Pak (4.7 cm) of the 3.Geb.D. had become immobile. This was also true of 12 12.2 cm mortars, as well as the pioneer flame throwers. Only 4 7.5 cm Pak were movable over good roads.[203]

This had major consequences. Thus, the German Gren.Rgt. 57 would be relieved by the Romanian 21. Geb.Jg.Btl., but on arrival the Romanians were found to have hardly any ammunition with them. As a result, the German regiment had to remain in position and provide its own ammunition from its own stocks. The 6th Romanian Jg.Btl. was deployed with the German Gren.Rgt. 116, but was not able to maintain its own supply either. A Romanian 'Reiterschwadron' had that problem too. The state of the Romanian uniforms was worrying as well. These were badly worn and the boots were in bad shape. According to the Ia of the German 9th I.D., 30 per cent of the soldiers of the 3rd Romanian Geb.D. no longer had boots! The division had reported this frequently and the 9th I.D. had done the same for its Romanian colleagues, but supplies from Romania were not forthcoming and the Germans had not provided them with any. The Ia concluded by saying that the Romanian leadership was doing its utmost to remain master of the problems, but that good will did not always win out over reality. In the opinion of the 9th I.D., the 3rd Romanian Geb.D. could not actually be deployed as a closed compound. The advice was to put parts of the division under the command of the 9th I.D. and evacuate the rest to the Crimea.[204]

The 9th I.D.'s call was only partially heeded. In the following weeks, many Romanian units were dispersed among German troops. This gave the following picture: At 9th I.D. the Romanian 2./Gr.Rgt.420, Geb.Jg.Btl. 94, 1./ Jg.Rgt./ 207, 4./F.A.R. 616, 2./Geb.Jg.Rgt.13, 6. Geb.Jg.Btl., 21.Geb.Jg.Btl and 22nd Geb.Jg.Btl. In artillery, several Romanian batteries served from May 1943 with the 9th I.D. (2.A.R.37) and 7 Medium Pak. At the 97th Jäger D., 4 Romanian battalions served. Of I.R. 94 and 95 as well as artillery. Several battalions, including from I.R.96 and the independent battalion 994 served with the 101st Jäger.D., as well as artillery from A.R.42. Among the pioneers served the Romanian pioneer battalion 19, the so-called 'Gruppe Marincescu'.[205]

Retreat from Kuban bridgehead

The Stalingrad debacle was a turning point in the relationship between the two countries. In memory of the victims of the battle, a mass was celebrated in Bucharest Cathedral at which King Michael and his generals were present, including Ion Antonescu, Mihai Antonescu and others. The military chapel of the Guards Battalion was the company of honour. Funeral services were held in other churches across Romania at the same time.[206]

Hard work was being done to keep the coalition together. Leaning on the Romanian sense of mystique, a special form had been chosen to coordinate mutual affairs between the marshal's circle and German interests, represented above all by the German envoy Manfred Freiherr von Killinger. In the so-called M.A. club, senior German and Romanian representatives met on Wednesdays. There was free food and drink - from 'Judengeld' as one German police official wrote - and that's where business was done. Besides Von Killinger, Mihai Antonescu, armaments minister Gheorghe Dobre, police commander general Emil Palageanu, leader of the 'Judenzentrale' Radu Lecca, the head of the German embassy's information office SA-Oberführer Roedel, press-attaché Von Ritgen and Romania's secret service chief Christescu took part in the sessions. What the term M.A. stood for was not entirely clear; it was supposed to mean 'Mittwoch Abend', or 'Marschall Antonescu'. In any case, there was the parallel with the secret 'Mittwochgesellschaft'.

This *'club'* had been founded in 1863 and consisted of 12 regular members. These members in turn invited others. They were all people of influence, so that political power could be steered from the wings. The M.A. club also had 12 permanent members and served an equal purpose. With Von Killinger at the head, an old loyal party colleague of Hitler's from the very beginning was at the helm. Von Killinger was a former naval officer and had been a member of the

Ehrhardt naval brigade that had been involved in the 'Kapp-putsch' against the Weimar Republic in 1920. In addition, he had helped put down Kurt Eisner's council republic in Bavaria during the same period. He had served in the 'Reichstage' for the NSDAP, was a senior officer in the SA and SS, and had served as consul for Germany in the US before becoming ambassador to Slovakia. Bucharest would be his last post.[207] According to Böhme, Von Killinger leaned completely on the *'unreliable'* Lucca and Von Killinger had no real contacts with the Romanian top brass. Not much later, however, Böhme had to back down. Von Killinger, as a former party comrade, could not take his criticism. Even the fact that the head of the Romanian secret service was in the M.A. club, as did Mihai Antonescu, indicated that there were politically useful contacts here.

It seemed more likely that the conflict went back to the competence struggle of party versus the 'SS'. Boehme, as police commander, had the cover of the Reichsführer-SS Heinrich Himmler, while Von Killinger fell back on the party.[208]

Thus one tried to iron out the creases. One found support in a tirade by Romanian philosopher, professor and Minister of Propaganda Nichifor Crainic, who reiterated the opinions of Nazi propaganda minister Joseph Goebbels and Nazi ideologue Alfred Rosenberg regarding the barbarism of *'Jewish-Bolshevism'* and the fact that this was the decisive battle for Europe. Crainic was an ideologue of anti-Semitism and had been an inspiration for the ideas behind the Iron Guard.[209]

The fire of hatred still burned, but there was also doubt about the outcome of the war. The first time doubt arose was in the winter of 1941-1942, when the German attack for Moscow had stopped, and there had been setbacks on the southern front near the town of Rostov, where the Soviets were stubbornly defending. This had led to a crisis at the 'Heeresgruppe Süd', where in the Romanians were operating. When commander von Rundstedt retreated because one was *'at the end of his strength'*, Hitler had him telegraphed directly from headquarters the *Wolfsschanze* that he should *'stay where he was'*. Von Rundstedt still argued that it was not a retreat but a front reduction ('Frontbegradigung'). Nevertheless, he was replaced by Hitler. The withdrawal of the experienced Von Rundstedt led to worried reactions among the allies, especially in Romania and Hungary. The 'Heeresgruppe Süd', in consultation with General Halder of the OKW, therefore had a letter sent out to Bucharest and Budapest stressing that Von Rundstedt had been suffering from heart problems since November 1941 and had therefore requested Hitler's resignation on 3 December, which would have been granted to him in honour on his birthday.

General Von Reichenau was to take over from Von Rundstedt, but in January he was stricken with a brain haemorrhage and replaced by general Field Marshal Feodor von Bock. The declaration by the 'Heeresgruppe Süd' to remove the unrest among the Romanians was addressed to General Jacobici of the Romanian General Staff before Bucharest and was an attempt at damage limitation.[210] In practice, Von Rundstedt had dismissed Hitler's decision to stand firm as *'madness'*, which was the actual reason for the officer's resignation. Outwardly, however, appearances were maintained.[211]

After Stalingrad, a German loss became increasingly likely. That this was seen as such in Bucharest became clear from contacts between Finland and Romania. Both countries had the agreement that they were allies of nazi Germany and so there were common concerns. To his Finnish counterparts, Mihai Antonescu openly complained about the poor German attitude towards the *'smaller states'*. He concluded that Germany was no longer Romania's *'friend'*. In addition, he had doubts about the struggle in the east. He did not rule out the possibility of a new *'Molotov-Ribbentrop Pact'*; a peace in the east.

Furthermore, General Constantin Pantazi complained more or less openly about the deteriorating situation. He pointed out that the Germans were shredding the forces, partly because of fears of invasion in the west, while the western Allies were winning the battle for the Atlantic. He believed that the German position in the Mediterranean was far from strong. Bucharest took into account a British landing in the Balkans, which would have consequences for Romania.[212]

Another tail on Stalingrad followed in June 1943 and there was something of a sensation. The Romanian press, as well as the Italian, reported that contact had been made with Stalingrad survivors,

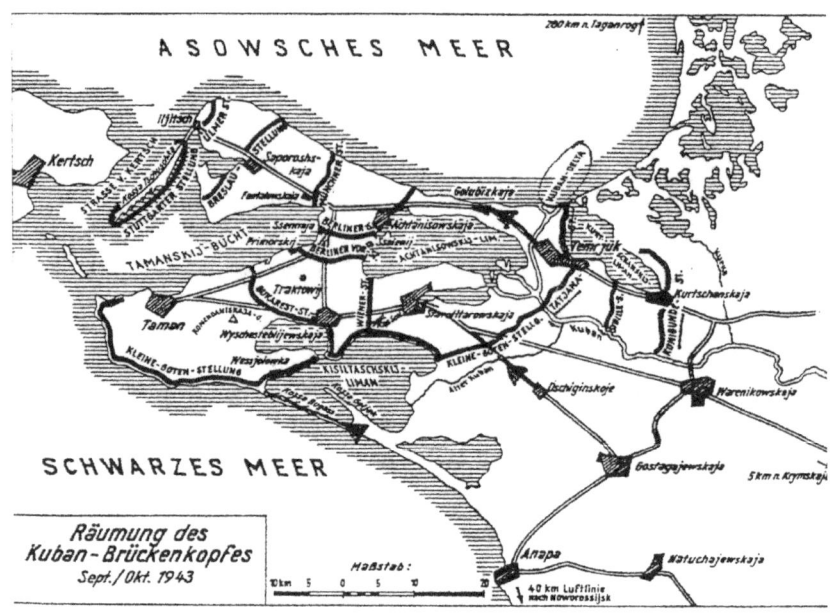

Evacuation of the 'Kuban-Brückenkopfes'.

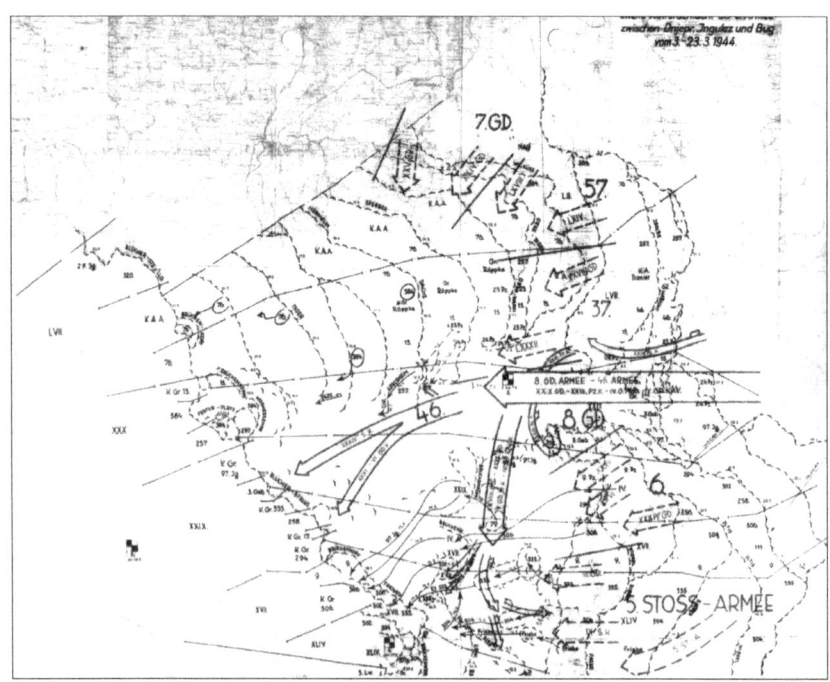

3 March 1944, The diverse German 'Stellungen' and front lines.

including Romanians and Italians, through the Turkish Crescent - the local branch of the Red Cross. These were said to be in prisoner-of-war camps east of the Urals in Siberia. This created a lively correspondence of relatives trying to make contact. In Germany, there was a reluctance to make contact. The final battle in Stalingrad had been memorialised as a heroic effort and people wanted to keep it that way. Soon messages did come through, via Major Dr Dobberkau and Generaloberst Heitz who had been taken prisoner by the Soviets. This showed that they were stuck in prisoner camp No 27, where Paul the commander of the 6th Army was also located. Since some of the officers defected to the anti-Nazi 'National- kommitee Freies Deutschland', this was an extremely embarrassing matter for Berlin.[213] Meanwhile, the Germans were trying to keep the Romanians on board.

The situation in 1943 was not too rosy. Bucharest had lost 2/3 of its troops, and by November 1943 the number of dead on the Romanian side had risen to more than 250,000 men. Despite this, they tried with simplified forces to rebuild the Romanian army, but their options were limited. On 12 April 1943, Hitler had received Antonescu at Klessheim Castle in Austria and tried to encourage him. Moreover, he had issued decrees reporting that the Romanian army had been treated with respect by the German 'Militär'. The fact that such a signal from Hitler was needed already spoke volumes. Antonescu was very concerned about the Romanian troops still on the front, which were mainly in the Kuban bridgehead and in Crimea. Hitler reassured him in that regard, but even so Romania sent out envoys to the western Allies and the Soviets about peace. This went through Italy, the Vatican, Bern, Lisbon and Madrid, and at the end of the year with the Soviets still through Stockholm. Meanwhile, the fighting continued.[214]

The omens were no longer good. A 'Stimmungsbericht' from the Ukraine of 12 April 1943 reported dulled apathy in the areas, people were simply trying to survive. The Ukrainian propaganda department that drafted the message believed that the Ukrainian people were lead to wonder whether they were enslaved by Bolshevism or enslaved by National Socialism. Three days later, the battle plan for the summer of 1943, Operation *'Zitadelle'*, in the front arc around the town of Kursk, was drawn up. Even this offensive did not bring the decision and had to be aborted prematurely due to Western Allied operations against Italy (Allied landing on Sicily) and Benito Mussolini's shaky position.

In an attempt to optimise mobilisation, the Germans had begun, with the consent of the Antonescu regime, to recruit 'Volksdeutschen' from Romania for the German army. On a smaller scale, recruiting for the Waffen-SS had already taken place in the past, and to this end Gottlob Berger, of the SS-Hauptamt, had urged Himmler to recruit the popular 'Volksdeutsche' Romanian general Arthur Phleps for the Waffen-SS, which had happened in the summer of 1941. It was hoped even then that this would have a pulling effect.[215]

Andreas Schmidt and the 'VoMi' also made efforts to win recruits. In doing so, they were so energetic that they more or less started *'stealing'* soldiers from the Romanian army. These were then branded as deserters by Bucharest. At Schmidt's insistence, nearly 1,000 men had defected to Germany, to enter German service. Like the so-called 'season workers' in agriculture, they had been taken by boat via the Danube to the 'Reich' and recruited there. Under pressure from Berlin, Schmidt and the 'VoMi' were eventually pushed back to avoid diplomatic riots. Outside the official offices, however, Berger continued to encourage Schmidt to continue. The pressure was often so great that the volunteer principle, which applied to joining the Waffen-SS, came under increasing pressure. People spoke of 'Beutedeutsche'.[216] On 30 July 1943, Gottlob Berger, chief of the SS-Hauptamt, reported that 41,560 men had been recruited, of whom over 17,000 were for the Waffen-SS. The lion's share went to 'Ersatz' units, which in turn distributed the 'Volksdeutschen' to various units. The SS Geb.Jg.Ausb.u.Ers.Batl. 7 and the SS-Gren. Ers.-Batl, 'Ost' were allocated the most troops with 4829 and 3262 troops respectively. The first unit was attached to the 7.SS-Freiwilligen Gebirgs-Division 'Prinz Eugen' which operated on the partisan front in occupied Yugoslavia. 510 'Volksdeutschen' were assigned to the newly created 'Bosniaks' division, composed of Bosnian Muslims, the 13. 'Waffen-Gebirgs-Division' the 'SS Handschar'. About a thousand men joined German concentration camps like *Buchenwald, Dachau, Mauthausen, Neuengamme, Sachsenhausen* and *Stutthof*. Different police battalions in Iglau, The Hague and Maastricht were assigned troops as well.[217]

Himmler was very pleased and complimented Berger on the result. *'You have done infinitely much for the fatherland and the Führer with this, and also with what you all did before this'*.[218] In practice, the integration of the Romanian 'Volksdeutschen' into the ranks of existing units proved not so easy. Several hundred eventually joined the Dutch Waffen-SS in the area of the 'Heeresgruppe Nord'. *'There is little affinity. They adopt an introverted and distrustful attitude. Food is not distributed. Among themselves, they spoke in Romanian,'* one Hague volunteer characterised the new cooperation.[219]

From the ranks of Volksgruppenführer Andreas Schmidt, pressure was mounting for Romanian 'Volksdeutschen' to choose the Waffen-SS in particular. Not all 'Volksdeutschen' thanked him for this. Another front man of the 'Volksdeutsche' community, Hans Otto Roth, spoke up for his son Herbert Roth, who served in the Romanian army and wished to stay there. Andreas Schmidt thereupon publicly called Roth *'Drückeberger'* and *'Feigling'*. This only escalated things further and, via two Romanian generals, an open request for a duel was handed to Schmidt, which he wisely declined. Thereupon, the Roths chose the legal route and took Schmidt to court for defamation. It did not come to a trail during the war.[220]

By July 1943, most of the Romanian army was within the framework of 'Heeresgruppe A', mainly in Crimea and in the so-called Kuban bridgehead, which had been formed in February 1943 after the German withdrawal from the Caucasus conceived as a springboard for renewed offensive to the oil fields. But it came to nothing. In late August, early September 1944, Soviet Marshal Tymoshenko's Soviet North Caucasian Front launched the offensive against the Kuban bridgehead, over which the German 17th Army, commanded by General Erwin Jaenecke, held sway next to Crimea. The attack, carried out by three armies with four corps, 21 divisions and five brigades mainly hit the Vth and XXXXIVth Corps. It was a frontal rush, supported by landings in the back of the German troops. This produced dangerous situations, but the landings were repulsed by the regiments *'Biermann'* and *'Babel'* (Rgt. 123 and 666) of the 50th and 370th I.D.[221] The battle for the Kuban bridgehead led to a retreat in stages, roughly from Krymskaya to Novorossiejsk, to Anapa and to Temrynk and slowly to the coast on the Kerch Strait. In September 1943, several Romanian units served on this front, the 1st and 4th Geb.D. as part 3l of the Vde Corps, as well as 9 Kav.D. and 19th I.D. in the Romanian Kav. Corps and the 10th Romanian I.D, within the XXXXIX Geb. Corps.

Pressed by the situation elsewhere on the front, Hitler belatedly gave the order to clear the Kuban bridgehead on 4 September 1943. The Germans retreated from position to position. Thus, those days the 50th I.D. crossed the Kerch Strait westwards on 27 September via the *Tatjana Stellung*. In the months before, superfluous soldiers and civilians had already been flown out and across on a daily basis, dispersing the crowds and enabling logistics to cope. Motorised units had been shipped as a priority. These were needed on the *Mius front* and could only play a limited role in the scaffolding war anyway, in which the battle for Kuban had ended. On 4 February, the shipment of the 13th Pz.D. had already been initiated, with the troop going first, so that a 'Schatten-Division' was already in Crimea when the last armed units came over. This made the division immediately deployable elsewhere.[222]

Among the retreating units was the 19th Romanian I.D. commanded by General Lacatusu. On 19 September, it embarked on the retreat to the *Kleine-Gotenstellung*. The unit was divided into several 'Marschgruppen', such as the 'Gruppe Oberst Florescu' (I.R. 96), 'Gruppe Oberst Gaspar' (I.R.95) the independent Inf.Btl. 994 and pi. Btl. 19 and a series of smaller sections. In the *Kleine-Gotenstellung*, the lines were reformed. The 19th 'Police Company' had taken up positions at key street junctions and assigned the units the new positions. The artillery and Pak were given central positions. They had learned from Stalingrad. As a reserve, small combat groups were formed behind the various sectors, such as the Pioneer Com- pany and 2 platoons of Bandenjäger (partisan fighters) behind Oberst Florescu's positions (I.R. 96, A.A. 19, 2 platoons of anti-tank artillery (Pak) of Pak company 19.)

While the 19th Romanian I.D. together with 4 German divisions of the XXXXI- Xth Geb. Korps held the *Kleine-Gotenstellung,* other divisions crossed the Kerch waterway behind them. First to go were the German 125th I.D., the 101 Jg.D. and the 9th I.D. followed by the Romanian 1st Geb.D., the Romanian 4th Geb.D. and the Romanian 10th I.D. On 3 October, a further retreat towards the *Bukarester-Stellung* and towards Taman followed for the units covering the retreat. Apart from some Soviet air raids, things remained calm at the front, so the 19th division could eventually be shipped out as well.[223]

In the retreat, the Germans destroyed the oil installations and everything of any strategic value in the area. The port of Noworossijsk was also destroyed so the Russian fleet could not use this and many other facilities for the time being. The narrow waterway through Kerch and the Sea of Azov was blocked by sunk ships. Civilians who could be used by the Red Army were deported.[224] On 8 October, the last units, troops of the 4th Geb.D. and the 97th Jg.D., withdrew to the 'Breslau Stelling', and at 03.00 initially went unnoticed by the Soviets in a final jump to the coast. After this, it came to some fierce fighting, with nastotting Soviet infantry and tanks. Yet under cover of artificial haze, provided by the Regensburg-born General der Nebeltruppe Hermann Ochsener, the last units were embarked at Iljitisch. A last-minute Soviet tank attack near Saporoshskaya was geno- erated by the 'Nebelwerfer' under heavy fire. Possibly 23 of the 30 attacking tanks were knocked out.[225]

By 9 October, the retreat from the Kuban bridgehead had been concluded. This had truly been a logistical undertaking of stature for the 'Heeresgruppe A' of Field Marshal Von Kleist and General Jaenecke of the 17th Army in cooperation with the 'Befehlshaber Strasse Kertsj', General Förster. Existing documents show that already by 26 July 1943, more than half a million people, almost 100,000 horses, 53,000 vehicles and 250,000 tonnes of goods had been transported from Kuban across the Kerch Strait. The closing report on 9 October reported the evacuation of 177,355 German servicemen and 50,139 allies - most of them Romanians. 28,436 'Hiwis' were also evacuated, 42,899 horses brought to safety, 1,815 pieces of artillery and 72 'Sturmgeschützen' and tanks retrieved. To top it all off, 109 locomotives and 1150 wagons had even been transported. People did not want to leave anything behind for the Soviets.

The evacuation was well organised, *'reibungslos'*, as one German document stated. The crossing had succeeded in part because the evacuation of *'superfluous'* troops had begun on time. These units had been systematically evacuated every day since March, even before the 'Führerbevel', partly by boat, partly via the pioneers (emergency bridges, cable cars) and partly by plane. The pioneers had done the lion's share (up to and including May 1943) with over 181,000 evacuated, followed by over 71,000 men via the navy and over 10,000 men by the 'Luftwaffe'. The evacuation was celebrated almost as a *'victory'*. Oberst Henke, of the 'Pioniers-landungs-Regiment' 770, was awarded the 'Ritterkreuz' for his work, and the 'Kommandeur des Oberbaustabes' 23, general Bacher, who had organised the port facility and quays, obtained the 'Deutsches Kreuz im Gold'. According to the 'Heeresgruppe A', the morale of the troops had not suffered from the retreat. Due to the tight organisation, the troops were still confident and felt superior to the Red Army. Apart from this logistical success, the battle had been a drain. Relative to Soviet losses, 41,271 'counted' dead troops, but estimated around 250,000 losses in dead, wounded and missing between 01.02.1943 and 09.10.1943, German losses were small but still significant. During the same period, the Germans lost, according to the Ia 'Meldungen' of the 'Heeresgruppe A' (dated 09.10.1943) 11,606 troops died, and 1896 Romanians troops passed. 43,489 Germans were wounded, against 7264 Romanians, and 4368 Germans went missing as well as 806 Romanians. In addition, over 14,000 Soviet soldiers had been taken prisoner of war, and 863 tanks and over 2,000 aircraft shot down. What received no public attention was the fact that military justice should have regularly intervened against forms of defeatism at the front.[226] After the successful retreat, the (emergency) bridges were destroyed.[227]

At the same time as the perils surrounding the Kuban bridgehead, fighting on the Mius-Donjet front, later the Dnieper front and then in the Crimea, was sharpening. In August 1943, the Mius front ignited. The Germans faced the same problem everywhere. The front lines were too long and the troops too few for overall coverage of the front. Many units that were there were risked in offensives (Operation *'Zitadelle'* near Kursk) or spent on maintaining redundant fronts (Kuban). Strategic front reductions were not made either. This left troops missing in the hinterland who could strike back *'aus der Nachhand'* as reserves. This limited the operative possibilities for the German army. This was due to Hitler clinging to every metre of terrain. With this, the German army lost many opportunities and would eventually lead to the dismissal of two very capable strategists, Von Manstein and Von Kleist, whom he had had at his disposal on the Southern Front.[228]

Mius and Wotan Theorem

On the day of the closing report on the Kuban evacuation, the diary of the 'Heeresgruppe A' for the 6th Army reported: '*Virtually all along the front the Red Army launched the attack*', as if seeking revenge for the escape of the 17th Army.[229] But the operations were separate. The Soviet South-West and South Front faced the German 1st Pz.Army on the Doniets and the German 6th Army on the Mius. On 17 July, the Soviet offensive had erupted. In the north at the 1st Pz.Army, only a breakthrough followed, with Stalino as the thrust direction. The Soviets did not get that far but the bridgeheads were a fact. The intention was to combine this with a breakthrough from the *Mius front* to create an encirclement of the German army group in the so-called Donjets balcony. After an artillery bombardment, which took place at 05.00 began, the Soviets attacked. A breakthrough followed which, against Soviet custom, was exploited during the night to break through further through the front area of the German 111th I.D near Kalinowka. By the next day, this had created a kilometre-wide gap in the front, where the Red Army's 5th shock army rolled forward. As a result, the stationary German front was out of alignment. Mobile units of the 13th Pz.D. tried to cushion the attack in the open terrain. Although the Soviets had already lost 114 tanks on the 20th, the Germans were unable to close the *Mius front* immediately.

In fact, there was only one chance left to save things and that was a direct and well-organised counterstrike by units of the 13th Pz.D. More mobile reserves the southern army group did not have, except for some smaller units in the Crimea, but their transport to the front would take too long.[230] [231] However, papers of a Soviet officer had fallen into German hands and these showed that the tank units of the 4th Ukrainian front were smaller than was assumed previously. Perhaps there was another chance. On the 20th, the battle group assembled within the framework of the XXIX Army Corps for the counter- thrust, which began at 2pm.

Surprised, the Soviets were thrown back and Ssemenowski was retaken, as was Heubel 188.4 km south of this place. The 4th Ukrainian front realised what was at stake. If the Germans could again entrench themselves in their lines, a tough battle of positions awaited. Tanks were directed forward. In a few hours, 43 Soviet tanks were destroyed, which was symbolic of the heaviness of the fighting. From the south, the 6th German Army thrust north and from the north, the German 1st Pz.Army tried to reach out to them and squeeze and surround the Soviet breakthrough. Corps XXIX and XVII came to hearing distance from each other. The grenadiers heard the exchanges of gunfire on the hills 175.5 and 188.4 but they lacked the strength for the final thrust. *'The Russian supremacy was too great,'* noted the war diary of Major Dr Franck, attached to the 6th Army. To avoid encirclement, the German units had to fall back.

In a last attempt to restore the important position via *'offensive'* defence, a second German attempt was made on 23 August. Before that, reinforcements arrived from the Crimea, but they were weaker than expected. The 13th Pz.D. was by no means at full strength. The aim was to destroy the Soviet units gathered around Krinitschka by surprise. To that end, the combat group, *Kampfgruppe Picker,* had to recapture hill 188.4. The XXIX Army Corps was to support this attack with a thrust to the north. On the eve of Picker's push, the infantry situation at the front deteriorated to such an extent that here and there positions were lost and supplies were endangered. Even the 111th I.D., which was hit right at the start of the fighting, had to cling tenaciously to the Uspenskaya bridgehead. Picker's attack initially met with success. However, around hill 157.3 near Alexejewka, the attack stalled. Exhaustive fighting ensued and the battle group quickly lost tanks. The final thrust of six km. could not be bridged.

As soon as darkness fell, the 13th Pz.D. was taken from the front and moved south via Kuteinikowo. Here they again tried to tackle the Soviets in the flank, together with the 'Kampfgruppe' Von Bila. The battle undulated up and down: *'Whoever stays on the battlefield a minute longer than the opponent wins,'* the army group mused. *'As usual, the Soviets did not shy away from losses,'* noted the chronicle of the 13th Pz.D. after the war. There were local successes, the 13th Pz.D. captured several hundred prisoners and a lot of equipment. However, the locals turned against the Germans and the gap in the front remained. On the 26th, the 298th Red Army tank was fired, but the bottle neck could not be closed. And this was the beginning of the encirclement and breakout of the XXIX Army Corps at Taganrog and the fall back to the *Schildkröten-Stellung*, between 27 August and 4 September 1943.

The average occupation rate of the German front was still 86 men per km of front line, and the German army was up against an eightfold superiority. The quarter-million man troops that Hitler had left more or less senseless in the Kuban bridgehead were now missed. When their evacuation began on the 7th, the *Mius front* was already beyond rescue. On the night of 3 to 4 September, the retreat on the *Schildkröten-Stellung*, which ran roughly from the area east of Mariupol across Makejewka to Konstantinowka, was completed.[232]

Once the front was moving, it also became clear that the *Schildkröten-Stellung* could not be sustained. The Germans decided to take their losses in an attempt to get the 'Heeresgruppe Süd' behind the *Dnieper Line* in one piece. Since the number of armoured and mobile troops was small, the retreat was phased and from position to position, so that they fell back- via the *Krokodil-Stellung* and the *Salamander-Stellung*, which was reached on the 9th, to the *Natter-Lurch-Stellung* around the 14th and 15th of September, which ran roughly from the Sea of Azov across Kuibyschewo along the banks of the Gaitschul. The Soviets constantly tried to break through and get to the Dnieper earlier than the Germans. At various times, this resulted in dangerous situations, such as fighting between the Soviet vanguards and the German 17th I.D. who narrowly held out in the *Krokodil-Stellung*.

This was followed by the retreat to the *Panther-Wotan-Stellung*, which was meant to be a line running practically the entire length of the eastern front and was the German answer to the lack of offensive options. The line extended from the mouth of the Narva River along Lake Pepius to the Black Sea. Largely, the line south of Lake Pepius

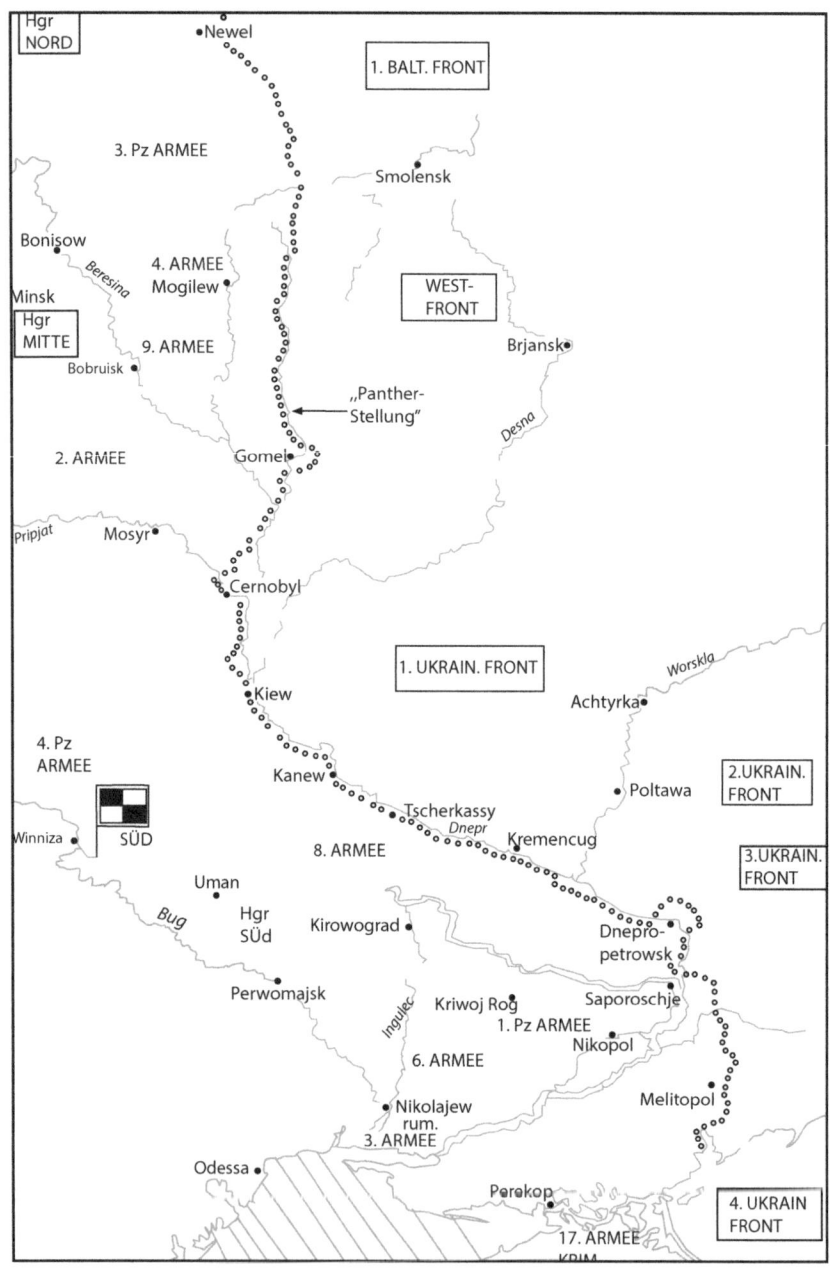

Panther-Stellung.

(the *Wo- tan-Stellung*) followed the banks of the Dnieper. However, since they wanted to protect the Crimea and the Dnieper curved to the west there, the line had been extended to the area east of the river. The area north of Peius, which was marked as the *Panther Line*, had been extended back longer . As many as 50,000 construction troops and Baltic civilians had worked on the 700km-long and built about 3,000 bunkers, as well as endless kilometres of barbed wire and minefields.[233] Ernst Friderici, the leader of the stage area ('Korpsrückwärts'), had indicated that, in addition to 10,000 guard troops, he would need another 220,000 workers to get the job done.[234] This was an impossible project in the time frame available. South of Pepius, therefore, they had not come far. Besides the lack of the waterway, this was the weakest link in the German defences. From 16 to 20 September 1943, the 'Heeresgruppe Süd' had retreated on this position. The Soviets had made a spectacular terrain gain. The Germans had literally had to run for their lives without it becoming a disorganised flight. Marches of 120 km in 48 hours were no exception. The Red Army too paid a blood toll for the battle with 492 tanks lost in the battle between Mius and *Wotan-Stellung* alone.

Roughly speaking, the new front ran from Tscherkassy over Krementschuk to Dniepropetrowsk - Saparoshje to Melitopol on the Black Sea. Above all, the *Wotan-Stellung*, also called the 'Ostwall', was more of a political *'tool'*, rather than a military solution to the problem. To keep the Soviets off the politically sensitive Crimea, a 130 km front had been drawn right through the Nougat steppe. In this treeless, hilly and coverless land, German troops were in practice at the mercy of the Soviets. Artillery was in the open. Under these conditions, the *Wotan-Stellung* was situated as best it could along the banks of the Molochna, a small stream that flowed into the Black Sea. In the process, the units had become weakened. In August alone, the German army had lost 218,000 men in the east, of which the 'Heeresgruppe Sud' had lost 133,000. Reinforcements were brought in via the Saparoshje - Melitopol - Genitschesk railway line, but to replace more than 77,000 men was simply not possible.[235] However, as of February 1943, the towns along the line had already been reinforced here and there and provided with Kampfkommandanten.[236]

On 9 October, fighting broke out around the *Wotan-Stellung*. The main concentration was on the front near Meolitopol as well as at Saporoshje, where the Soviets stormed unimaginatively every day. Near Oktoberfeld it came to a tank battle between the 'Kampfgruppe' Von Gaza of the 13th Pz.D. and broken-through Soviet units in which 62 Soviet tanks went up in flames. This put the Russian offensive on hold until the 17th of October.[237] This was no cause for relief. There were disturbing reports coming from the front. For example, the 16. Pz.Gren.D. reported their experiences of cooperation with the 'Tiger-Abteilung' 506 in the Saporoshje bridgehead. It turned out that the Soviets now had grenades that could pierce the tanks. Through propaganda, the 'Tiger' had always been portrayed as indestructible. Now it could be seen that the tank could be pierced by a frontal shot from 500 metres away and from the sides from 1,500 metres. The 'Tiger' proved more vulnerable than thought. It was also a *'great cabinet'* at over 3 metres high, which *'stood like a lighthouse in the country'* and drew fire.[238]

General Eberhard von Mackensen, whose corps represented the front at Saporoshje, asked Hitler for permission to abandon the bridgehead, despite the initial defensive success. Hitler did not agree, but some time later it became clear that Von Manstein shared this view. Hitler then decided to contact Von Kleist of the 1st Pz.leger north of Von Manstein to ask whether he could take over the Saporoshje bridgehead with 'Heeresgruppe A'. Von Kleist was willing to do so only if he received an extra one or two divisions as reinforcements. These would have to be taken from the *Crimean front*. This was unacceptable to Hitler and so he decided, as always, to stand firm. As a result, the first Soviet troops were on the west bank of the Dnieper on 14 October. A major hatch in the front had been created between the XXIXth and XXXXIVth Army Corps.[239]

Soviet Marshal Tolbouchin then opened the attack on Melitopol where heavy house-to-house fighting broke out, with the 111th I.D. of General Recknagel having to abandon the city after a 12-day siege. On 23 October the city fell into Soviet hands. It was the beginning of the advance of the Dnieper to the entrance to Crimea, Perekop, between 24 October and 3 November 1943. Besides the retreat of the German army, this brought new, large streams of refugees, from 'Volksdeutschen' but also Caucasians, who collaborated with the Germans. Furthermore, it brought Russians who could be of value to Moksou. It was a veritable movement of people. In total, some 885,000 people were deported. In the end, the *Panther Line*'s preliminary security counted 541,000 who had actually arrived.[240] On the Romanian side, it was the 4th Romanian Geb.D. that was dragged into the debacle. The unit had been assigned to the German 370th I.D. on 25 October and was in the Akimowka area that day.[241]

Between Dnieper and Bug

The ford at Melitopol and also at Kriwoj Rog up to across the Dnieper was a new sign. With this, important industrial areas had also been lost. The Germans had invested heavily in this coal basin. Stalin had destroyed and flooded the iron and manganese mines on the retreat in 1941. The Germans had tried to restore the industry with tens of thousands of slave workers. The German *Hoerder blast furnaces* had taken care of the Stalino and Rykowo blast furnaces, *Hoesch AG* was involved in mining at Kriwoj Rog, *Klöcker Werke AG* managed the Mariupol blast furnaces and *Krupp AG* the *Asow steel mills*. But everything was shifting.[242] On 25.10.1943 in the evening, the 'Heeresgruppe A' already feared a sudden appearance of Russian vanguards at Perekop. By 11pm in the evening, a Führer order arrived at the army group to stop the Russians west of the town at all costs.[243] That same day, Hitler summoned General Kurt Zeitzler and discussed the future situation in the Crimea. Here the final decision was taken not to evacuate Crimea but to hold out. This was in some ways contrary to the measures that had been taken. One of the last strong German units in Crimea, the 50th I.D., was rushed in to the 6th Army front. This had left the German front, especially near the strait of Kerstj, extremely vulnerable. This was partly because the KTB of the 'Heeresgruppe A' on 27.10.1943 reported a lot of intercepted radio traffic which pointed to reinforced shipping activities on the Soviet side, which were preparing a landing from Kuban. Still, Hitler felt he had no choice. The only way to prevent the cutting off of Perekop was for at least the *Friesen-Stellung* to hold west of the town. This was at that time being built on support points headlong. The 6th Army still consisted of 20,000 fighting troops but, according to the 'Heeresgruppe' itself, was at the end of its strength. *'If reinforcements did not arrive immediately, all hope was lost,'* the bequeathed documents read. This led Hitler to decide to fly in (parts of) the

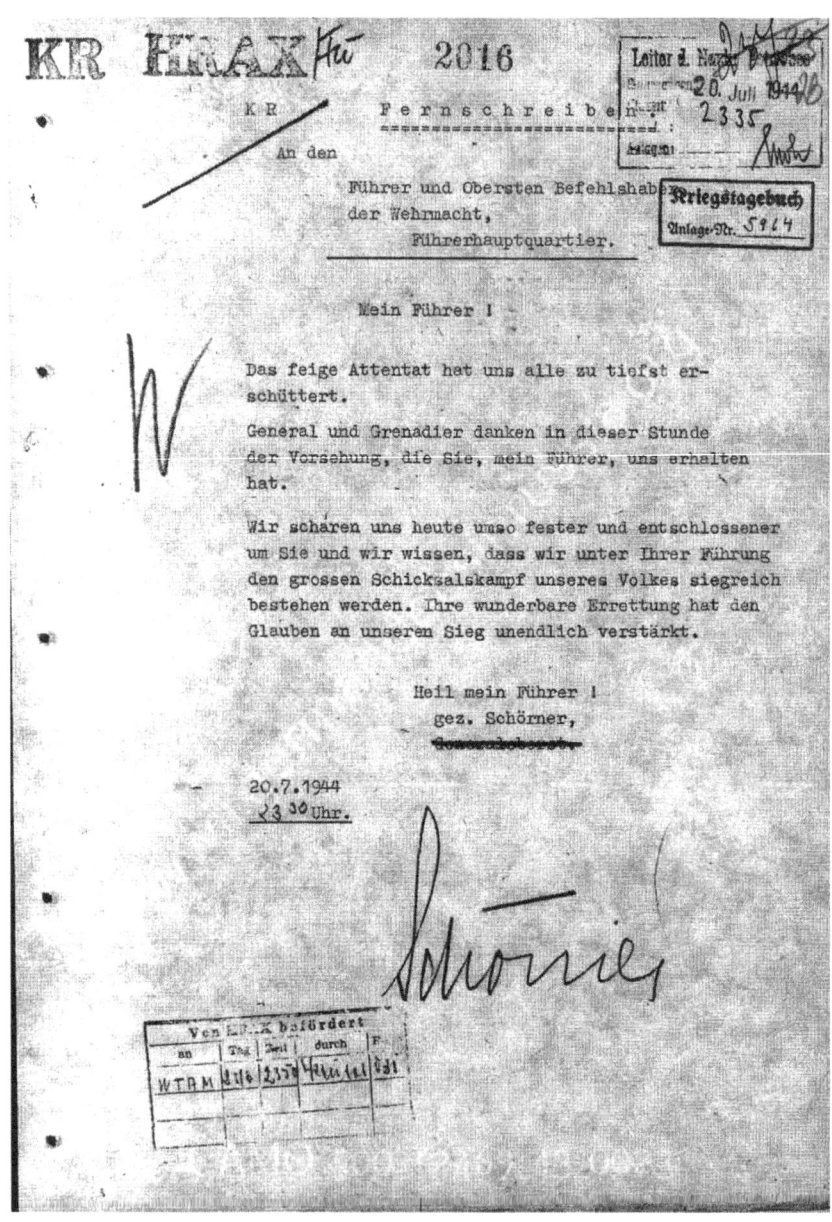

General Schorners' reaction to the Von Stauffenberg attack.

indispensable 50th I.D., from the Guben and Züllichau area, to the 6th Army after all.²⁴⁴

Besides informing Zeitzler of his decision to retain Crimea, Hitler also contacted Antonescu. He asked him to support Germany as best he could, because every Romanian division freed up a German division for a counterattack. Antonescu, however, had been briefed by his own confidant General Steflea, who indicated that the situation with the German 6th Army on the *Dnieper front* was not good. Crimea was expected to be cut off from the outside world soon. At the time, there were seven Romanian divisions in Crimea and one weakened German division. Romania would not be able to absorb a second Stalingrad, Antonescu argued. Hitler immediately sent the urgent message that Crimea was also vital to him to Antonescu by plane. It should not become the springboard to the Balkans and the Soviets could threaten the strategic oil area around Ploesti from Crimea. These oil fields were vital to the Third Reich, so Antonescu could count on full German support in Crimea.²⁴⁵

In Bucharest on 26 October 1943, the pressure was further increased when the leader of the DHM Romania General Erik-Oskar Hansen was summoned by General Steflea. The latter immediately made it clear that he had understood from the commander of the 3rd Romanian Army, General Dumitrescu, that there was a crisis at the front. Steflea pointed him to the breakthrough at Melitopol and that the German 6th Army was in no position to stop it. Steflea told Hansen that it was not his intention to interfere in tactical matters, but that he wanted to report that the situation for Romania was very serious. Bucharest could not afford a second Stalingrad and it was assumed that a closure of Crimea had become inevitable. Without movable armoured reserves, Steflea considered the preservation of Crimea impossible. Without proper German support, the Romanian divisions would feel *'abandoned'*, the Romanian general argued, and German reinforcements were therefore indispensable if they were to hold out. Should the Germans not be able to reinforce Crimea, Steflea urged the evacuation of Crimea.²⁴⁶

Two days later, Marshal Antonescu addressed Hansen too, pointing out that the Germans had solemnly promised that the Saparosje-Melitopol bridgehead would hold. Now that this was not the case, they feared the worst. Both ports of entry to Crimea (via Perekop and Kerch Strait) were barely defended. Antonescu was more than concerned. It was pointed out to the Germans that the best Romanian units were in Crimea. If armoured weapons and anti-aircraft guns were made available, the Romanians could be of more use, the Romanian supreme command believed.[247]

On 2 November 1943, a repeat of moves took place. General Steflea again pointed out the imminent situation to the Germans. That same day, Steflea also sent a three-page letter to Antonescu in which he more or less, but very politely, reminded him of his responsibilities. The Romanian unions in Crimea were the last *full* divisions of the kingdom and were in danger of being lost. He further pointed to the situation at the front and believed that the southern flank of the German 6th Army had *'disappeared'*.[248]

In an undated letter, Hitler responded directly to the new unrest. In doing so, he stated that in the Melitopol-Saporoshje-Dniepropetrovsk area, a 'Gross Bereinigung' would be set in motion. Should that fail, the German 6th Army would at least bar access to Crimea for the Red Army. Crimea itself would be reinforced with new units, including from the 'Luftwaffe' and the navy. Should everything still go wrong, Crimea would be evacuated to at least save its people. This was how Hitler tried to reassure Antonescu. He informed him that he *'understood and shared'* the marshal's concerns. Here we saw Hitler at his diplomatic best.[249]

In December, Foreign Affairs intervened in the issue as well. Civil servant Wiehl stressed the importance of maritime supplies to Crimea and the capabilities of the German navy in the area. A plea was made to open a U-boat base in Konstanta on the Black Sea.[250]

All political and diplomatic exchanges notwithstanding, the situation had created its own logic. It was Hungarian outsider Jenö Ruszkay who kept an eye on things from a distance. He simply noted that Romania, at least Antonescu, had long since had no choice but to persevere to the bitter end. *'He is German-friendly, but he cannot be otherwise,'* Ruszkay concluded. Antonescu rode the tiger and could not dismount. The lion's share of generals and Romanian youth still supported the marshal. The economy had become completely intertwined with Germany's. There was no turning back.[251]

The solution Hitler had in mind did not translate to the battlefield. The *Wotan-Stellung* had been breached and a large-scale counteraction proved unfeasible. Efforts were made to entrench troops in the *Friesen-Stellung* further to the west and also to develop the more northern town of Nikopol into a bridgehead. Reinforcements trickled in, including the 50th I.D., a Slovakian division and Romanian units. Both the Slovaks and Romanians, which the 'Heeresgruppe' had at its disposal here, were not held in high regard militarily by Major Dr Franck. Everything now flowed back west. At Cherson and other places, over 15,000 trucks and as many horse-and-carriages crossed the Dnieper. Troops of the XXXXIVth Army Corps caught the German troops and the mass of Romanians in the *Dnieper line*.[252]

Between 26 and 28 February 1944, Hitler and Antonescu had a meeting in *Klessheim* Castle near Salzburg. At this, Hitler informed Antonescu that he no longer trusted Hungary and was considering a possible occupation of the country. Hitler told Antonescu this to prevent this modification of the status quo from oxygenating Bucharest's territorial disputes with Hungary. Hitler wanted to preserve Hungary's territorial integrity and, by intervening, better mobilise the country for the fight against Bolshevism. What Hitler did not mention was that German strategists had been working on a plan (Operation *Margarethe II*) for the military occupation of Romania since January 1944.

Meanwhile, measures were being taken. Thus, from February 1944, Romanian-occupied Transnistria came under German military administration. This was necessary because the Romanians were very keen on the area and this nationalism was not allowed to interfere with German war interests. The Romanian governor of the area, General Potopeanu, who had succeeded the first governor Professor Alexianu, therefore had to tolerate the German Generalleutnant Aulub next to him. Of particular strategic importance to the Germans was the Shmerinka - Christinowka railway. Furthermore, there were concerns about the Ploesti oilfield, which had been bombed by the Allies since early April. Antonescu provided 20,000 troops with reinforcements for active- and passive-air defence of the area.[253]

In the meantime, the front of the 'Heeresgruppe Süd' was being pushed further and further west. By early March, Nikopol and Kriwoj Rog had been cleared and the great retreat from the Dnieper River to the Bug River had begun. Here too, the army group tried to prevent an escape and fell back from position to position and in organised operations towards the west, such as 'Unternehmen Tauziehen'. However, this could not prevent a Soviet breakthrough between 3 March and 8 March 1944 at Nowyj Bug. A fall back to the Iltis-Riegel was the answer. They fell back elsewhere from position to position too: the *Falke-Stellung*, *Wissun-Stellung*, *Wolf-Stellung* and many others. Sparse tank units, such as the 3rd and 24th Pz.D. tried to prevent overly large breakthroughs. Korück 539, meanwhile, built up a new 'Siche- rungsfront' on the Igul, and the Bug was expanded for defence. In the field near Sergejewka, it came to an armoured battle in which the Germans achieved another defensive success on 13 March. At the same time, the 6th Army definitely fell back on the west bank of the Bug, retaining the bridgeheads

Nikolajew commanded by General Von Förster, commander of the LXXIIth Army Corps, and Woshnjessensk commanded by Oberst Weikinn, an artillery officer of the XXXth Army Corps. Both places had been designated 'Festen Platz'. This marked the beginning of the final phase east of the Bug River. Cherson was cleared on 14 March and on the 21st of that month, the eastern bridgehead of Woshnjessensk was also retaken. It took the army group three weak divisions to hold that area and these troops were simply no longer there. That same day, the last bridge, the railway line near Trichaty, was blown up by the Germans, after the last units of the 9th and 335th I.D. had passed the Bug. In any case, the Germans had managed to escape destruction between Dnieper and Bug with the lion's share of troops. Both units on the stabilising Bug front belonged to the Romanian Army, as did the 4./24th I.D. deployed as part of the LXXIIth Army Corps.[254]

Drama Sebastopol

The successes on the Bug made it possible for Soviet Marshal Tolbouchin to attack Crimea. By then, Hitler had fulfilled his promise and strengthened Crimea somewhat. On paper, work had been going on since 24 May 1943 to develop Crimea into a 'Festung'. However, paper was patient and resources limited.[255] All in all, this involved some 200,000 troops. In principle, that was a decent fighting force, but there was a lack of everything. A February report showed that most divisions were between 20 and 30% undermanned, with the 3rd Geb.D. leading the way with 27% missing officers, 66% non-commissioned officers and 40% missing men. Units were missing no less than 2844 light machine guns (the MG. 34 and 42) and 165 heavy, as well as 159 Pak. This particularly affected Sebastopol on the northern side of the front, where there were few natural obstacles. In this so-called 'Freie Raum', if Soviet tank units broke through, there would be little hope for the garrison. Commander Jaenecke had barely been able to defend this area in forward form. The 'Tatarengrab' had been in Soviet hands since 3 November 1943.[256] Last-minute units had been provided with troops returning from leave, such as the 370th German I.D. which was allocated 2,500 'Urlauber'. The 73rd and 111th I.D. were without their artillery in Crimea. The 6th Army had ceded the 336th I.D. to Crimea, but this division too had no artillery and had only four battalions of infantry at its disposal.[257]

Jaenecke himself was an unusual figure. As commander of the 389th I.D., he had been trapped at Stalingrad earlier in the war. Here he had openly urged Paulus, the commander of the surrounded German 6th Army, to disregard Hitler's orders and break out. Jaenecke thus knew what it meant to be surrounded. Paul ignored Jaenecke, who was wounded and flown out of Stalingrad on 17 January. Later, Jaenecke was directed to the *Kuban* front and thus became commander of the 17th Army. In Crimea, he had to operate in a rather unclear command structure, as the 'Befehslhaber Krim' General Friedrich Köchling still had a finger in the pie as well. Air force and navy had their own lines too, and, including at the defence of Perekop, units of 'Bergmann' served with the 17th army, which fell under the 'Dienststelle der Freiwilligen-Verbände' and which consisted of 'Osttruppen'; mainly Turkmen.[258][259] A depth defence had been built up as best as it could be.

They had even dug up Russian mines again and set up new minefields from them. The extra miners requested from the army group did not arrive. Jaenecke let it be known that he wanted Crimea cleared, which of course went against Hitler's orders. In response, the historian David Zabecki opined that Jaenecke was acting *without any urgency* in defending Crimea and was mainly concerned with plan 'Michael', as the evacuation was referred to within the 17th Army.[260]

The question is whether Zabecki paints a justified picture of Jaenecke here. The German commander knew from experience around Stalingrad how the game had to be played. Right decisions had to be enforced. He did what he could to secure a timely evacuation, trying to direct the OKW towards a fait accompli. Yet, at the same time, he set himself up for the final battle in Crimea itself. A document dated 1 October 1943 makes this clear. It is the *Befehl für den Arbeitseinsatz der Zivilbevölkerung auf der Krim* which was signed by himself. In it Jaenecke characterised himself as a ruthless, ruthless commander who did not shy away from fully exploiting the civilian population for the German war effort. This involved the 'Erfassung' of the labour-suitable sections of the population. The attached order outlined the population of Crimea: 730,000 inhabitants of whom 350,000 were employable. Of this potential, 80,000 had already been put to work in the 'Wehr- machtdienststellen', the 'Reichsbahn', Todt's construction troops, RAD and other organisations. Jaenecke now wanted to mobilise the other forces as well and instructed the 'Wirtschaftskommando Krim' ('Wirtschafts-Kommando' 105) to strictly supervise this. For this purpose, the peninsula was divided into several 'Bereichen': the Bereich Kerch, Feodosia, Yalta, Sebastopol, Bakhshissaraj, Simferopol, Dshankj and Eupatoria. As assignment number one for deployment, Jaenecke chose scaffolding, which was not surprising given the terrain conditions in Crimea as well as his own background as a pioneer general. 'Korück' 550 was tasked with ensuring order and surveillance of the various construction sites.²⁶¹

The fact that Jaenecke could push hard had become apparent during the retreat from the Kuban bridgehead. Here he had ordered drastic measures to be implemented. Everything of value had been taken or destroyed. Labouring sections of the population had been deported. Later in Crimea, Jaenecke continued the scorched earth tactics. A *'dead zone'* was created on Kerch, where there was basically nothing left. In this way, they tried to make it difficult for attackers. Jaenecke made frank statements to the Soviets here after the war. Nowhere did he argue here that he had actually not wanted to defend Crimea, as was suggested. In cooperation with General Von Kleist, he had meticulously executed all destructive orders relating to Crimea. Another salient detail emerged here, when the Soviets asked him about the deployment of gas against the two partisan groups operating in Crimea. This would be the gas asphyxiating. Jaenecke confirmed that such a special command had come to Crimea on the orders of Von Kleist and the 'Heeresgruppe'. It would have been the same type as deployed against the *Maginot Line* in 1940.²⁶²

While Jaenecke's measures were running, preparations for evacuation were already under way at the same time. Jaenecke chose a two-track policy. It had already been decided that the Romanians would be evacuated first. many of the Rumanian units were at half strength anyway. In total, some 65,000 Romanians in Crimea.²⁶³ An organised evacuation by sea - which was eventually codenamed operation *'Gleiboot'* - and a forced evacuation; operation *'Adler'* - were prepared. The 17th Army still had hopes of choosing between different scenarios, but things turned out differently. Indeed, part of the Soviet offensive moved up the northern edge, heading for the 'Freie Raum'. The northern front was defended by the XXXXIXth Mountain Army Corps, within which the 10th and 19th Romanian infantry divisions also operated. In addition, there were seven Romanian battalions in Sebastopol.

The Soviet attack of the 4th Ukrainian front, commanded by General Tolbouchin, with 16 divisions and two armoured corps (278,000 troops and 6,000 artillery pieces) on 8 April struck above all the German 50th I.D. with full weight. Additionally, the Soviets were active on Kerch as well, with 143,000 troops. The attack came by surprise. There was no stopping it and the front tore across some seven km. The 10th Romanian infantry was initially on the periphery. In the afternoon, the centre of gravity shifted to the Romanians, who received a huge salvo of rockets. Between 600 and 800 men were wounded in one fell swoop as a result. This was followed by a tank attack on the Romanian positions. The 10th Romanian infantry division was practically destroyed in the process. The German pioneer battalion 111 that tried to jump into the breach suffered the same fate. The 'Jäger-regiment' Krim, from Feodosia, was rushed towards Tomaschewk to close the gap, but they too were overrun by the tanks, with grenadiers sitting on them. Barely 25 men escaped. In the gap, the army advanced to the Dsankoi - Jahun road. The 17th Army was now fighting for existence. Seven German battalions and three Romanian ones were successively thrown into the breach, but consumed by the fire. Even twenty-five 'Sturmgeschützen' could not stop the Soviet advance. On 12 April, the message came through that Operation *'Adler'* had been authorised. The evacuation could begin.

This meant a rush back to Sebastopol. One had to arrive there before the Soviets. This was easier said than done. The Red Army deployed large numbers of tanks. The 17th Army reported 750 tanks of which 464 were fired between 8 April and 14 April. Most of the tanks were of the older model KW1. These numbers did give a clear understanding of their material superiority.[264] Jaenecke constantly appealed for the fastest possible evacuation. This led Hitler to replace him with General Hans Allmendinger; the commander of the Vde Corps. Allmendinger was a very experienced officer, lecturer at the 'Divisionsführerlehrgänge' in Berlin and, through his experiences in the Demjansk pocket on the northern part of the Eastern Front, had experience of encirclement as well.[265]

The German and Romanian navies, as well as Hungarian ships, did what they could to save the Crimean garrison. Boats sailed to and fro, such as the 'Charlotte' which on one of its voyages took nine officers and 590 soldiers from the *'allies'* (read; most probably Romanians), as well as 135 German soldiers and 220 tonnes of goods, and then immediately reloaded to supply Sebastopol; coal, 300,000 pieces of German and Romanian munition and 304,000 kilos of food and field mail (12,000 kilos) as well as fuel. On one of its voyages, the 'Danubius' brought back 355.5 tonnes of material to Romania, with two German officers, eight German soldiers, two civilians, two Hiwi's, 569 captured civilian and 39 allies. The 'Kaswa' brought back more than 500 tonnes of goods and delivered back 575 tonnes, including tobacco and field mail.[266]

Until 8 May, 64,553 men were evacuated, 9424 wounded, 11358 civilians and 4260 prisoners of war; altogether 89,575 people. Many ships sailed on the port of Konstanza. Over 31,000 more men followed in the days that followed. Navy ships sailed to and fro, but after 13 May there was no one left to evacuate. Sebastopol had fallen. A later count put the total number of evacuees at 127,000. 'Admiral Schwarzes Meer' General Helmuth Brinkmann assumed 130,000 evacuees (and 21,457 by air) on 23 May. A report signed off by Admiral Dönitz of the German Navy stated that 190 warships and merchant ships had taken part in the evacuation and that the Romanian skippers, like the German ones, had shown great bravery. In all, some 6,000 men remained at sea.[267] Hitler insisted that as far as Romanians were eligible for decorations, this should be completed as a priority.[268] The former commander Jaenecke came off less happily. Hitler ordered an investigation into his actions and commissioned Heinz Guderian to do so. This experienced tank general had better things to do at that point in the war and delayed the investigation, allowing Jaenecke to escape. He later fell into the hands of the Soviets, who first demanded the death penalty and converted it into 25 years of hard labour. In 1955, after Chancellor Konrad Adenauer visited the Soviet Union, he was finally released. Karl Allmendinger was evacuated with his troops, but was not given a new post.[269]

From Odessa to the Pruth

Besides the drama in Crimea, the war also rolled on towards the west. The Red Army's *Dnieper-Carpathian* offensive brought the war to Romania's borders. On 28 March, Nikolayev was liberated and in April the Red Army approached Odessa. For the Romanians who had been closely involved in the 1941 capture of the city, this was another sign of impending doom. Attempts had been made to hold the city via the so-called *Brückekopf-Stellung Odessa*. Units of the 5th Luftwaffe feld.D. and small units of the 24th Romanian Infantry Division - reinforced with artillery from Artillery Regiment 150 - had been released to the 'Ostriegel' in defence of the city. The Romanians had moved into their headquarters at Kujalnik station. In defending northwest of the city, troops of the 21st Romanian I.D. had been deployed, working with the German 304th I.D., Lds.Schtz.Btl, 552 and 'Ostruppen', namely the I.Ostrei- ter Rgt. 454, which was deployed at Karpowo station. Moreover, there were some 'Sturmgeschütz' units on hand, the 'Sturmgeschützbrigade' 259, reinforced by the 'Sturmgeschütz-Abteilung' Hupe (about 15 'Sturmgeschützen').[270] This little army thrown together was, of course, incapable of defending the Black Sea port permanently. On 10 April, the city was liberated. Odessa had been occupied for 907 days and in that time 82,000 people had lost their lives and were 78,000 residents deported to Germany as workers.[271]

At the time of the fall of Odessa, the entire further southern front was already on Romanian soil. Marshal Antonescu used the moment to express his concerns towards the 'Heeresgruppe'. What further worried him was the fact that many 'Osttruppen', i.e. peoples from the Soviet Union in German service, were now stationed on Romanian territory. Apparently, Antonescu assumed a dark scenario in terms of their consequences and demanded their removal from Romania. The 'Heeresgruppe', which as we saw above at the *Brück-*

enkopf-stellung Odessa, made full use of the 'Osttruppen', and had no means of replacing him. Antonescu subsequently announced that he would make Romanians available.[272] On 20 July, the day of the *Von Stauffenberg attack*, the 'Heeresgruppe Südukraine' informed Oberst Ivanescu that the 'Osttruppen' were being taken from the *'Romanian area'*. This involved 4,000 men of Soviet volunteers working south of the Danube in supply depots and storage warehouses.[273]

One sometimes marvels at the priorities certain issues had. Antonescu's reticence possibly had to do with the large flows of refugees Romania had already had to deal with. Germany evacuated hundreds of thousands of 'Volksdeutschen' across the Danube River, to the west. Even young men fit for military service had been deported en masse. On top of this were the large transports from the Crimea and other threatened front areas.[274]

The deployment of 'Osttruppen' had begun in December 1941. At that time, the creation of national legions had begun, targeting the Caucasus and then it involved Georgians and Armenians. Tatar units were established in early 1942. The Germans used Russian and Ukrainian nationalists who had distanced themselves from communism and turned against Moscow in the ROA (Vlassov Army), among others. Muslim minorities were recruited as well, including with the help of the Grand Mufti al-Husseini from Jerusalem. Thus, on 4 July 1942, the order was given for the drafting of the so-called Turk battalions, made up of Turkmen. The SS followed with its own plans, leading to the establishment of the SS formation (later division) 'Neu Turkestan' and Islamic Waffen-SS units in the Balkans.[275]

The Romanians played another role of their own in the creation of these unions. In February 1943, a request was made to the Romanians by the 'Deutsche Heeresmission' in Romania to look in their POW camps for 'Ostvölker' who were suitable for German military service. Thereupon, the camps in Bucharest (camp I to III), in Braila (IV and V) in Jassy (VI and VII) and in Cernavoda (VIII) were searched. Apart from deployment in legions and battalions, many 'Osttruppen' were also employed as 'Hiwis' (Hilfswilligen) Soviet citizens in German military service, who could be found in most German divisions and without whom the machinery would hardly work.[276]

The following day, 21 July 1944, another awkward dispute came to an end, when German troops replaced Hungarian units on the front in Bukovina around Kuty. This too was very sensitive.[277]

However, in addition to Antonescu's concerns about the 'Osttruppen' and Bukovina, attention was focused on the front around the Pruth River. During new visits in March 1944 by Antonescu to Hitler, and subsequent extensive correspondence, the plan had arisen to halt the Soviet attack here. German troops had been given a free hand on Romanian territory, and storage depots and field hospitals with 20,000 beds were already ready for the coming battle. Over their heads, meanwhile, Allied air forces flew, targeting both the oil refinery near Ploesti and the capital Bucharest, as part of a psychological and economic war effort. A first bombardment took place on 5 April, followed by 24 April and 5 May 1944. It was a huge air duel. No fewer than 28 heavy, 11 medium and 9.5 light batteries opened fire on the overflying air force. A German 'Jagdstaffel' and 2/3 Romanian staffs tried to counter the attacks from the air. Despite heavy losses to the Allies, some of whom flew from Italy and landed again in the Ukraine (shulltebombar- dement), considerable damage could not be avoided. In the attack on 5 May 1944, 25,000 tonnes of fuel went up in flames. To this was added the problem of transport. Logistics - via rail and the Danube - were under heavy fire too, so the total loss was in fact 114,000 tonnes. The OKW therefore spoke of a catastrophe. Meanwhile, the air force was supplied from an emergency supply and many divisions at the front were only mobile by *'black supplies'*.[278]

To reverse the negative trend, Berlin promised to do even more. Additional anti-aircraft artillery (Flak) was promised, adding another 17 batteries to the cannons already in place, including nine heavy ones. Four mobile Flak batteries with 10.5cm Flak were also promised. More deliveries were planned for August. The air force, 'Luftflotte IV', was to be reinforced. Berlin promised 40 new fighters, as well as night fighters.[279] A special envoy was also sent to Ploesti by the OKW to keep production going. This was the Sonderbeauftragter des OKW, Major D.G. Dereser, 'Bearbeiter für Treibstoff-fragen in WFStab'. This worked with General Alfred Gerstenberg, who was to be appointed on 4 June as 'Deutschen Kommandanten des Rumän.

Erdölsgebiet' in which a system was devised to protect the refineries from bomb splinters. Due to this approach, the main refinery that had been hit, *Astra Romana*, would have been out of operation for 'only' two months.[280]

Labour was needed to rebuild the damage suffered. There was a growing shortage of these too. This again generated tensions with the Romanians regarding the 'Osttruppen' and 'Hilfswilligen' ('Hiwis') the Germans had recruited from Soviet residents. The 'Heeresgruppe Südukrain' indicated that the 'Osttruppen' were fighting for Romania as well, but Antonescu saw them mainly as a danger and feared *'gang formation'*. He took issue with the establishment of POW camps on Romanian soil too. Antonescu's antipathy went so far that he personally took to the road Ploesti-Kronstadt and stopped a column of organiser Todt consisting of 'Hiwis'. He complained bitterly to the German authorities about this. This put the Germans in a quandary. It had become clear during the bombing of Ploesti that the Romanians would run off at the slightest hint. The lethargic 'Ostvölker' were much more indifferent to the bombings and were thus more reliable workers.[281] On 1 June 1944, Antonescu visited the oil refineries and acknowledged the problems occurring there.[282]

So alternative work forces had to be found. General Gerstenberg, who had been assigned this task, sought help from SS-Obergruppenführer Richard Hildebrandt, the HSSPF Black Sea. Hildebrandt was a Nazi of the first rank, veteran of the 1923 Munich 'Bierhallenputsch', in which Hitler made a grab for power. Later, he was adjutant to the be-known SS general Joseph (Sepp) Dietrich and HSSPF Danzig and Böhmen und Mähren. Ukrainian men were supplied and put to work under SS-Brigadeführer Horst Hoffmeyer.[283] As the Romanians had forbidden the German land forces to involve 'Hiwis' in the work, the 'Luftwaffe' was diverted and the Ukrainian men operated under their flag. This was, of course, a purely theoretical evasion of the Romanian protest, but functioned again for the moment and with united forces they went to work, which was necessary, as the Allies had, among other things, mined the Danube and other waterways that were important for the logistics of oil from the air.[284] The Germans reined in this by appointing a *'Sonderbevollmächtigter des*

Führer für die Donau', Generaladmiral Wilhelm Marschall. Marschall was a former U-boat commander from World War I (UC 74 and the UB 105) and had later been commander of the battleship *Admiral Scheer*. After a conflict with Grand Admiral Erich Raeder, he had been sidelined for some time, but made amends with this post. On 20 June, his official authority began.[285]

The jumble of agencies and appointments surrounding Ploesti's oil production did lead to major tensions among the German agencies. This had resulted in several conflicts, which ran so high that the Reichsführer-SS Heinrich Himmler and the leader of the 'VoMi' ('Volksdeutsche Mittelstelle') SS-Obergruppenführer Werner Lorenz had to get personally involved.[286]

At the heart of the problem were the *'long toes'* of the HSSPF Hildebrandt. His confidant Oberst Grahamer was retired. This officer had been Hildebrandt's eyes and ears in the Ploesti area and Hildebrandt accused his competitors, especially Gerstenberger, of being the evil genius behind the inactivation. Gerstenberger informed Lorenz, who was told by the Reichsführer-SS to investigate, that Grahamer simply could no longer cope with the growing tensions and had therefore been relieved of the position. Things were even harsher between SS-Brigadefüher Hoffmeyer and Hildebrandt. The latter regarded the Ploesti area as his territory and did not allow another SS officer to call the shots there.

In the summer of 1944, the quarrel ran so high that angry letters went back and forth and one appealed to the Reichsführer-SS to thwart the other side. Hildebrandt called Hoffmeyer to the carpet and lectured him. Hoffmeyer, however, was not intimidated and took an *'unsolidaristic'* stance, as an agitated Hildebrandt put it. Hoffmeyer, however, invoked specific orders from Himmler and that he could exercise his authority by proxy. Hildebrandt then put pressure on the police units at Ploesti through his BdO SS-Brigadeführer Ernst Konrad Hitschler, causing Major Büttner of the 'I. Polizei-freiwilligenbataillons Schwarzes Meer' was not allowed to accept orders from Hoffmeyer. *'The prestige of the SS has been damaged to the bone in the Wehrmacht,'* Hoffmeyer angrily informed Lorenz, who in turn reported back to Himmler.

The Reichsführer-SS wrote an angry letter to his SS generals. That, of all people, these veterans had nothing better to do in this difficult year of war than to bother him (Himmler) with such petty matters, the Reichsführer-SS found extremely disappointing. Even after this letter from Himmler, the quarrel did not end, and on 18 August 1944 Lorenz again reported to Himmler about his intervention in the matter, which ended with a *'good talk'* between Hildebrandt and Lorenz.[287]

Furthermore, the railway network was strengthened. New equipment was supplied by Berlin. There was some backlog in this area, and 'Chief of Transport Wesen' General Gercke tried to catch up. Rudolf Ernst Otto Gerke was an East Prussian veteran of World War I, where he had served as a staff officer in the 'Heeresgruppe Kronprinz Rupprecht'. He had later become a staff officer in the OKH and was appointed 'Heeres- transport chief beim Oberkommando des Heeres' on 26 August 1939. Especially the Bucharest - Craiova - Foscani - Tecuci route deserved special attention. In Craiova, they were trying to expand a locomotive production workshop, while 300 German locomotives were promised for the Romanian railways.[288]

The battle had moved from the Bug River to the Romanian border. There were all kinds of urgent consultations. On 22 March, Antonescu flew to Berlin and on 30 March, German generals Von Kleist and Von Manstein were sent packing and the 'Heeresgruppe Süd' was transformed into 'Heeresgruppe Nord Ukraine' and the 'Heeresgruppe A' into 'Südukraine'. In reality, however, Ukraine was already back in liberated territory and even the dismissal of these (very experienced) generals could not change things at the front.

In the immediate hinterland of the front of the 'Heeresgruppe Südukraine', commanded by General Ferdinand Schörner from 1 April 1944 to 25 July, there were also problems. The Germans tried to supply and care for the 'Heeresgruppe' from Romania, but this went with great difficulty. Romania was in financial difficulties and a voucher system, agreed with the farmers, did not work. German envoys Carl Clodius and Oberst Dr Krull were deployed to solve these problems, but they soon concluded that Antonescu had no understanding whatsoever of economic issues. He left these entirely to

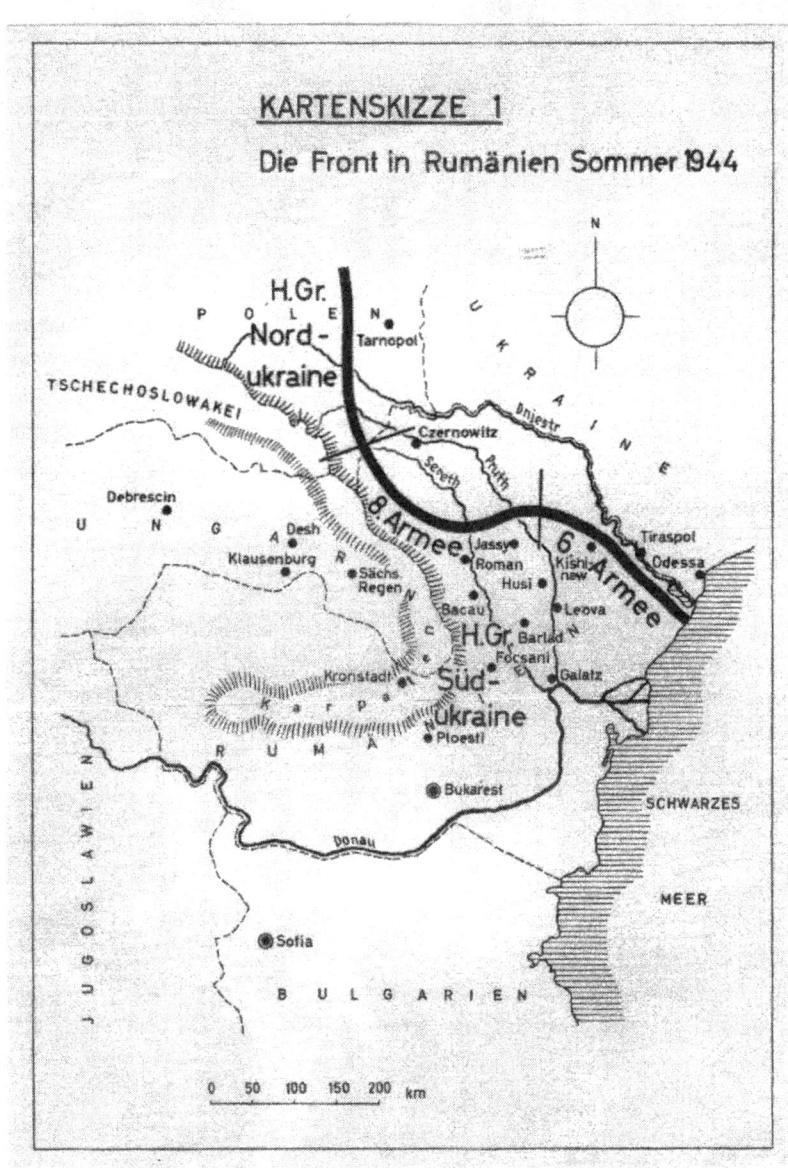

his namesake Mihai Antonsecu, whom the Germans described as *'a clever lawyer'*, and this was not a compliment. They saw him mainly as someone who eagerly looked out for opportunities to get Romania out of the war via the Anglo-American line. *'Apart from the contribution to the front, there was no serious Romanian contribution to be seen,'* the envoys believed after protracted negotiations.

Opinions about the Romanians at the front differed considerably. In general, it could be said, Schörner endorsed, that the Romanians were decent soldiers when properly trained and armed. As for the armament, Nazi Germany promised better. It was promised that Romania would receive 10 7.5 Pak 40, 10 light 'Feldhaubizte' (FH) monthly and that the number of 'Sturmgeschützen' would be increased from 10 to 20. Under the code names 'Olivenbaum' and 'Blei', the stuff would be delivered. Moreover, they were trying to rebuild the 4 Crimean divisions, which had largely lost their equipment. In order not to set the bar too high, a 70% re-equipment rate was sought.[289]

Generalkommando IV. Armeekorps
Der Kommandierende General

57o/44 g.Kdo.

K. Gef. Std., 14.8.44.

Durch Offizier geschrieben!

2 Ausfertigungen
1. Ausfertigung

An

den Oberbefehlshaber der Armeegruppe Wöhler,
Herrn General der Infanterie Wöhler.

Über die Stimmung in Rumänien berichte ich:

1.) Unter der Bevölkerung, besonders unter den Juden der Stadt Jassi, sind Gerüchte im Umlauf, wonach der Krieg am 2o.8.44 beendet sein soll. Teils wird dies mit einem Regierungswechsel in Rumänien, teils mit einer angeblichen Verlobung des Königs Michael mit einer englischen Prinzessin in Verbindung gebracht. König Carol sei bereits im Lande, die neue Regierung sei schon zusammengestellt. Die Verhandlungen würden in Rom geführt. Die rumänischen Offiziere seien nach Jassi befohlen worden.

Ob es sich hierbei um Nachrichten ausländischer Sender oder um Flüsterpropaganda handelt, konnte bisher nicht ermittelt werden.

2.) Aufschlussreicher erscheint folgendes:
Am 13.8. fand eine Abendgesellschafft beim Komm.General des rum.IV.A.K. ,Generalleutnant Stoenescu statt, an der ausser mir 2 deutsche und 5 rumänische Generale sowie der neue Chef des Stabes des rum.IV.A.K., Oberst Tautou, teilnahmen. Im Laufe des Abends sagte mir Gen.Stoenescu, dass er vor wenigen Tagen einen Brief von Gen.Eberbach erhalten habe, der jetzt eine Panzergruppe im Westen führe. Anknüpfend hiervon lenkte ich, da Gen.Stoenescu mir an diesem Abend aufgeschlossener als sonst erschien, vorsichtig das Gespräch auf

German document about the Jews in Jassy August 1944.

The decisive breakthrough at Jassy

Meanwhile, there was a strange lull before the storm in the country. In some cases everything seemed like business as usual, such as at a friendship meeting between the German organisation 'Kraft durch Freude' with its Romanian counterpart Munca si Lunina in Sibiu (Hermannstadt) at which the Romanian Minister of Labour Odagescu, acted. In Deimrich, in the west of the country, Culture Minister Ion Gheorghe gave an uplifting speech in an attempt to boost morale. He spoke purposefully about the upcoming showdown at Jassy. Moldova's ancient capital was to be defended as a *'city of culture. The battle is the touchstone of our prowess. There are those who believe that you escape a danger by bowing to it. That is a big mistake and especially now. The world has become so much worse'*.

Several Romanian periodicals, such as *Curentul, Ecoul, Viata* and *Tiumpul,* painted a vitalistic picture of a Romania preparing for battle. However, one read between the lines and saw the seriousness of the matter. The world was in the grip of systems, which *'do not tolerate contradiction',* and were fighting to the death. The 'Volksdeutschen' were mobilised as well and held large rallies where they declared their allegiance to Hitler and the Romanian nation. In attendance were the German ambassador Freiherr Von Killinger, the leader of the DHM General Hansen, the Landesgruppenleiter NSDAP/AO ('Ausland Organisation') Kohlhammer and the Volksgruppenführer Andreas Schmidt. Attention was paid to the Allied landing in Normandy too. Some commentators expected a quick peace to follow this. Others mainly commented on the western Allies and especially their bombing raids over Romanian territory, both from Italy and the Soviet Union. These were said to have hit civilian targets especially in Jassy, where historical buildings went up in flames. Twenty Romanian civilian workers in the Ploesti oil industry were awarded the Order of the German

Eagle for their brave and tireless efforts. This was how they tried to keep their spirits up.[290]

Meanwhile, the Soviets had made their preparations for the thrust to the west. The front was around the line Frumos - Jassy - Petresti - Kishinjov and then deflecting southwards through Jermoklija to the Black Sea coast near Kaloglej. The 2nd Ukrainian front commanded by P.J. Malinowksi and the 3rd Ukrainian front commanded by T.I. Tolbouchin had assembled for the attack, a total of 920,000 troops. The battle plan initially consisted of two concentric attacks. Northwest of Jassy, a thrust towards Birlad was to be achieved, followed later by an attack further west at Pascani to widen the front. The 3rd Ukrainian front was to attack with the 57th and 37th armies mainly from the area just south of Tiraspol and march towards Leowa. This would create two pockets. To these were pushed through in depth, which would trap the 3rd Romanian Army on the western flank and separate it from the German units.

On the German-Romanian side, since 25 July, the 'Heeresgruppe Südukrain' had been under the command of General Johannes Friessner, who had previously led the 'Heeresgruppe Nord'. Friessner had impressed Hitler with his unadorned way of reporting on matters at the front. With this, Hitler saw Friessner as a 'Tatmensch' he needed on the threatened southern front with its important oil fields. Friessner did not shy away from harsh measures in the past. A year earlier, when the town of Karatschew in the front field of a German line was *'in the way'*, large parts of Karatschew were razed to the ground at the behest of Friessner and Orel's town commandant, General Haman, including an electricity work, a water work, the 'Durchgangslager' ('Dulag') 185 and a large series of other buildings.[291]

Friessner's new position came at an unusual time. On 20 July, the *Von Stauffenberg attack* had taken place, in which a group of officers around General Ludwig Beck and Claus Schenk von Stauffenberg tried to liquidate Hitler by bombing. On the day in question, General Eberhard Kinzel excitedly burst into Friessner's office saying that he had just received a call from Berlin from Oberst Von Stauffenberg.

The latter had informed him that Hitler had been killed in an attack that day and that orders from now on would be given by Generaloberst Beck. '*Who is Von Stauffenberg?*' asked Friessner in amazement. The attack came as a complete surprise. That Beck would now call the shots was a wonder, as Beck had been inactive for some time.

Even before they could call the OKH for information from the 'Heeresgruppe', Hitler's right-hand Field Marshal Wilhelm Keitel hung up the phone and announced in no uncertain terms that Hitler was alive and would address the German people by radio. '*We waited, and a subdued mood prevailed,*' Friessner wrote in his memoirs. It turned out that Hitler was indeed still alive and, as is well known, the coup quickly collapsed. Friessner rushed to the front to see how the men reacted. According to Friessner, there was only one sound among the men, disappointment and condemnation of the attack. According to Friessner, German troops had long since ceased to be purely under orders on the Eastern Front. Everyone feared an overthrow of Germany by the Soviets and therefore fought to the bitter end. The Allied call for unconditional surrender, formulated at the Yalta consultations, did not help either.[292]

Ferdinand Schörner, still on the letterhead of commander-in-chief of the Südukraine army group, also put his loyalty to the Führer in writing:

'*This cowardly attack has affected us all deeply. General and grenadier thank providence that you have been spared. We rally around you all the more and know that under your leadership we will win this battle of fate ('Schickalskampf'). Your miraculous rescue has strengthened our faith in victory. Heil mein Führer!*'[293]

That same day, he wrote a long letter to Hitler pointing out that there were untapped opportunities and food reserves in Romania that could be put to good use by Germany. Due to '*Romania's rigid hold*', this had not yet happened. He concluded his Romania experience by saying that he was convinced that Marshal Antonescu was still behind Germany but that it was important that he meet Hitler again soon. Antonescu needed support to push through against subversive forces.[294]

On 23 July, Schörner also wrote an internal memo to his generals, thanking them. But he drew their attention to the mental attitude of the troops as well, who wrote home that '*the war would soon be over*'.

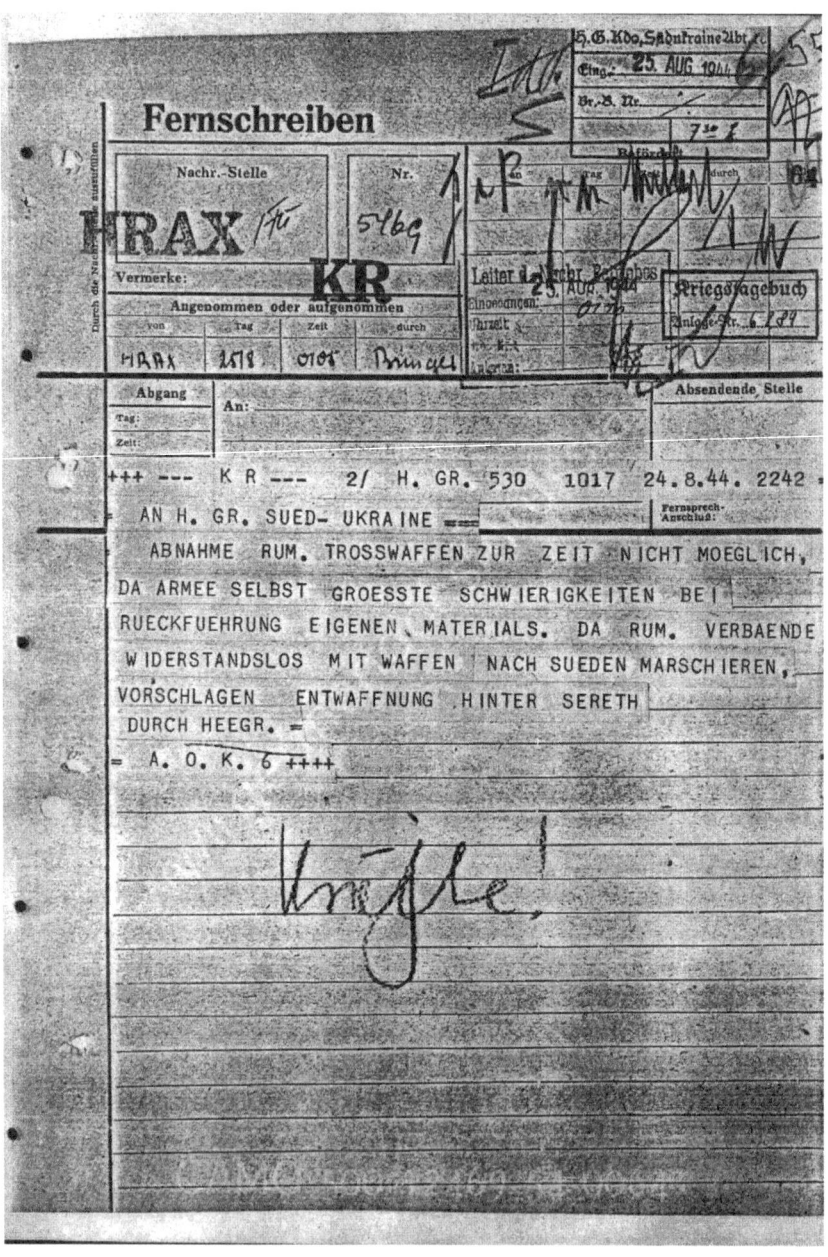

Romanian troops leave for the West without complaining.

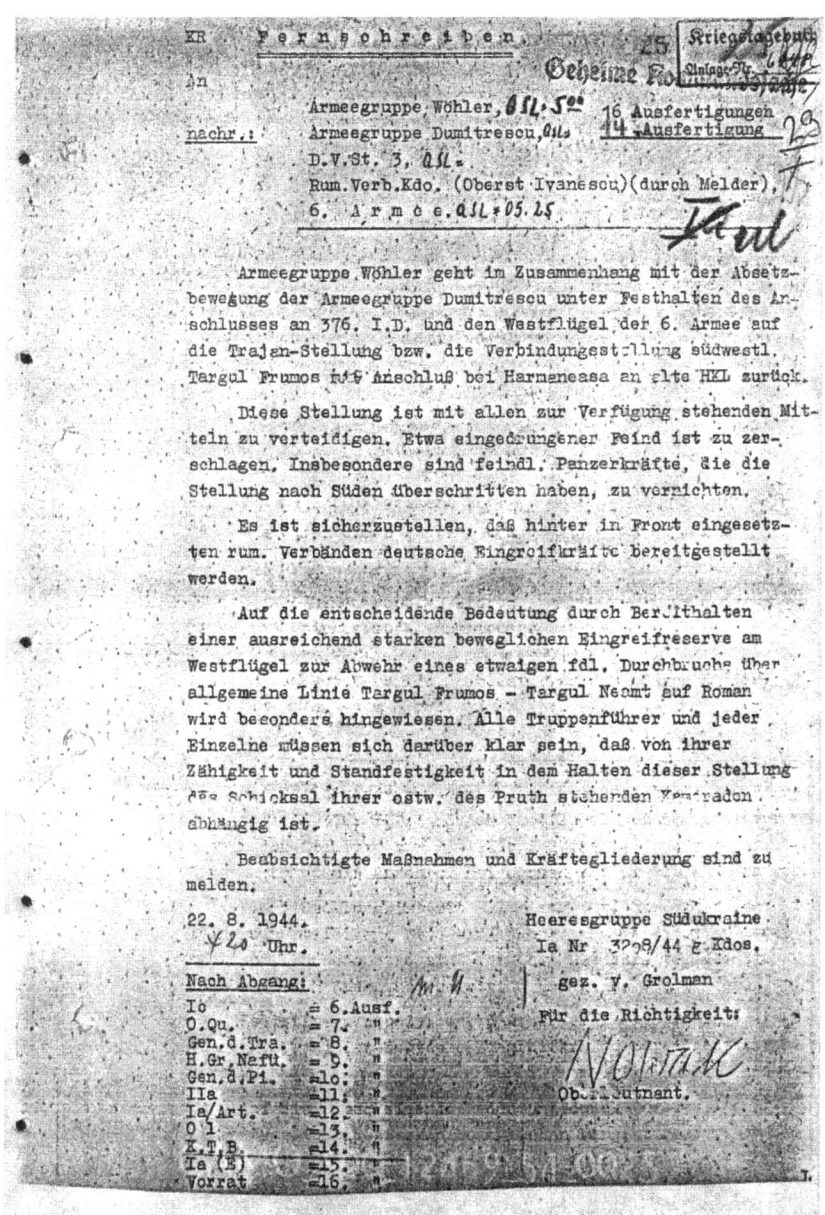

The German general Otto Wöhler withdraws the troops to the Trajan-Stellung, 22 August 1944.

Schörner found this dangerously defeatist. Everything had to revolve around the 'Endsieg'. Moreover, he was worried about the 'Volksdeutschen', who in his view were seen too much as second-class Germans and thus could not be expected to make the utmost effort.[295]

After the war, Friessner admitted that the purely bitter reaction to the *Von Stauffenberg* attack was a one-sided reaction. However, at the time, it was felt this way by troops at the front. It also brought distrust between officers and soldiers, but the German soldier stayed at his post and the war soon lapsed back into the daily pattern. Allies were stricken too.

Friessner met Hitler shortly after the attack and the latter received him *'very seriously'* but was *'friendly'* towards the general. Hitler reminded him that Friessner's change of command towards the 'Heeresgruppe Südukraine' was not a sign of distrust or disapproval. About Antonescu, Hitler reassured him the marshal would remain loyal to him.[296]

In his current duties, Friessner had at his disposal the German 6th Army and 8th Army (Armeegruppe Wöhler) and the two Romanian armies, the 3rd and 4th. The 3rd Army had at its disposal the II.de and III.de Romanian Army Corps (9th I.D., 110th I.Brigade, 2nd I.D., 15th I.D.), 21.I.D. and 4th Geb.Brigade, in addition to some German units. The 4th Romanian Army had the Vth Romanian Corps, Ist Romanian Corps and VIIth Romanian Corps, consisting of the 5th I.D., 1st I.D., 13th I.D., 101st Geb.Brigade, 4th I.D., 1.Garde D., 6th I.D. 20th I.D., 103rd Geb.Brigade and the 104th Geb.Brigade, in addition to German units. In addition, the IVth Romanian Corps served with the German 8th Army with the 5th Kav.D., 102nd Geb.Brigade, the 7th I.D. and the 3rd I.D.[297] Braila and Focsani were initially declared 'Festen Platz', but the army group withdrew this on 29 July 1944. After all, the Germans did not have complete control over these areas and respected Romanian authority. Right on the eve of the Soviet offensive, on 19.08.1944, there was no more time for diplomacy and the 'Heeresgruppe' revoked the decision after all, making the places 'Festen Platz' once again.[298]

Lines were being built out and on 23 July there was a planning lecture at 6th Army headquarters on the further expansion of the *Tra-*

jan-Stellung, Stefan-Stellung, Ferdinand-Stellung and the *Carol-Stellung*. Building materials were in short supply, so it was decided to demolish 40 buildings in Targul Frumos and then use the material for the construction of positions.[299] In the previous month, the 'Heeresgruppe' had tried to make some front corrections, which should make the defence line stronger. This led to 'Unternehmen Michael' on 22 July 1944. The operation took place at Rascaeti and was carried out by the XXIX Army Corps, within which the 21st Romanian I.D. and the 304th German I.D. operated. The operation was initially planned for early July, but was postponed on 11 July. The reason was that there were objections to the plan among General Dumitrescu's 3rd Romanian Army. It was feared that the advantages would not outweigh the disadvantages. It was known that the Russians were well entrenched. In the end, the Germans pressed ahead anyway. On the 22nd, the order was given and on 23 July the attack began.

A preliminary artillery bombardment of about 15 minutes followed. Sixty artillery pieces from the divisions supplemented by artillery from the 13th Pz.D. and the 9th I.D. took the Soviet positions under fire. Grenadiers and 'Sturmgeschützen' then came into action. The attack was initially successful. The 700 metres that had to be bridged to the new line along which the HKL was intended to run was hastily bridged and Soviet soldiers were taken prisoner of war. The first positions were abandoned by the Soviets shortly afterwards, except for a few soldiers who resisted. To the Germans' surprise, the Soviets had managed to place some mines in the abandoned positions with lightning speed.

The position itself was well built out with an average depth of 180 to 200 metres. The Red Army soon recovered and launched a massive counterattack. As always, they did operate with too many men in a small area, so the Red Army suffered bitter losses. We read from an internal German report that the Soviet soldier barely reacted to hand grenades and had no fear. Very different was the deployment of flamethrowers and 'Panzerfäusten', which had also been used with the Romanians and for which they were *'sehr empfindlich'*.[300]

At 'Zielpunkt' 390, heavy hand-to-hand combat occurred between the Red Army and pioneers of the 304th I.D. At a tank trench, in front of which the Soviets had constructed a minefield, the attack of the Ist Battalion of Romanian Regiment 24 stalled. The 'Sturmgeschützen' and the pioneers managed to penetrate two lines deep into the Russian positions. Here, two 'Sturmgeschützen' ran into landmines and burned out. The grenadiers of regiment 575 were now trapped behind the 'Sturmgeschützen'. The 'Sturmgeschützen' shot point blank into the Russian positions, who answered fire from there with Pak. One 'Sturmgeschütz' received a full hit and could no longer move forwards or backwards. It was hitched up with chains and towed backwards.

A real battle ensued on the small patch of ground, with the deployment of Soviet air power, which ended with the German-Romanian units being thrown back on their starting positions. During the retreat, the 6th company of the 304th I.D. became temporarily surrounded. At that moment, 'Stukas', German dive-bombers, appeared over the battlefield. This gave some air. However, the Soviet anti-aircraft defence was so heavy that the 'Stukas' were only able to drop part of their bombs and had to turn off again. At 15.00, a 'Kampfgruppe' of the 304th I.D. arrived with some 'Sturmgeschützen' who eventually relieved the trapped 6th company. By 17.00, every-one was back on the exit line, under heavy cover from its own artillery that relentlessly kept the Soviet positions and the no man's land under fire.

'Own losses are heavy,' noted the diary of the 'Heeresgruppe Südukraine'. There was little focus on the battle scene in the daily reporting of the army group. Probably everything was still under the influence of the experiences surrounding the 20th of July, the *Von Stauffenberg* attack. It did not take away the fact that the 304th I.D. counted almost 100 men killed, 400 men wounded and 100 missing, while the 21st Romanian I.D. counted almost 150 men killed, 500 men wounded and 100 men missing. To these were added some smaller losses, including 278 men of the 'Sturmgeschützbrigade'. Fifteen 'Sturmgeschützen' had been shot at and damaged, three of which were lost permanently. In barely one day, the 'Heeresgruppe' had lost 1,000 men to no avail. General Bechtolsheim of the XXIX Corps blamed it mainly on the Romanians, whose lack of non-com-

missioned officers meant they had not performed well. This does not seem very fair in this case. This mission, as Dumitrescu had pointed out, had little chance of success from the begin. For instance, the Romanians wanted to go in with three battalions, but the front sector and operational space was so limited (by mine fields), that they had to settle for one battalion in the first line. However, it was *'morale unimpaired'*, Bechtolsheim thought, and the Romanians were eager to *'take revenge for their fallen comrades'*.[301]

After 'Unternehmen Michael', the situation was and remained somewhat subdued and German-Romanian relations not without tension. There were Romanian defectors here and there, often Romanians from areas already in Soviet hands.[302] Friessner was worried about his allies. Romanian units were of varying quality. For example, an internal report dated 31 July 1944 noted that the 4th Romanian I.D. was *'poor in scaffolding'*, while the 1st Romanian I.D. was labelled *'good'* with regard to this work. Also worrying was that the Romanians, as well as the forward observation posts, were sorely lacking in radio equipment. This adversely affected reaction capability, especially with the artillery.[303]

The commanders of the 5th Romanian Kav.D. and the 7th Romanian I.D. were described as *'slick'*. The latter division had still been involved in fighting in March and had not done well. The 'Heeresgruppe' did note, however, that the Romanians had to defend a front sector that was too large. Soldiers from the 13th Battalion had defected to the Soviets at the time. The 5th Kav.D. was a unit with some good regiments, but General Carp was not trusted. The unit's artillery had been reinforced with units of the German 3rd I.D. and the positions were poorly built out. The 'Heeresgruppe' was positive about the commander of the Romanian 11th I.D., 'Ritterkreuzträger' Radulescu, who was characterised as *'deutschfreundlich'* and *'tüchtig'*. The division was characterised as good, as was the scaffolding construction. General Racovita of the 4th Romanian Army was also described as *'deutschfreundlich'* and honest, as was the Romanian commander of the IVth Army Corps, General Stoanescu, who was seen as *'intelligent'*, although more of a theorist than a man of practice, which could well be true as he was a former finance minister and confidant of

Marshal Antonescu. About Germany's own units, the 'Heeresgruppe' mentioned that the 46th I.D. was *'very good'*, the 376th I.D. likewise. The 79th I.D. had been hardened in the earlier fighting at Jassy, prior to the major offensive. One of the town's cemeteries alone held 800 of the division's dead.

The town of Jassy itself also remained a concern of the 'Heeresgruppe'. A relatively large Jewish community still lived in the town, about some 30,000, who were a *'grosse Gefahrenquelle'* according to the 'Heeresgruppe'. One listed four points, which gave a nice insight into how a German army unit viewed the Romanian-Jewish issue: the city was *'völlig verjudet'*, and there were *'numerous Jewish brothels in the city'*, it was *'a hotbed of espionage and agents'* and the *'cause of many venereal diseases'*. The proposal of the 'Heeresgruppe' was to completely evacuate Jassy, *'in the interest of the troops'*. General Karl Stingl had been appointed city commander of Jassy.[304]

Friessner's armoured units were limited. In this respect, the defence was mainly formed by army 'Sturmgeschütz brigades'. These were the brigades: 228, 286, 239, 243, 286, 905, 911, 1008, 1052 and 195. On paper, this seemed bigger than it actually was. The latter three brigades had only nine and twice eight 'Sturmgeschützen' at their disposal on 28 July 1944. The best-equipped brigade was the 'Heeres Sturmgeschützbrigade' 243 with 25 'Sturmgeschützen' deployable.

Ironically, Friessner's best-equipped unit in terms of quantity of material was the 1st Romanian Pz.D. (from 29 July to be named in 'Gross Rumänien')[305] with 52 PzKpfw IV, long-barrel (L) tanks combined with 31 'Sturmgeschützen'. This also showed how much Berlin did its best to keep the Romanians there. The *'own'* 13th Pz.D., for example, had 31 PzKpfw.IV. L tanks and no 'Sturmgeschützen'. The diary of the 'Heeresgruppe' noted on 29 July that they were trying to get the division fully deployable. To this end, training troops of the 20.Pz.D. were present with the unit in Bacau. The commander of the division was described by the Germans as *'very good'*, although somewhat *'schematic'*, to which *'French school'* was added in brackets.[306] On 03.08.1944, however, a complaint came from Marshal Antonescu that many 'Sturmgeschützen' had been deprived of the division again. These had been transferred (back) to 'Sturmgeschützbrigade

905'. This would have left the 1st Romanian Pz.D. with only 9 'Sturmgeschützen'. General Hansen tried to accommodate Antonescu on 02.08.1944 by transferring 10 'Sturmgeschützen' provided for the 2nd Romanian Pz.D. to the 1st. Antonescu, however, demanded restoration of at least 26 'Sturmgeschützen' for the 1st Romanian Pz.D. The German LVII.th Corps, within which the 'Sturmgeschütz´ unit operated, stated that the unit was needed in an operation in the Targul Frumos bridgehead. 'Sturmgeschütz´ support would have been emphasised in earlier orders by both the marshal and Ferdinand Schörner. Thereby, the German side stressed, all troops were part of the 4th Romanian Army. On 4 August, another letter came from Antonescu via Steflea, showing how sensitive things were. Antonescu spoke of the *'soldiers honour'* and feared too much German influence on the division (and decline of tanks at the moment suprême). The latter, incidentally, happened to the 2nd Romanian Pz.D., also in line-up, which gave up its tanks to the Germans on 22.08.1944, after the Soviets had broken through at Jassy. At the time, these were mainly 'Sturmgeschützen' from 'Sturmgeschützbrigade 905' and material taken over by the 20th Pz.D.[307]

In terms of armoured troops, the *Armeegruppe Dumitrecsu had* 63 tanks and 146 'Sturmgeschützen' available and 28 'Sturmhaubitzen', and the *Armeegruppe Wöhler had* 52 tanks, 137 'Sturmgeschützen' and three 'Sturmhaubitzen'.[308]

On 3 August, Friessner had sent his 1.Generalstabsoffizier Von Trotha to Hitler's headquarters to draw attention to the specific problems on his front. Of great concern to him was the growing stream of reports indicating a Romanian betrayal. Furthermore, he feared the coming attack and pleaded with Hitler to retake the front on the more defensible stilt of Galatz - Focsani and the edge of the Carpathian mountains. He had prepared a six-page 'Denkschrift' in duplicate, one for Hitler and one for Heinz Guderian (OKH). In it, he reported that, as commander-in-chief of the 'Heeresgruppe Südukraine', he felt responsible for the situation behind the front as well. It was vital that German-led forces remained in power. He further stressed that he had only few mobile reserves, two medium-strength German Pz.D., an armoured grenadier division and the Romanian 1st Pz.D.

```
SSD                 Fernschreiben.
```
                                                    Kriegstagebuch
                                                    Anlage-Nr. 6036

An   **Geheim**

Armeegruppe Dumitrescu,
6. Armee,-

nachr.: D.V.St.3 (Oberst i.G. v.Uckermann)
        Rum. Verb.Kdo. (Oberst Ivanescu) d.Melder

Die auffallend hohen personellen und materiellen
Verluste der deutschen und rumänischen Verbände des
XXIX.A.K. bei dem Unternehmen Rascoeti am 23.7. lassen
den Schluß zu, daß schwere Führungsfehler bei Anlage
und Durchführung des Unternehmens vorliegen.

Armeegruppe Dumitrescu beauftragt 6.Armee mit der
sofortigen Einleitung einer Untersuchung der Vorgänge,
soweit sie deutsche Truppen betreffen.

Die Armeegruppe wird ferner gebeten, eine ent-
sprechende Untersuchung bei den beteiligten rumänischen
Verbänden durchzuführen.

Das Ergebnis der Untersuchungen ist der Heeresgruppe zu melden.

26.7.1944   gez. Prießner
20²⁵ Uhr   Generaloberst und Oberbefehls-
                                haber der Heeresgr.Südukraine.

                                Ia Nr. 8547/44 geh.

Nach Abgang:
IIa/Abt.III
K.T.B.
Ia (Entw.)

                                                        Gr.

Assignment 'Michael'

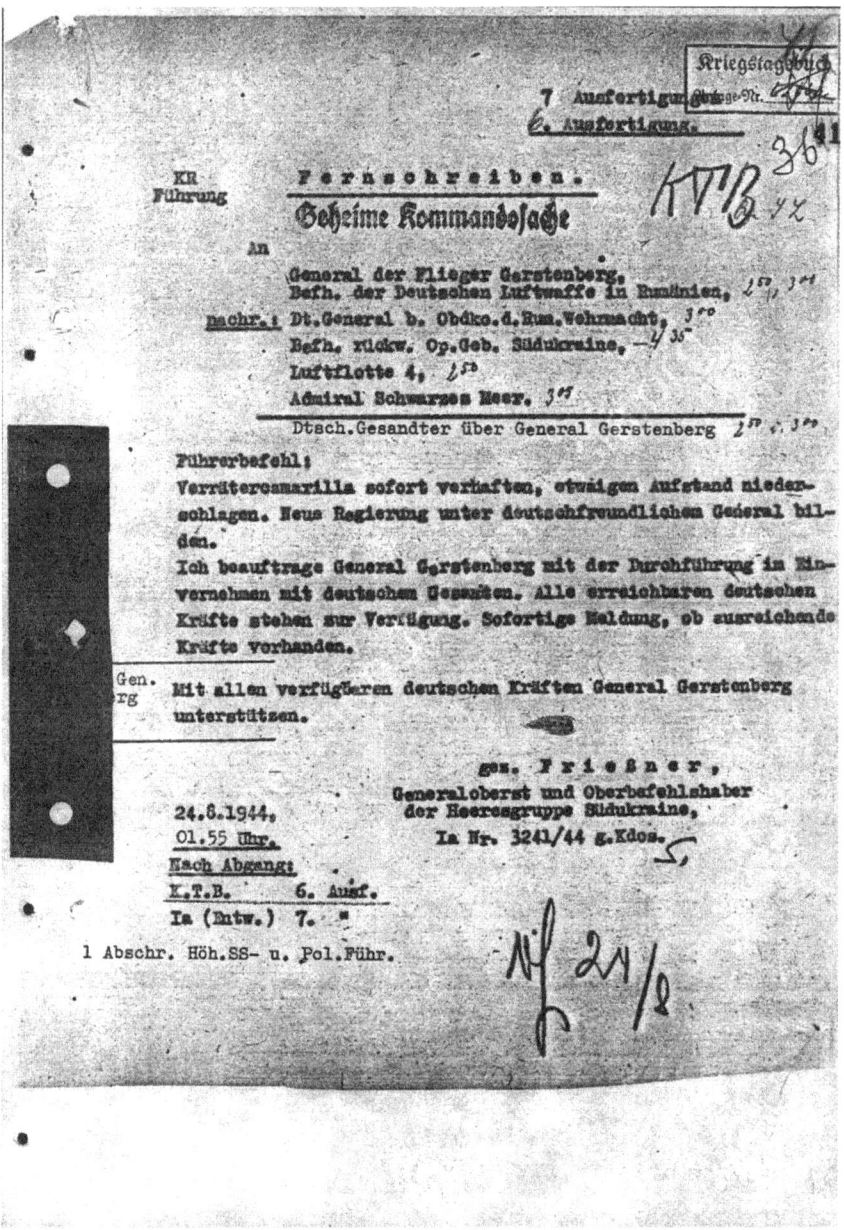

Anti-German putsch in Bucharest.

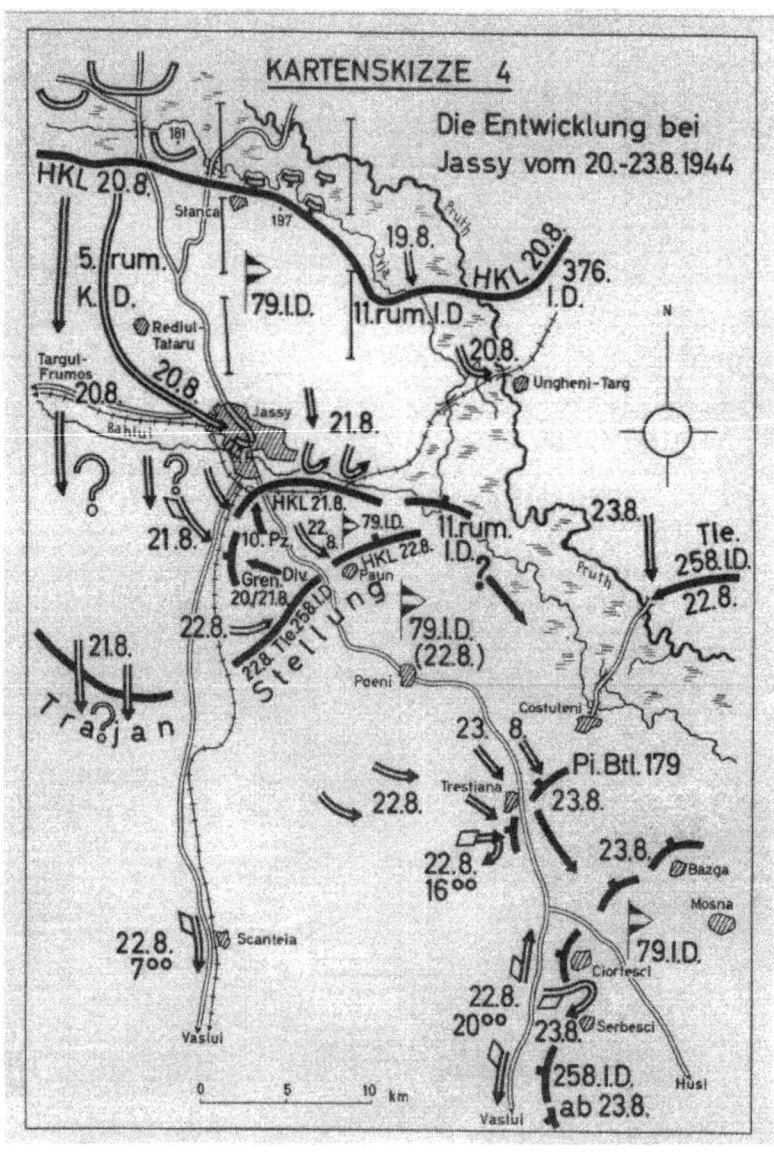

Jassy breakthrough

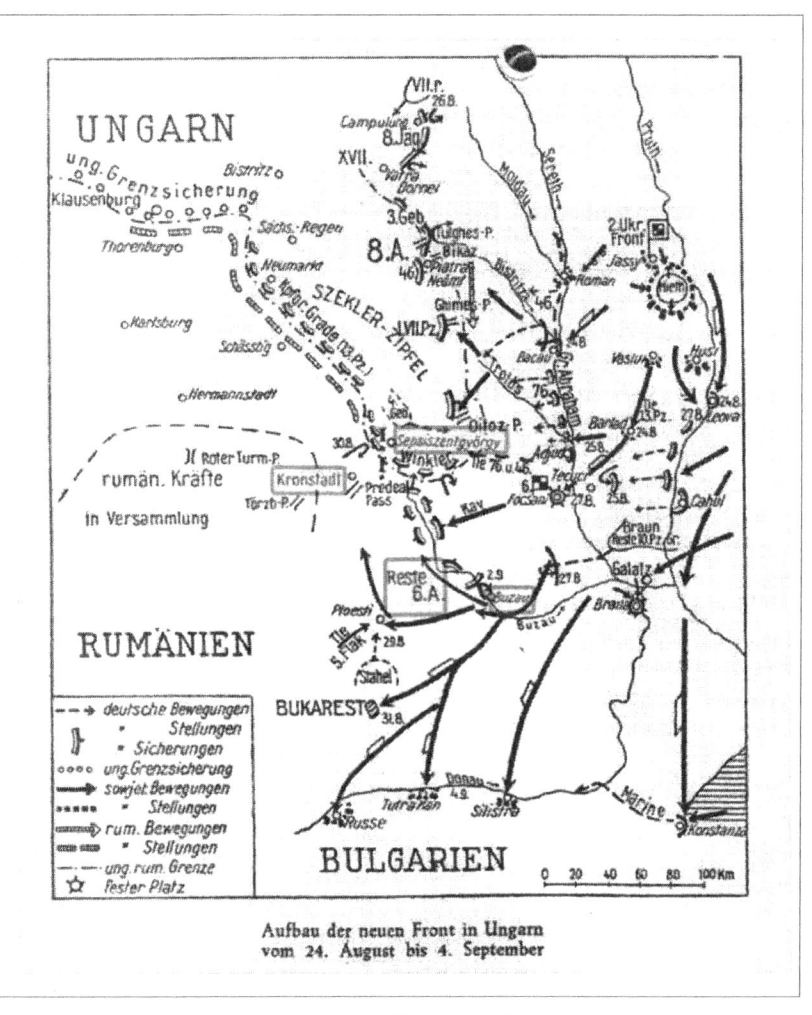

Soviet breakthrough, between August and September 1944.

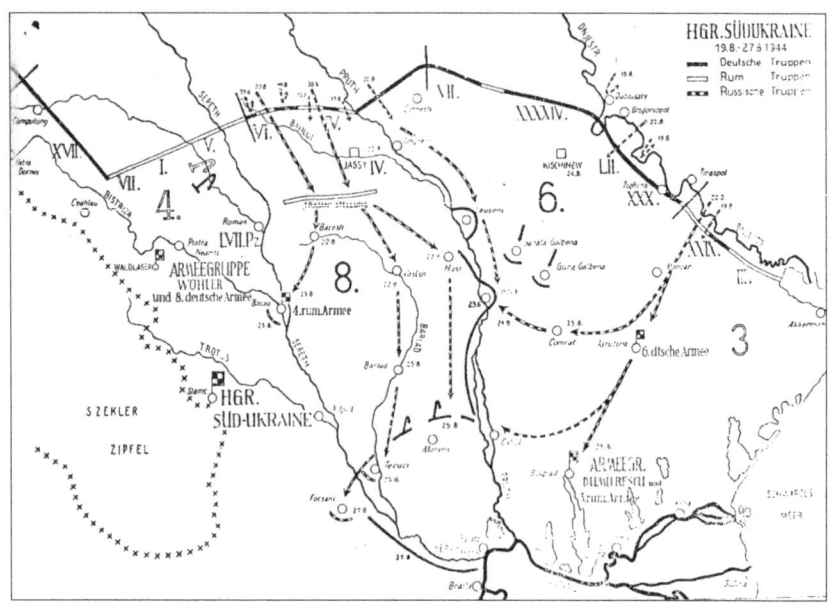

Jassy breakthrough 19 August 1944.

For the protection of the Ploesti oil fields, he urgently requested 140 additional fighter aircraft.[309]

Von Trotha returned on 8 August, but he had got no further that handing Friessner's 'Denkschrift' to Heinz Guderian. Friessner understood that he was on his own, together with his Romanian *'friends'* and the Hungarians under his command. This was an additional challange, as the Hungarians and Romanians hated each other. Still, the main concern was the increasing number of movements at the front. On 7 August, mass movements were observed at the Pruth River. This was confirmed by the German air force. Something was clearly going on. The Germans soon recognised ballooning movements at Jassy and Tiraspol. Even though they had been warned, they were still stuck in the blood-hot treeless steppe of Bessarabia and could not move.

The next day, Ia Oberst Von Trotha, Chef des Stabes General-major Von Grolman and several other officers joined Steflea and Ivanescu to update the Romanians. They pointed out that, through the commitments of the OKH and Guderian, Germany was in the process of drafting 40 divisions from the 'Ersatzleger'.

As soon as these would be available, the 8th and 20th Pz.D., which at that time were being refreshed and belonged to the 'Heeresgruppe Südukraine', could be freed-up for an offensive elsewhere and replaced by enough other troops. This would give Nazi Germany new scope for offensive action. Moreover, there was talk of expanding lines and the new German bunkers (type 'Tobruk') that could take point blank hits from 15.2 cm artillery.[310]

In addition, German troops in the front line sensed changes among their Romanian allies. From the beginning of August, soldiers of the German 79th I.D. (Generalleutnant Friedrich August Weinknecht), part of the IV Corps, 8th Army, which was 12 km north of Jassy, already gained the impression that the Romanians were no longer on the German side. Romanian soldiers spoke openly to the Germans that there would soon be a new government, which would make peace with the Soviet Union. These messages were relayed to *'up-stairs'*, where it was declared that they were ready to intervene should the need arise.

The 79th I.D. had already inconspicuously mapped out the storage depots of supplies of the 11th Romanian I.DS. and the 5th Kav.D., which lay next to them on the front at Jassy, and had their minds on how to capture them from the Romanians as soon as possible. This marked the problems of coalition warfare. The 79th I.D. was a good division, and regiments 208, 212 and 226, commanded by officers Rittner, Poehl and Plagemann, were well entrenched in their positions, which consisted of three lines of reception and were supplied with excitation wire and mines. Von Wolf's artillery regiment 179, and the added II./A.R. 40 ('Heeresartillerie'), provided additional support. Villages and farms had been built out as support points.[311] The picture matched that which German General Maximilian Fretter-Pico, commander of the XXXth German Army Corps, had already heard from General Dumitrescu in July 1944. The latter argued that Romania would lose even more territory if it withdrew from the war.[312]

German artillery preemptively fired into Red Army rallying points, but this could not prevent the movements from continuing. On the night of 18-19 August 1944, however, calm returned. The movements had been completed and this was just the calm before the storm. The following day, the violence was unleashed. These involved aggressive reconnaissance, at company and here and there at battalion level. Nonetheless, at the Romanian 21 I.D. near the town of Rascaeti, when a local breach of the front occurred. The 6th Romanian I.D. at the 'Armeegruppe' Wöhler beat off an attack.

At the 11th Romanian I.D., right next to the 79th I.D., an all-Soviet jet battalion had passed undetected through the Romanian lines and tried to take control of the railway bridge over the Pruth by surprise. As a precaution, a small German combat group from the pioneer division of the 79th I.D. was stationed there, and prevented the strategic bridge from actually being captured. It was another sign of things to come, both in terms of the reliability of the Romanian units and the fact that the offensive was coming.[313]

The attack hung in the air. There was no surprise. On the 18th of August 1944, Friessner sent a roll call to all German and Romanian commanders. In it, he stated that the attack was expected in the coming days. It was of the utmost importance to hold the main defence line ('Grosskampf HKL') at all costs. The following day another major meeting took place in Slanic with the main commanders, Friessner, Grolman, Von Trotha and Buntrock of the 'Heeresgruppe', Gaedtke of the 6th Army, Reinhardt of the 8th Army, Engele of the liaison staff with the Romanian 3rd Army and and Schulz of the 'Luftflotte 4'. The attack at Jassy was anticipated and the 6th Army expressed suspicion that it would come to a 'Grosskampf' with them too.[314] On 20 August, *'Black Sunday'*, the time had come. From thousands of artillery pieces, drumfire opened in the early hours of the morning on the 'Heeresgruppe Südukraine'. The centre of gravity was immediately clear on the first day: south of Tiraspol, north-west of Jassy and with centre of gravity on the Romanian units. Soon after the start of the offensive, there were two deep breakthroughs on both main attack lines. *'The Romanian units were surprisingly unsteadfast,'* was written in the diary of the Südukraine army group. On both fronts, the situation was *'serious'*.[315]

Concentrating first on the Romanian units, we see that the Soviets managed to separate the Germans and Romanians in the area of the 3rd Army. An attack on the right wing of the XXXth Army Corps achieved this. Some five Russian infantry divisions, supported by some 100 tanks, broke through the lines. The 4th Geb.Brigade was subdued, leaving the Romanian 21st I.D. to falter as well. Rascaeti was taken by the Red Army. The front began to slide, with the German 9th and 306th I.D. now taking on the full burden of the offensive. The German13th Pz.D. was deployed to halt the attack, but met with little success. *'The total weight of the defence lies on German shoulders,'* mused the army group's diary.[316]

Furthermore, things went wrong at the Wöhler 'Armeegruppe'. There, the front of the 7th and 5th Romanian I.D. was attacked between Rodi Mitropoliei and Erbiceni. These units left their positions almost without a struggle and went on the run. The towns of Vultur and Rediu lui tataru were lost as a result. Friessner, in his memoirs, spoke of a *'surprisingly rapid breakthrough'* by the Soviets. The front of the 11th Romanian I.D. and the German 79th I.D. initially remained intact. The 79th division was the neighbouring division of the Romanian 5th. It was disconnected from the unit and corps almost as soon as the drumming began. As a result, the 79th hung isolated on the front northeast of Jassy. Reconnaissance units were sent to the Romanians on the left flank, but no real picture was obtained. This changed when they picked up uncoded messages from the Red Army. The Soviets reported finding the Romanian 5th I.D.'s positions deserted.

This gap in the front was the beginning of even more bad news. Shortly afterwards, reports came in that the Soviets had already entered Jassy behind the back of the 79th I.D. The Soviet attack had started early that day and by 10.00 in the morning they had already reached the outskirts. There were few German troops in Jassy and the town commander Generalmajor Stingl met them with armed construction troops. At the large concrete bridge in the town, it came to an encounter. Stingl was no match for these Soviet shock troops and the city occupation sought refuge in the university buildings nearby. From there, there was bitter fighting with the Red Army.

Divisional commander Weinknecht of the 79th I.D. immediately understood the need to move in. The Germans had been scared to death since Stalingrad *'eingekesselt'* (surrounded) and a battle group was assembled to come to Stingl's aid. The Ist battalion of regiment 212, supported by 'Sturmgeschützbrigade 825', joined in. From the north, they advanced towards Jassy. What the Germans did not know was that the Soviets were already advancing south around Jassy, so the disengagement force encountered relatively little resistance. At 16:00 on this first eventful day of combat, Stingl's battle group was relieved and Romanian soldiers who had been made prisoners of war were freed.[317]

However, here the capabilities of the disengagement force also stopped. The one battalion was totally insufficient to really fight the city free. To the west of Jassy, stronger Soviet units had taken hold and would not allow themselves to be driven out. During the evening, fighting at Jassy flared up again. It was the German 10th Pz.gren.D. that intervened in the battle. The unit had crossed the river from the east side of the Pruth and was placed under the command of the IVth Corps in order to restabilise things at Jassy. Along the banks of the Bahlui, the unit had pushed up to Jassy and was now fighting with the Red Army. This was good news for the 79th I.D., but also indicated that the reserves were already fully deployed and the battle for the HKL was on. In quick succession, the 'Heeresgruppe' tried to form a new mobile reserve, taking armoured vehicles from the 2nd Romanian Pz.D. (with Antonescu's agreement) and - under Major Braun's leadership - converting them into the 'Kampfgruppe Braun', consisting of parts of the 20th Pz.D. and 'Sturmgeschützbrigade 905'. By the very next day, it was clear that Jassy could not be purged. The 79th I.D. lay intact in well-built positions, but hung in the air entirely on the left wing. Small remnants of the Romanian 5th Kav.D. seeped into the German positions in the north of Jassy the next day. They told the Germans that the war was over for them. They had been *'sent home'* by their officers. The Germans were stunned. It became clear that the 79th I.D. could not stay in position. Although there was hardly any contact with the corps, the actions of the Soviet air force gave an insight into where the front lay, and it already seemed to be playing out at *Trajan-Stellung*, some 20 km or so south. The positions that had been built up over four months had to be abandoned. The aim was to get the bulk of the troops behind the Bahlui River and meanwhile preserve the southern part of Jassy, through which the river flowed.[318]

The situation looked bleak for the 'Heeresgruppe Südukraine'. Soviet targets were already clearly drawing in. Tank units and grenadiers would push forward into the depths to take control of the bridge crossings on the Pruth river. In this way, the bulk of the Romanian army, the 'Armeegruppe' Dumitrescu, would be rolled up. According to Friessner, the breakthrough went down so successfully due to the failure of the Romanians, especially at the 'Armeegruppe' Wöhler. Here, four to five Romanian divisions had simply gone up in smoke and had been threatened by the 306th and 15th I.D. in their flanks. This had prevented them from concentrating on their main tasks and the 13th Pz.D. was too small to compensate for the loss. Wöhler, in consultation with Steflea, ordered the *Dacia-Stellung* to be abandoned and fall back to the *Trajan-Stellung* on the first day. At the 'Armeegruppe' Dumitrescu had lost the 4th Geb. Brigade and the

21st I.D.. Radio messages from the Red Army were picked up from which the isolated dramas became clear. For instance, the Russians reported that in the area of the Dumitrescu army group near Hadgimus, there had been heavy fighting with an isolated German company which was *'heroically resisting'*. Such heroism notwithstanding, the beginning of the Soviet offensive showed a *'catastrophic result'*, Friessner said.[319]

Soon after, Antonescu appeared at Friessner's headquarters in Slanic. It was the first time the men had seen each other, but it became a *'soldier to soldier'* conversation. Antonescu was surprised by the failure of the Romanian forces. He had often visited the positions and had been under the impression that the troops were steadfast. Friessner pointed out to him the political intrigues that might be running. Antonescu wanted nothing to do with that. Friessner was appreciative of his Romanian colleague, whom he saw as a military talent; a learnt man of stature.[320] Both agreed that the centre of gravity of the battle would be in the Pruth-Moldau area. Friessner believed that an encirclement was still avoidable, but one had to be able to build on the Romanians. That was a tough precondition. *'We are on a boat in the storm,'* Friessner wrote, *'and whoever disembarks now endangers not only their own country but the whole European world'*.[321]

But the ship was sinking, the 22nd August proved. The Soviets penetrated even deeper on the flank of the 6th Army. The town of Comrat was liberated. The XXXth German Corps was now in real danger. The Soviets lost 92 tanks at very heavy defences, but the front was not tenable. A retreat was out of the question; they had to fight back. They tried to keep the bridgehead at Leova open. The Romanians, more to the north in the *Trajan Stellung*, now also had a hard time. Here, the 101st Romanian Geb.Brigade was still fighting doggedly. A Soviet tank attack was repulsed, with 12 of the 20 Soviet tanks going up in flames.[322] That same day, permission to retreat behind the Pruth river finally arrived, in the so-called *Ferdinand-Pruth-Stellung*. The 11th Romanian I.D., together with the 79th German I.D., was breached several times that day and no longer had a united front.

On the 23rd, the Red Army's spires, east of the Pruth river, reached the area near Comrat. Parts of it turned south and took Tatar Bunar and Furmanca, 24 km north of Kilia. Parts of the Romanian III Army Corps became encircled as a result. The German 9th I.D. was ordered to break out to the southwest. The 6th Army retreated, organised as best it could. At the 'Armeegruppe' Wöhler, the Red Army penetrated the city of Roman. The 46th I.D. defending there had to turn back towards Trifesti. The following day, the Red Army pushed on to Bacau, which was overtaken. The general retreat was a race for safe shores. The Germans had to brave the north-south flowing Pruth, Barlad and Sereth. On the 24th, the diary of the 'Heeresgruppe Südukraine' reported that only the Romanian 20th I.D. was still in the positions and fighting properly.[323]

Hitler wanted to stand his ground. Friessner shrugged, *'völlig Situationsfremd'*, he noted about the 'Führerbefehl'. The IVth Corps meanwhile cleared Jassy. The Romanian 4th Army had already started the retreat on its own initiative and could only be halted again under great German pressure. It came to huge arguments between German officers and their Romanian colleagues. Army commander Racovitza of the 4th Romanian Army again invoked Antonecsu's orders. Elsewhere, Romanian cannons were simply hitched up and left the battlefield. Marshal Antonescu reappeared in Slanic with Friessner. It was his last visit to the 'Heeresgruppe'. The marshal was at his wit's end: *'If the Russians get past the Focsani-Galatz line, all is lost,'* he stated.[324]

The collapse of the Antonescu regime

'The Führer will eat more carpets now'
(From a translated report by the OSS of bugged German officers, September 1944)

On 23 August 1944, a message arrived from the 'Deutsche Heeresmission' in Romania that something was *'up'* with Marshal Ion Antonescu. Shortly afterwards, at 10pm, the king announced that an armistice had been concluded with the Soviet Union. What had happened? There was growing hesitation about Romanian role in the war. Even Antonescu was unsure. On the 22nd, he had talked to opposition parties about an even- tual ceasefire. Through his foreign minister, Antonescu sent a courier to Stockholm to contact Moscow. However, opposition circles did not want Antonescu to lead them out of the war. When Antonescu came to the king to inform him of his new moves, he was simply deposed. This was preceded by a conversation in which young king Mihai (Michael) indicated to Antonescu that peace should be signed. Antonescu struggled with the issue that he had given Hitler his word. He then came up with a counter-proposal to withdraw Romanian troops into the Carpathians and continue the battle there. The king could not agree; this would turn the whole country into a ruin. Subsequently Antonescu, Mihai Antonescu, the defence minister, Contantin Pantazi, and the interior minister Vasiliu, were arrested.

Antonescu knew there was opposition to continuing the fight and, in fact, it was as old as the Romanian crossing of the Dnieper, into Soviet territory. Marshal Antonescu still regarded the king as a child and the measure must have taken him by surprise. The king then handed Antonescu over to his communist enemies around Emil Bodnaras, a communist politician and Soviet agent who had been spying for Moscow since 1935 and had even spent years in prison in Brasov before that. Bodnaras later unceremoniously handed the marshal over to the Soviets without further consulting the king. Once the leader of the Romanian secret service noticed that Antonescu had not returned from the king and the German envoy Manfred Freiheer von Killinger was alerted. The M.A. club's contacts were still working.[325]

The die was cast and Romania abandoned the sinking ship. Friessner immediately called the leading Romanian generals. Dumitrescu, who knew Friessner as an old serious soldier, announced that he was completely surprised but could not damage the king's confidence. General Steflea informed that he had to *follow the instructions from Bucharest*. Next, the 'Heeresgruppe' was in contact with Hitler. The latter informed Friessner that he must *immediately deal with the traitor clique and form a new government*. This was not a typical assignment for a soldier and Friessner let Hitler know that too. The latter then thought that a reliable Romanian general should be found to take over the government.

While all this played out, the front collapsed and the troops were fighting for their lives. The situation of the 376th I.D., which had previously been destroyed at Stalingrad and rebuilt at the *Trajan position* east of Jassy, was typical of the whole.[326] The 376th I.D., together with the 11th Romanian I.D. and the German 79th I.D., was part of the IVth German Army Corps, the 'Gruppe Mieth', as part of the 8th German Army ('Armeegruppe' Wöhler). The division had lost contact with the Romanian 11th I.D., which was west of the division, shortly after the start of the Soviet offensive. On 22 August, the Russians were barely 500 metres in front of the division's headquarters. The trench system the division had built had proved its worth, but was simply no match for the masses the Soviet army deployed. Shortly afterwards, the headquarters of regiment 672 became surrounded. A relieved offensive was immediately carried out by Fuselier Battalion 376. The 'Sturmgeschützbrigade' 238 intervened as well. On the 25th, the division commander Generalleutnant Otto Schwarz gathered his officers around him. The 'Abfall' of Romenia was discussed. He predicted tough days for the German army and people had to try to *'keep their nerves in check'*. An *'exemplary attitude'* of the troops was expected, despite the difficult situation. Schwarz ordered the falling back from the *Tarjan position* to a line around the town of Ghermanesti. The troops had to fight their way there. Along the way, they were all joined by fleeing soldiers from the 106th Rhineland I.D., which had been broken up. They included Oberst Carl Ringenberg, the unit's commander. The unit's lousy situation was remarkable, considering that before the offensive, the unity was well regarded, with excellent morale. The division's material equipment had been in order too.[327]

The 106th Division, which was part of the VIIth German Army Corps of the 6th Army, had been completely overrun and was to be officially disbanded in October 1944, the same fate that awaited the 376th I.D. Many officers of the 106th I.D. had been killed or wounded, such as the commander of the pioneers who was replaced by Hauptmann Eder. Soon the line at Ghermanesti proved unsustainable as well and they had to fall further back. As the troops were hardly motorised, it became a rush hour race. This was made worse by the fact that the connection with the 79th I.D was also lost and there was a tank breakthrough by the Soviets on 26 August. On that day, headquarters was moved to Duda. By now there was only radio contact with the corps and Regiment 315. The anti-tank units of Pz. Jg.Abt. 376 with their 7.5cm Pak tried to stop the Soviet tanks as the order came in to advance towards the more southern XXXXI- Vste Corps, which had become surrounded. In an attempt to fight them free, the 79th and 370th I.D. attacked, while divisions 376 and 258 tried to cover the north wing.

In this chaotic fighting, news arrived that regimental commander Oberst Riedel of grenadier regiment 315 had been killed. The division's Ia, trying to connect with the division's other units, drove its small convoy into a Russian tank breach. The Ia narrowly escaped, but other staff officers were captured. On 27 August, an order arrived from the corps that was actually tantamount to saving who can save themselves. The 376 I.D. was in an extremely difficult position. Husi, where they wanted to go, turned out to be occupied by the Red Army. No more normally passable roads to the west were available. The troop vehicles were disabled and even the radio equipment of 'Nachrichten Abteilung 376' was destroyed. Deaf and blind they

Nationalkomitee
„Freies Deutschland"
Bund Deutscher Offiziere

RUMÄNIEN IST AUSGESCHIEDEN!

An die Offiziere und Soldaten der 23. Pz. Div.!

Ihr kommt aus Rumänien und habt in Jassy gelegen. Dort war es „ruhig"—also schnell hierher ins Karpatenvorland, wo es brannte. Jetzt ist auf dem Balkan der Sturm losgebrochen.

Am 23. August begann die russische Offensive. In wenigen Tagen wurde die deutsche Armee zerschlagen, 4 deutsche Generale gefangengenommen und die Städte JASSY, FOKSCHAN, RIMNIKUL, SULINA, GALATZ, KONSTANZA u. a. besetzt.

Das rumänische Volk hat Antonescu gestürzt und die rumänische Armee

The comittee 'Freies Deutschland' points out the hopeless position of the As-armed forces to them.

now moved on through the terrain towards Cretesti. The seriously wounded were left behind with Oberarzt Dr Stephan, in the hope that the Red Army would follow conventions to protect the wounded.

This was not a foregone conclusion on the Eastern Front. At Cretesti, elements of the 376th I.D. encountered remnants of the 79th I.D. that still had a radio. Here contact was made with the corps. In Siscani, the new headquarters was moved into. General Schwarz was so physically spent that he was replaced by Oberst Schulz, who now led the remnants of the 376th I.D. At Siscani, the remnants of the 79th Division and the 370th I.D. now also gathered. From the corps, orders were given to blow up all vehicles and fight free. At 04.00 in the morning, they tried the breakthrough towards Vutcani. The 376th I.D. was with the 'Kampfgruppe' Dreyer (regiment 672) in the 09.00 am group. One reached the vicinity of Orgoest, but the hills near Vutcani turned out to be strongly occupied with Red Army soldiers.

Southwest of Vutcani, under the command of corps officer Major I.G. Bucher, troops managed to get a bridge across the Barlad (Barladul) into German hands. The 376th I.D. tried to join this. There was no longer a large overarching command. To the west of the Barladul, the survivors gathered. Two new 'Kampfgruppen' were formed with men from different units of the IVth and VIIth Army Corps. Heavily wounded were left behind and continued towards the Sereth River, which was crossed 50 km south-east of Bacau on the 30th. A new 'Kampfgruppe' commanded by Generalmajor Hülsen was formed on the west bank. The 370th I.D. Ammunition was redistributed and the troops continued on their way.

In the Trotosul valley, any organised breakthrough to the west came to a halt. The valley appeared to be occupied by Soviet troops and survivors who broke out later reported that in one village the commanders of both the 370th and 376th I.D. had been overrun by the Soviets. With their own lines in sight, Oberstleutnant I.G. Heinz of the 376th I.D. stepped on a landmine and was captured by the Soviets. By this time, all the division's regimental commanders had been killed or captured. The 376th I.D. had ceased to exist.[328]

Obituary of a German 'Ritterkreuztrager', who fell at the Romanian front August 1944.

The Western Allies announce the occupation of Bucharest.

The 258th I.D., the 'Eingreifreserve' behind the front near Jassy, suffered the same fate and also had to cross the Barlad near Vutcani. The Pomeranian-Mecklenburg division, which had been at the front since 1939, had been replaced by the 282nd and 62nd divisions at the front on 19 August, to act as a reserve. To this end, the unit had been assembled at Milestii Mari, as part of the VIIth Army Corps. As soon as battle broke out, reports trickled in that the 7th Romanian I.D. and the 5th Kav.D. had been pushed out of their lines and that the 79th I.D. had been compromised. The 258th I.D. was ordered to close the impending gap at Jassy and was rushed to the front.

In trucks, they continued their way to the threatened zone. Divisional commander Oberst Hilscher was updated on the situation at the divisional headquarters of the 10.P.zD. There was great unrest everywhere. Jassy itself was in danger of being taken and the first available units were required to march out immediately. This was the so-called 'Kampfgruppe' Sann, led by Major Sann, which consisted mainly of the Füs.Btj. 259, a number of pioneers and a company from regiment 479. The unit was brought as close as possible to Jassy, but the town was already in danger of falling. Some isolated German units still held out near the railway station in the town. 'Kampfgruppe' Sann had to fall back to the town of Poeni, and on the 22nd there were consultations at divisional headquarters in Cortesi, southeast of Jassy. There it became clear that there could be no more talk of closing the front. The Soviets had already penetrated the depths left and right with tanks and motorised infantry. The Jassy - Moldovenii - Vasluiui road was already in the hands of the Red Army. Soviet fighter pilots controlled the skies above the battlefield.

Around Poeni, the nage units of the 258th I.D. were now captured too, including the artillery division. The centre of gravity now shifted from a thrust towards Jassy to a breakout towards the west. Divisional headquarters was shifted to Pocreaca. Regiments 479 and 387 assembled there. The latter regiment was already pretty shaken up by the turbulence. There was not a moment's rest. From Pocreaca it continued back to Pietris, heading southeast.

On 24 August, it became clear that the Soviets were already at Dolhesi with tanks. Hilscher moved the division's headquarters to

Armaseni. Regiment 387 led the breakthrough further south. Armaseni, Rosiori and Averestie were broken through and cleared of Soviet troops. At Plopi, the attack came to a halt. About 15 Soviet tanks blocked the road here, as well as Red Army infantry. The pressure on Plopi intensified. Eventually most of the Soviet tanks withdrew, but five unmovable tanks, which were manned, remained behind and posed a threat. It went hard against hard. During the night, Oberst Hilscher gathered his officers around him. A concentrated breakthrough was prepared and the next morning, 25 August 1944, both to the left and right of Plopi, a surprise attack was launched. The Russians were taken completely by surprise by the balled-up deployment of forces. A Russian column of trucks was overrun. A unit of motorcyclists unsuspectingly drove into the German line and was completely destroyed by Pak and Flak. A Soviet double-decker reconnaissance plane accidentally landed among the German troops. Supplies, including tyre dust, were captured. While advancing towards the southern edge of Hosi, Plopi was cleared by major Sann's 'Füsilier Bataillon'. The 'Kampfgruppe' was then deployed to keep the road from Husi to the southeast clear for the retreating unit. In the process, Tatarani was captured. Soviet resistance was broken with Pak and Flak. Soviets then shelled the place with rocket launchers. Russian fighters were frequently used. Losses could not be avoided. The Ia and Iia of the 258th division, Oberstleutnant Von Bila and Hauptmann Drescher, were wounded.

A new, feverish consultation took place in the evening. Food supplies had practically run out and troops were weakening rapidly. The overall situation was completely unclear to the division. There was no longer any direction at corps or division level. About the position of the Romanians, the men of the 258th I.D. were completely unaware. They saw with their own eyes that at least some Romanian units were still fighting on the German side.

The next day, the breakout continued and units of the 258th I.D. reached the town of Kurdugui, where heavy fighting broke out. In the process, the division quickly ran out of the last remnants of ammunition. Oberstleutnant Tech of regiment 478 was appointed Kampfkommandant of Kurdugui. On the following day, the division became more and more entrenched. The town was under very heavy Soviet artillery fire and burned down completely. The men of the 258th I.D. now had virtually no cover. The situation was becoming untenable. The final breakthrough had to take place now. Oberst Hilscher reported that there were still five groups of Germans in the area trying to break out to the west. They were trying to streamline somewhat and come to a common breakout. The last heavy weapons, which ran out of fuel, were blown up. At 4pm, Kurdugui was abandoned. One penetrated as far as four km west of the town. The Soviets immediately followed and heavy rearguard fighting ensued. One continued roughly in the direction of Vutcani. There was no more organisation. The few 'Sturmgeschützen' who had accompanied the affair had run out of ammunition. The troops thronged together and the Soviets fired into the crowd. The losses were terrible. There was no longer an overarching command. Oberst Hilscher was hit by Red Army fire in a maize field west of Vutcani and died. On 29 August, the Barlad bridge was passed ten km from Vutcani. The remnants of the 258th I.D. flowed westward without any cohesion under the fire of Stalin organs (Katyusha). The 258th I.D. had gone into battle as a well-equipped unit and was completely dispersed and defeated in barely a week.[329]

Lieutenant Lange and Wachtmeister Fromm reported on the fate of the 370th I.D. In September, they reconnected with the German troops and were questioned. The 370th I.D. had been on the Jassy front, as a neighbouring division of the 106th I.D. and the 376th I.D. of the XVIIth Army Corps. Lieutenant Lange served with I.R. 668 and Fromm with the artillery regiment 370. On 21 August, the order had been given to detach from the Red Army and begin the retreat. The men also took part in the retreat, within the lines of regiment 668, commanded by Major Marheinicke. As by no means all equipment could be taken along, 60 to 70 wagons (!) of ammunition, mostly Pak grenades, were blown up. In hilly countryside, the retreat was laborious and slow. The roads were extremely bad. The Russians closely followed the retreat. At Hisporani, the unit tried to reassemble, but before this position could be reached, the column was broken up by concentric Soviet attacks. In a forest, near the route, the units of the 370th I.D. took refuge.

This forest was then heavily shelled by Soviet artillery, with serious consequences. In the process, hundreds of vehicles became trapped on the narrow forest paths. Panic ensued and German troops went on the run. Staff officers were no longer there. An officer breakout group, with some soldiers, had tried to fight their way through the Russian lines, but whether they had succeeded was not known. On 24 August, Lange was at the head of several dozen soldiers breaking out in a southeastern direction. The roads were full of Red Army soldiers everywhere. The German group roamed the country, searching for a way out. Rivers were swum and after a 400-km (!) foot march towards Broscheni, they finally found themselves rejoining their own troops. The exhausted men were met by the 13th company of the Geb.Jg.Rgt. 144 of the LVIIth Corps.[330]

In Führer headquarters, people were, out of necessity, making plans for a major retreat. There was already heavy speculation about building a new deterrance front in Hungary. At a certain point, the Soviet supply lines became too long and there was a lull, which had to be exploited. In the meantime, Hitler demanded military intervention against the new rulers in Bucharest via a 'Führerbefehl'. There had been reports of open hostilities between Romanian and German troops from the Carpathian front on 24 August 1944. Here, men of the 3rd Romanian Border Guard Regiment had fired on soldiers of the German 3rd Geb.D.. In general, Romanian troops seemed to avoid confrontation.[331]

As the front cracked, Hitler ordered General Alfred Gerstenberg to intervene. There were rumours that the embassy was surrounded by Romanian tanks and that General Christian Hansen was also trapped there. In case Gerstenberg was unable to intervene, SS Brigadefüher Hoffmeyer was probed for the same assignment. The always fanatical Hoffmeyer immediately started gathering troops stationed around Ploesti. From his 'Waldlager' near Bucharest, he rather optimistically announced that he would be able to intervene within an hour and a half. Even before that happened, the DHM was contacted at 03.05 and it was reported that General Hansen was in consultation with Racovita, the new Romanian Defence Minister. The latter made it clear to the Germans that they should refrain from countermeasures and that otherwise hostilities would ensue.

At 04.05, the 'Heeresgruppe' managed to get in touch with General Hansen himself. The latter informed that it was not a small *'traitor clique'* they were facing, but that there was support from the population and from the military apparatus.[332] General Gerstenberg, Dr Clodius, General Hansen and Von Killinger agreed that the German forces were insufficient to intervene. At this, Hitler sought refuge with Luftwaffe chief Hermann Göring, who then contacted General Gerstenberg with the unholy plan to have 'Luftflotte IV' bomb Bucharest. This would seriously overcomplicate matters. A kind of truce was now in force, under which the Germans could withdraw without a fight and the Romanian forces would take up positions behind the Braila - Fopcsani line. At 04.35, there were feverish consultations with the 'Luftwaffe'. It was not yet too late to make the deal without unnecessary bloodshed. At 05:00, however, reports came in that Hitler stood by his decision. On the 24th, Hitler had ordered to bomb Bucharest. It was pure revenge with no military purpose. 'Stukas' had taken off from the Baneasa base and then fired on the Royal Palace and government buildings. In response, the king diverted to Oltenita (Oras).[333] Gerstenberg rushed from Bucharest to the 'Waldlager', from where he helped coordinate. Some 6,000 men had been assembled by SS-Brigadeführer Hoffmeyer, who marched against Bucharest at 07:30. At 11.30 it became clear that Romanian opposition was fiercer than expected. Reinforcements were flown in and two 'Landschutzenkompagnies' from Focsani were to be rushed to the capital. New battle groups were assembled from the 5th Flak Division commanded by Julius Kuderna, who was responsible for the anti-aircraft defence around Ploesti. In addition, they scraped together units at Constantza, such as a company from the 'Brandenburg' regiment (4. Rgt.'Brandenburg') and the Pz.Späh.Kp. 468 and the '2. Sturmgeschütz-Brigade 201'. These were all very small units and they could not make a turn. Romanian general Iosif Teodorescu beat off the German attack. In Bucharest, the German units gathered around the freshly appointed Rainer Stahel, a Flak officer from Bielefeld, who had previously been commander of the 'Festen Platz'

Wilna and briefly also of Warsaw. He too could do little. Things were rapidly deteriorating for the Germans. On 26 August, Gerstenberg's and Hoffmeyer's units were surrounded by the Romanians. The next day, Gerstenberg informed Friessner that a direct attack on his weakened 5th Flak Division at Ploesti could be expected at any moment. *'We will fight to the last man,'* he informed. At 4.40pm the report came that the refinery lines had been captured by the Romanians. In Bucharest, too, the Germans were becoming increasingly outgunned. Near the city, the Romanians had 26 German-made 'Panther' tanks and the 'Gruppe Stahel' had shrunk to 1,900 troops. He telegraphed to Friessner asking if reinforcements were still on the way. When these failed to arrive, a breakthrough towards Mizil or Ploesti was considered.[334] On the 28th, the last German units were driven out of Bucharest. Among them were General Gerstenberg and the just appointed Kampfkommandant Bucharest, General Rainer Stahel.[335]

By now, it had become clear that no Romanian units at the front were obeying German orders any longer. The consequence of Hitler's bombing of Bucharest was that the neutral Romanians had now become Germany's enemies. The declaration of war followed on 25 August 1944. Things went from bad to worse. At the front, the 3rd and 4th Romanian Army marched westwards towards the Focsani-Braila line. *'The floodgates were open,'* Friessner wrote.[336]

Back it went, everything flowed westwards. The Carpathian roads, along which troops escaped to Hungary, were narrow and clogged. Nobody could move forward anymore and there was general confusion. Ammunition depots were blown up, as were oil tanks. The next major battle unfolded around Ploesti, where the various Flak divisions had formed into battle groups and had to repel attacks from all sides. The falling German armies formed themselves into 'Kampfgruppen', such as those commanded by General Friedric von Scotti and Walter Winkler. Places like Braila and Focsani were eventually designated 'Festen Platz' after all, an order with which Hitler tried to use them as a *'breakwater'* against the advance. In practice, these measures amounted to little. The diary of the 'Heeresgruppe Südukraine' of 23 August indicated the occupation of Braila by 1800 men and that of Focsani by only 300.[337] Flak units of Oberst Simon's

15th Flak Division were now directly at the front. How heavy the fighting was was shown by the losses their guns caused in these days: 112 aircraft, 96 tanks and 82 artillery pieces. In Constantza, the port was blown up and the coastal battery *Tirpitz* went up in flames. The oil area of Ploesti was lost. German troops there fought both Romanians and Russians. Hitler suggested at the last minute the idea of deploying SS paratroopers who were active on the Yugoslav front at the time, but this plan was not viable. Meanwhile, British agents were flown in from London because of the strategic importance of the oil fields near Ploesti. In fact, the harbinger of the coming Cold War was already at play here.[338]

Divisions fell apart, men were overtaken by Russian troops and tried to reconnect with the German lines alone or in groups. Some even went out in civilian clothes. Their experiences were mixed. *'The Romanians gave us food and showed us the way'*. Others complained about the Romanians reporting them to the Russians or even shooting at them. About the Hungarians, people were generally more polite. They were more friendly towards the German soldiers. Where the Romanians had become acquainted with their 'liberators', however, the atmosphere turned. The Russians were notorious for their behaviour and Germans were *'rehabilitated'* to some extent as a result. *'They showed us the safest roads again'*, stated NCOs Kuhnel from Golitsch and Punkes from Richterstatt in their raport after reaching the German lines again.[339]

The Jassy-Kishinev battle, as the drama entered the history books, lasted from 20 to 29 August 1944. The consequences of the large-scale Soviet breakthrough were enormous. Germany lost Romania as an ally, Bulgaria followed on 24 August 1944, there were uprisings in Slovakia and Finland abandoned the sinking ship in September. So the consequences were huge. Historian Silviu Miloiu argued that Romanian secession from Nazi Germany had been widely debated in the Finnish press, and that this also affected the situation in Finland.[340] Turkey had already severed diplomatic relations with nazi-Germany on 2 August. Antonescu had feared this all along. What to do if Turkey opened the waterways to the Allies? After the breakthrough at Jassy, there was no longer a stable south-east front.[341]

The German front of the 'Heeresgruppe Süd'[342] fell back on Hungary, where new, very heavy fighting awaited. Additionally, the Red Army penetrated Yugoslavia and threatened the German 'Heeresgruppe F' in south-eastern Europa. A Reuter report from Moscow on 3 September had calculated German-Romanian losses at 238,000 men; other sources spoke of 250,000 to 280,000 men. The official Soviet report later assumed 256,000 losses on the German side, of which 150,000 had been killed.[343] Some of the German POWs had been captured by the Romanians. This would include some 50,000 troops, nine generals and 652 officers. Among them General Gerstenberg. SS-Brigadeführer Horst Hoffmeyer committed suicide in Russian captivity at Krapovo camp. A large number of other senior officers were made prisoners of war, such as Stanislaus von Dewitz, the city commander of Kikschinev, Ludwig Müller, commander of the XXXXIVth Army Corps, Julius Kuderna of the 5th Flak Division, Friedrich August Weinknecht, commander of the 79th I.D., Hans Simon, comman- dant of the 5th Flak Division, Georg Postel, commander of the XXXth Corps, Karl Stingl, commander of Jassy, Karl Spalcke, the military attaché in Bucharest, Botho von Hülsen, commander of the 370th I.D, Otto Schwarz, commander of the 376th I.D., Erich Buschenhagen, commander of the LIIth Corps, Friedrich Bayer, commander of the 153rd F.A.D., and Hans Troe- ger, commander of the 13th Pz.D., who ended up in Bulgarian captivity. General-major Walter Gleininger committed suicide and General Friedrich Mieth of the IVth Corps died on 29 August 1944, as did artillery colonel Paul Kohwalt. [344]

The collapse of the Jassy front brought new problems for Nazi Germany. On 9 September, Friessner was in Budapest. After Antonescu, there was a new ally to be kept happy. Admiral Miklos Horthy wielded the sceptre there - until October 1944 - and had naturally followed developments in Romenia closely. The consequences were directly felt by Hungarians too, due to the Soviet push into Transylvania. Border units and paramilitary militias, some 20 Szekler battalions, had marched towards the Soviets, but were just as quickly dispersed. It became a difficult conversation for Friessner in Budapest, especially as it was not limited to military matters, which were complicated enough in themselves. Members of the Hungarian cabinet agreed to a return to the Honduran core country; others wanted to keep the precious Transylvanian land at all costs, because *'the best Ungarntum'* lived there. In doing so, the Hungarians made high demands on the German military.[345] Like Antonescu, the Hungarians demanded a line on map behind which they would be safe. But Berlin had long since stopped dictating how things looked at the front.

The front was moving and difficult to stop. Until the last moment, OKW and OKH tried to restore their grip on the situation through all kinds of interventions. On 15 September, for example, orders had gone out that any soldier who destroyed an enemy tank with a 'Panzerfaust' or 'Panzerschreck', a hand-held anti-tank weapon, could count on a holiday from the front. Soldiers who shot two tanks with their Pak 7.5 cm got the same reward. The heavier 8.8 Flak had to make do with four tanks. The leave was for 10 days. The reason for this measure, apart from the disastrous situation for Nazi Germany at the front, was the fact that the enemy tank losses were out of all proportion to the large numbers of (hand-held) anti-tank weapons available to German troops. The order had been signed personally by Friessner.[346]

Besides the above emergency measure, they further tried to rearrange things organisationally. In the absence of sufficient motorised units, they tried to reinforce tank defences ('Panzerjäger') on the German side. This freed up the 'Sturmgeschützen', which were largely trapped within the infantry divisions - often like a corset bar to which the infantry clung - and could be used as a mobile reserve. As a replacement, the Pz. Jäger-Sturmgeschütz 38 T 'Hetzer' had been developed. Each division was to consist of 14 examples and each 'Hetzer' was to be equipped with 1,000 'Panzergranaten' and 1,000 'Sprenggranaten'. This weapon would be the best answer to Soviet panzer supremacy. The divisions would have to be closed to deployment. The 'Panzerjäger' was built on a Czech chassis. *'Fighting to the bitter end is the only combat mode for the Panzerjäger'*, the 'Führungsgrundsätze' stated, *'No weapon may fall into enemy hands undamaged'*. The 'Panzer- jäger' was strong, cheap and effective, but came too late to cause a change. After the war, the Czechs and the Swiss absorbed the 'Hetzers' (or variants thereof) within their own armed forces.[347]

Moreover, they tried to recapture the scattered German infantry that fell westwards. On 19 September 1944, 'Feldjäger' were organised to catch these falling back units along the Oradea line (Grosswardein) - Szatmar - Nemeti - Nyiregyhaza - Eger to the area north of Budapest. From there, troops were to be forwarded by the Feldjäger-Kdo.I on- der command of General Müller to assembly points organised by unit. Thus soldiers of the 8th Army went to Bethlen, 6th Army to Szilagysomly, 'Heeresgruppe' staff to Hadju-Szoboszto, 15th Flak D. to Valea-lui-Mihai, 'Luftwaffe' personnel to Debrecen, Navy to Budapest, militia-like units to Valea-lui-Mihai, DHM-Rumänien to Kis Ujscallas and 'Hiwis' to Szaniszlo.[348]

In a discussion with the commanders of the 6th and 8th armies in Szatmar Nemety, Friessner stressed that every effort had to be made to keep obedience high. This had to be clear from the highest commander to the simplest soldier. *'If an officer is ordered to defend a certain front area he must stand there and die. One must not swerve'*. The big scare was the French front, where German soldiers with their officers surrendered with white flags. That was not allowed to happen in the east. There were concerns about the large number of suicides as well, which were only allowed if one's own *'honour'* was at stake. Yet, as long as there was *'another German soldier standing next to another'*, they had to fight on.[349] All German efforts notwithstanding, on 25 October 1944 the last Romanian town of Carei was liberated. With the collapse of the Romanian front at Jassy and the turn that Romanian politics took, the front had moved almost 500 km to the west in a very short time. Heavy scars were left behind. Romanian losses on the front amounted to 500,000 men. However, Rumania had been spared much fighting by the turnaround. A traditional occupation had also been omitted as a result. In the process, the Romanians turned their artillery and were now fighting on the Allied side.

With the matter lost both politically and militarily, Berlin searched diligently for a substitute for their staunch ally Antonescu. The first choice was the Romanian ambassador to Berlin, General Gheorge, but he had little desire to board a sinking ship. In this, the alternative scenario was chosen. Horia Sima, sentenced to death in Romania but sheltering in Germany, was put in the starting blocks. One fell back on the old guards, who had been put under a spell by Antonescu in early 1941.

Along with other leaders of the Iron Guard, Sima had, after January 1941 and the 'putsch pogrom' in Bucharest, been detained in the 'Arbeitslager' Bergenbrück near Frankfurt am Oder. Since then, there had been an internal struggle in Germany over how the gardists should be treated. There was a hard line (foreign ministry) and a soft line ('Reichssicherheitshauptamt').[350]

The lack of direction so unsettled Sima that in December 1942 he tried to defect to Italy, where he hoped for more understanding from his Fascist counterpart Benito Mussolini. However, not long after, he was back in German custody. Horia Sima was in the 'Sonderlager' Fichtenhain, an 'Aussenlager' of Buchenwald near Weimar, and was given 50 Reichmark *pocket money* a month from February 1943 by the Reichsführer-SS Himmler, which was used to try to alleviate the conditions under which the gardists were held. His adjutant Traian Borubaru and 11 others also received this allowance.[351]

In practice, it corresponded to a mild house arrest, but this way Sima and his supporters could no longer get in Antonescu's way. Now they were given a second chance. The diplomat Erich Haas, himself from Transylvania and formerly working at the embassy in Bucharest, was assigned by Berlin as translator and 'protokollarischer Bertreuer'. In a New Year's message on 3 January 1945, Sima called for a fight against the *'barbarian enemy'*. He stated that the Führer was watching over the fate of Europe *'calmly and with determined energy'*. The former governor of Bessarabia, Vladimir Christi, stated that *'the Romanian government would not rest until, together with the German army, they had liberated Romania from Bolshevism'*.[352] Sima made weighty claims about the following he would still have in Romania and believed that 60,000 to 80,000 men could be mobilised to fight against communism as partisans. In practice, however, it soon became clear that many gardists considered the cause lost and decided to cut their losses. Two regiments were eventually formed, one of which was still being developed in Poland when the Red Army approached, Sima's exil government was transferred from Vienna to Alt-Aussee and simply disbanded by the Germans in May 1945.[353]

With the retreat of the German units, agony began for the 'Volksdeutschen'. They were ill-prepared for events. Since any doom-and-gloom was tantamount to defeatism, there was no script. Andreas Schmidt, the leader of the Romanian 'Volksdeutschen', was not even in the country when the change of power in Romania took place. His mode of operation came under increasing criticism from the SS, and Himmler believed he had to *'rehabilitate'* himself.[354] There were wild plans for the liquidation of Romanians, regardless of their ethnicity, who would collaborate with the Soviets. One SD foreman believed that one could mobilise units of the Romanian army and 'Volksdeutschen' in the Carpathians, who, supported by paratrooper units, could continue to offer resistance. It was somewhat similar to the 'Werwolf' organisational plans that continued in the west and were initially led by SS-Oberstgruppenführer Hans-Adolf Prützmann. Parts of the SD had developed a *'stay-behind'* strategy, in which sabotage and terror went hand in hand. The murder of 'Werwolf' units of Aachen's new mayor Franz Oppenhoff in liberated territory, on 25 March 1945, was the best-known example of this.[355]

Initially, the 'Volksdeutschen' were urged to remain calm and wait and see. Yet when the German troops withdrew, some residents simply joined them. In the process, the new government announced measures against both the 'Volksdeutschen' and the Hungarian minority in the country. The official offices of the 'Volksdeutschen' were immediately closed. Prominent people were arrested, although in many cases they were teachers and the like who did not actually hold political office. Some 2,000 to 3,000 people were reportedly involved, some of whom went to Targu-Jiu camp, on the edge of the southern Carpathians. They were generally treated reasonably.

On 5 September, SS-Obergruppenführer Otto Phleps, himself from the region, gave the go-ahead for a large-scale evacuation. This involved enlisting the 'Kreisleiter' from the regions. Thus, on 7 September 1944, 'Kreisleiter' Andreas Schell of the 'Ortsgruppe Botsch' received the go-ahead for the 'Wagentreck' from Phleps.[356] Phleps' official title was: 'Bevollmächtigter General für Siebenbürgen'. A huge stream of refugees arrived, often by horse and cart due to lack of railway capacity. Phleps indicated that he urgently needed troops to cover the exodus of some 350,000 people (the able-bodied men were all in the army, i.e. the elderly, women and children). Should they fall into the hands of the Red Army, Phleps told the OKH and Himmler, a *'völlige Vernichtung'* was to be expected.

As if Phleps did not have enough problems anyway, he was also confronted with unrealistic expectations from Himmler. The Reichsführer insisted on forming units from the 'Volksdeutsche' community that could go partisan hunting. Phleps firmly rejected this. People who had led a civilian peasant life for 800 years could not be so easily militarised. Besides, all able-bodied men (64,000 men) were already serving in the German armed forces.[357]

It was a race against time. They even considered flying in paratroopers to protect the road junctions. Parts of the 22nd 'SS-Freiwilliggen Kavallerie Division' 'Maria Theresia' in line near Budapest were deployed. Moreover, Phleps requested the release of his *'trusted'* division SS Mountain Division 'Prinz Eugen'. Furthermore, the message was let out that actions by Romanians on the 'Volksdeutschen' would result in reprisals against Romanian minorities in Hungary. The latter was possibly prompted by the latest German experience in Slovakia, where an uprising against the Axis powers had occurred on 24 August 1944. In this, the 'Volksdeutsche' population of Slovakia, under Schmidt's Slovak equivalent, Franz Karmasin, suffered terribly.[358]

It became an agony towards an uncertain future. Along the way, Allied fighters swooped down on them and strafed the unarmed columns. German troops tried to help them where they could and took escapees on their vehicles. In Transylvania, cavalry units of the '8th SS Kavalerie Division Florian Geyer' came to the aid of the refugees. At river crossings, carts and carriages gathered for the crossing and it became an unimaginable chaos. It came to serveral incidents, including with Hungarian units, which increasingly distanced themselves from the Germans.

The 'Volksdeutschen' who remained behind had their own problems. As soon as identity papers came into the hands of the Red

Army, 'Volksdeutschen' were called up as auxiliaries for the Red Army. Men came into work battalions, women had to work in the hospitals. The Romanian 'Volksdeutschen' thus got off lightly compared to the 'Volksdeutschen' from Yugoslavia, who were seen passing by on transport into the Soviet Union. Romania was not seen by the Soviet Union, as a result of the 23rd August, as an enemy nation. Nevertheless, Bucharest wanted to respond to the Soviet Union's call for labour. To this end, the 'Volksdeutschen' were still rounded up and deported. These included both men and women in the working age classes. The 'Volksdeutsche' areas were surrounded by politicians and the army and some 75,000 people went on transport, mostly to the *Donjets coal basin* where the Romanian troops had been a few years earlier. They were put to work in Stalino, Worroschilowgrad, Kriwoi Rog and Dniepropetrowsk. Conditions there were primitive and some 15% would lose their lives there.[359]

Many Volksdeutschen managed to evade deportation by going into hiding and hiding. They were often helped in this by their Romanian neighbours. Some spokesmen of the 'Volksdeutschen', such as the Siebenbürger Sachs Hanns Otto Roth and the Banat German Frank Kräuter appealed to the Romanian elite. Among others, the Jewish foreman Dr Fildermann was approached, but the door remained closed there.[360] More difficult for the Romanian authorities was the question of what to do with the 'Volksdeutschen' who had fought in the Waffen-SS. Most of these had been imprisoned near Kiev and were then transported to Romania in December 1950.[361] Once there, they were often stripped of their nationality. Many transporters went on to the GDR, which was created after the fall of Nazi Germany. Many 'Volksdeutschen', who had been 'umgesiedelt' to the parts of Poland occupied by Nazi Germany, were simply put back on the train to Romania by the new communist authorities. Some who remained behind were able to migrate to Germany in 1950.[362]

The follow-up battle is beyond the scope of this book, but is described in *Hungary 1944-1945, the Forgotten Tragedy*.[363] After a fierce battle in the Puszta, east of Budapest, from Christmas night 1944 the battle focused on the Hungarian capital Budapest, which had been bombed into a 'Festung'. There, German and Hungarian troops fought a battle doomed to failure until 13 February, the day the city fell and several hundred soldiers of the 72,000-strong garrison managed to escape. A trio of disengagement offensives, Operation 'Konrad' from the Gerecse-Pilis Mountains and the area north of Lake Balaton (Plattensee) ran aground before they could reach Budapest.

After the failed *Ardennes offensive* in the west, the 6th SS Pz.leger under the command of Hitler's confidant Jospeh (Sepp) Dietrich was transported to Hungary. After a limited offensive against the Gran bridgehead north of the Danube, the SS army was deployed in operation 'Frühlingserwachen'. Dietrich boasted that he would give Hitler the Ploesti oil fields for his 56th birthday, but the attack, which started on 6 March 1945, did not even reach the Donau. On 16 March, it had started to freeze and when the roads were passable again, the Soviets opened their 'Vienna operation'. The 6th SS Pz. Army was driven back towards the Austrian border. The hastily expanded *Reichsschutz-stellung* could not prevent the Red Army from also invading Austria, after which, after the fall of Vienna, the Nazi leadership retreated to the so-called 'Alpenfestung' and experienced the end of the war there. By then, General Friessner had long since been replaced by General Wöhler, the commander of the 8th Army, who in turn handed over the staff to General Lothar Rendulic. None of them were able to turn the odds of war anymore.

Romanian forces turned the guns westwards after the waste of Germany. In practice, to some extent, the same happened here as in the east. From the moment the last piece of Romanian territory was 'liberated', interest waned. The bulk of Romanian troops were put under the command of Marshal Rodi- on Malinovsky's 2nd Ukrainian Front. These included the 1st and 4th Romanian Army. There was also the volunteer division 'Tudor Vladimirescu' fighting within the ranks of the Red Army and commanded by Colonel Cambrea. The latter was wounded on 30 September and was replaced by Oberstleutnant Micea Haupt. Malinovsky faced quite a challenge. His troops were fighting in three countries, Romania, Hungary and Yugoslavia, and faced serious logistical problems. Large parts of the army were still in Bessarabia, including hundreds of tanks, while the front was already at Debrecen in Hungary, where there was heavy fighting.

The battle first concentrated around Debrecen and on 30 October 1944 the operation started towards Budapest. Cooperation between the Romanians and Russians was not without problems. Near Szolnok, Romanian troops went on a massive rampage during a German counter-offensive. The Red Army responded with summary executions. At the battle of Budapest, the VIIth Romanian Corps under General Nicolae Sova made an important contribution. Just before Pest was captured, Soviet general Afonyin directed the Romanians out of the city. It was clear that the Red Army did not want to share the impending victory with the Romanians. Romanian general Sova was white hot with anger. The Romanians had 11,000 men dead, wounded and missing in the hard street fighting, which was about a third of the combat value of the Romanian corps.

About the difficult cooperation between the Red Army and the Romanian army, we find an interesting report by a German SS-Hauptsturmführer Ing. Kurz (probably working in the 'SD'), who found his way through the lines to the German front: *'At Petri a Russian company, 200 men, all between 14 and 16 years old. They were well equipped [...]. A Russian officer told me that the Soviet Union was going to field a million such cadettes next winter. As new troops within the Red Army, I also saw Romanians from Transnistria, Bessarabia and North Bukovina. Mostly these were older annuals. [...] The fighting spirit of the Romanians is very small. They get no supplies, no newspapers, the regiment does not even have a radio. Nothing extra came at Christmas. Mail from the home front was 30 days in transit. Officers and soldiers scolded the war and the Russians. They feared the defeat of*

Germany, otherwise they would all have deserted by now. Russians are war-weary. They scolded Stalin. [...] In the stage I only saw ammunition and fuel [...] In the Romanian soldiers you can see the hunger in their eyes. [...] When Hungarian soldiers are taken prisoner of war they quickly let them go back into civilian clothes. There are many Hungarian deserters. The Russians realise this and demand that the Hongarian POWs be handed over to the Red Army'.[364]

Struggling with the demons of the past

'In Romania, no one believed in communism with conviction, at least not the murderous version of Ceaucescu. Fear was the only weapon.'

(Jeroen van Kan: Silence or Writing,
In conversation with Herta Müller)

Processing the past came with difficulty in Romania. This was due to several factors. Many Romanians preferred not to be reminded of the bad role the country had played in World War II and hid behind Nazi Germany. In addition, Rumania had come within the sphere of influence of the Soviet Union in 1944, so communist historiography prevailed. This historiography had little interest in, for example, the fate of the Jews, but concentrated mainly on the fate of communists and Soviet citizens.

Interestingly, this view of Romanian historiography was in fact in line with Antonescu's defence at his trial, along with 23 others, in May 1946. Not that people had much compassion for Antonescu, and as an anti-communist he ended up before the firing squad. However, Antonescu distorted Romania's role within the Holocaust. The reality was that no ally of Nazi Germany had dealt with its own Jews as thoroughly as Romania. Nevertheless, Antonescu presented an entirely different picture. In a defence plea on 6 May 1946, he argued that he had deported the Jews to protect them from Germans (the DHM apparently) and from anti-Semites (Iron Guard and others) in the home country. He did not deny that many deaths had occurred in the process, but he attributed this, among other things, to the unexpectedly harsh winter that had made the deportations so bloody. All this contrasted sharply with Antonescu's own words, who as recently as 6 September 1941 had informed the Romanian cabinet that Bessarabia and Bukovina should be completely cleansed of Jews. The various waves that characterised the Holocaust made it clear that the physical extermination of Jews was no problem for Bucharest. Only 'Kernrumänien' renounced this policy although Jews were victims of forced labour and discriminatory legislation.

Quite remarkably, in the whole concrete case of the murder parties in Odessa, following the bombing of Romanian troops, as we have already discussed, Antonescu pretended that he had only heard of this *'incident'* in July 1944. Since these massacres had been carried out by the Romanian army, this is more than unlikely. Antonescu claimed, however, that in the summer of 1944 he had been approached by General Pantazif who proposed to exhume the Jewish victims again and destroy the mortal remains, in order to avoid discovery of the mass murder.[365]

Antonescu's argument, hiding behind the army, the Germans or legionnaires, offered the Romanians perfect cover. Above all, the Romanians had chosen an opportunistic position in World War II, which, although it had proved fatal for many Jews, had not been an end in itself. It provided the country with a comfortable position.[366] Early sources, however, indicated that things were more complicated. Matatias Carp, general secretary of the Organisation of Romanian Jews, already published a number of books between 1946 and 1948, which included original documents surrounding the Romanian Holocaust. This publication proved very valuable in retrospect, as many of the documents Carp located disappeared over the years. There were even whispers from Hungarian sources that a *'looting campaign'* was underway from Bucharest worldwide to make Carp's books *'disappear'* on an international scale. Either way, it was clear that Bucharest was most comfortable with the *'follower'* explanation for its own actions. Explanations that were less in line with what Antonescu was all claiming on that 6 May - such as the fact that the Jews had little sympathy because of their role in the 'conspiracy' with the communists, that they were walking between the fronts and therefore had to be in the ghettos - were ignored.

A certain escapism regarding the fate of the Jews was and is also visible in today's Moldovan republic. Diana Dumitru published about this and argued that historians such as Paul Goma emphasise that behind Antonescu's Jewish politics there was no anti-Semitic worldview. As a result, the murder of the Jews could not be labelled under the term Holocaust. Iziaslav Levit came up with a response to Goma's work, pointing out to him the fact that it had been established (already by Carp) that the retreating Romanian from Bessarabia were indulging in pogrom-like behaviour as a result of the *'red week'*. In addition, he pointed out that many Bessarabian Jews were Zionist rather than Communist. How deeply the emotions run, even to this day, was shown in a debate by a writers' collective that wanted to publish a collection of documents on the Holocaust. They could not agree on what to include in it. One of the authors, Alexandru Moraru, claimed that the persecution of the Jews was not based on ethnicity and was therefore not part of the Holocaust. The selected documents brought him into conflict with co-editor Sergiu Nazaria, who accused him of *'selective choices'* and *'cherry picking'*. Eventually, the planned multiple work was published in one volume in 2005. In 2006, the first symposium on the Holocaust was held in the Moldovan republic.[367]

The debate about whether or not the Romanian persecution of Jews was part of the Holocaust has to do with the curious timeframe and of a certain arbitrariness (read opportunism) that was involved. The time frame shows a different picture from the Holocaust elsewhere. The authorities in the German-occupied and controlled areas first gathered the Jews in ghettos and from there they went to the death camps. In Romania, there were few ghettos and no one went to extermination camps. In the *'policy'* implemented by Romania, chaos was a regular component. Like Jassy's corpse trains, the murder of the Jews from Bessarabia and the other territories - conquered in 1941 - was planless rather than structured in nature. Historians Adina Babes and Alexandru Florian speak of a *'hasty approach'*. However, that did not make the deadly intention any different. Moreover, in deporting people to Transnistria, Jews were handed over to SD and SS execution units, which was an important component of what we understand as the Holocaust.

Opportunism was around the corner there, where Jews were needed (Hillgruber and Raul Hilberg pointed this out too), but it was no different in Nazi Germany (*Schindler's List*) when it was convenient. This mainly concerned Jews from the 'Altreich'. This slewing policy meant that even in Bessarabia, parts of the Jewish community survived, as we also saw in this book from German documents around the town of Jassy in August 1944. Even then, Jews were suspected of collaborating with the communists. The little systematic killing of Jews gives some historians reason to doubt intentions, but, as we saw earlier, Nazi Germany was no stranger to opportunism either, and there we talk of a de facto Holocaust. The victims generally do not care which ideology killed them, but a denial of anti-Semitism as a major police force within Antonescu's Romania is not a viable option.

Even before the fall of the wall, in the mid-1980s, the picture first swung in Romania, partly through the work of Jean Ancel, who wrote a 12-volume work on the Holocaust in the country, in which Romanian archival materials were ploughed in depth. This reinforced the picture of wider Romanian involvement. The (Romanian) work of Lya Benjamin also contributed to this, as well as Randolph L. Braham's study, *The Destruction of Romanian and Ukrainian Jews during the Antonescu Era*. The opening of new archives followed after 1989, including from Russia and Ukraine. This resulted in the Romanian government acknowledging responsibility for the Holocaust on Romanian soil and committed by the Romanian government for the first time in 2004. Only when the chances of war on the eastern front became more unclear did opportunism emerge. Bucharest had to reckon with a new pact, preferably with the western powers, and began to impose restrictions on itself with regard to anti-Jewish terror. Later, new studies followed that diversified the perpetrator group. Ukrainian militias and 'Volksdeutschen' had also participated. This automatically gave a place to the issue of the *'welfare worker'*.[368]

The fall of Antonescu ended independent Romania, which was swallowed whole by the Soviet sphere of influence. British Prime Minister Winston Churchill, who had visited Stalin in Moscow as recently as October 1944, later clarified that he was already happy if the West could keep Greece and Italy. King Michael had hoped to gain a place at the negotiating table with Moscow through the coup against the marshal. But Stalin had not yet forgotten Romania's contribution to Operation *'Barbarossa'*, and so the participation did not materialise. Romania was lost.

Antonescu's trial took place in the basement of the Interior Ministry in Bucharest. Journalist George Calinescu watched the marshal, who made an unbroken impression, despite his prison time in the Soviet Union after his arrest and his return to Romanian prison. He invoked the fact that he had served his country for 45 years and apparently felt he deserved a better fate. He sat up straight, an officer with *'solid nerves'*, as Calinescu described it. The man, an ascetic vegetarian, did not suffer from *'intellectual complications'* and had an *'authoritarian profile'*.[369] The sentence of death followed on 17 May.

At this, the lawyer appealed, Antonescu refused. Attempts were made to play on the king's feelings and an attempt was made to transfer Antonescu to the court in Nuremberg. However, the king was put under strong pressure by the Soviet military commander in the country, Marshal Fyodor Tolbouchin. The latter pointed him to earlier incidents during Independence Day on 10 May, when royalists had applauded King Mikhail. These were subsequently promptly arrested. The king felt he had little leeway. The appeal was rejected on this. King Michael invoked the fact that he was trying to avoid conflict. Requests of grace from Lita Baranga, the marshal's mother and his lawyer now landed on his desk. Furthermore, there were no more supporters of the *'leader of the nation'*. With this, the marshal's fate was sealed.

On 1 June 1946, the execution took place. In the early morning, authorities and relatives arrived at the Jilava prison. An Orthodox priest had come with them. The relatives were allowed to enter first and Antonescu received his wife with a large bouquet of red roses. The others present were his mother, his mother-in-law, Miss Nicolescu, and a niece of his. They all received a rose. Then the priest was admitted and the marshal and three other convicts, Gheorghe Alexianu, the governor of Transnistria, Constantin Vasiliu, the interior minister and Mihai Antonescu and the vice-president, went to the execution site. Antonescu led the way in black suit. Thirty policemen docked. The marshal's hands were not tied at his request and he did not wear a blindfold, as did the other prisoners. Mihai Antonescu threw his hat into the grass behind him just before the execution. Antonescu brought his hat forward, as a final salute. Then the shots sounded. Antonescu first fell on his side and rolled over onto his stomach. The commander of the police unit ran to the executed and gave them all another head shot just to be sure. Antonescu received a double shot.[370] Antonescu entered death with other leaders of his government. After this, the marshal sank into oblivion, but after the fall of the wall in 1989 and the execution of Ceaucescu, there was a brief revival. Antonescu was suddenly remembered again as an opponent of communism and gained hero status. Statues of Antonescu resurrected in several places in Romania, but this was relatively short-lived. Romania had to find its way in the new Europe and the veneration of a fascist leader could not meet with approval. After 2002, all statues of the marshal had been removed again and the Antonescu era disappeared once more behind the scenes of history.

The agony of Romanians on the Eastern Front was also not a theme in Romanian and communist historiography for many years. More recently, work by Adrian Pandea, Ion Pavelescu and Eftimie Ardeleanu, *Rommanii la Stalingrad* (The Romanians in the Battle of Stalingrad) has been published, to which this book pays attention as well. The debate on the exact number of casualties of this battle still continues and hovers somewhere between 149,000 and 158,000 men, the vast majority of whom were made prisoners of war. Attention was always given to the Romanians in POWs who defected to the communist camp, as they were grouped together in the 1st 'Tudor Vladimerscu' I.D., named after the Wallachian revolutionary. Several more divisions were added after 23 August 1944. As historian Viasan Miu Tudor argued, the Romanian campaign in the Soviet Union was in the communist era a blank page. The more objective studies came only after 1989, such as Constantin Kiritescu's work, published in 1996. After 1989, the correspondence between Antonescu and Hitler in Romania was also published, compiled by Vasile Arimia, Ion Ardeleanu and Stefan Lache. In the field of history of mentality, there was the publication by Vasile Soimaru, with interviews of those involved.[371]

Most of the German protagonists survived the war. Hans Friessner wrote his memoirs in 1956, *Verratene Schlachten* and died on 26 June 1971 in Bayerisch Gmain. Erik Hannsen of the 'Heeresmission' came out of Soviet captivity in 1955 and died in freedom in Hamburg on 20 March 1967. Sonderbeauftragter Hermann Neubacher spent seven and a half years in prison and wrote his memoirs, *Sonderauftrag Südost*, in 1953. Von Killinger, the man behind the M.A. club committed suicide in Bucharest. 'Volksgruppenführer' Schmidt was extradited to the Russians and died in captivity from an axe blow. Artur Phleps went on a reconnaissance mission as 'HSSPF Siebenbürgen' with some staff members on 21 September 1944 and fell into Russian captivity. In the chaos surrounding an air raid, he was shot dead by the Soviets. His disappearance initially caused suspicion among the Nazi leadership. Himmler even issued a warrant for his arrest. When personal items belonging to him were finally found, his true fate became clear. On 23 November, the 'Eichenlaub zum Ritterkreuz' was posthumously awarded through his son Reinhart Phleps, who served with the division 'Prinz Eugen'. The 'SS-Freiwilligen-Gebirgs- regiment 13' was renamed 'Artur Phleps' and the unit was allowed to wear an armband with this name.

The foreman of the Iron Guard fled to Spain after the collapse of the exile in Vienna. There, in the Cold War, they suddenly rediscovered him as an anti-communist and it seems to have come to some secret collaboration. Like Hitler, the Western Allies apparently hoped that Sima would still have a certain constituency in Romania, on which an anti-communist opposition could be built. In 1953, rebels were reportedly dropped over Romania, but the plan proved unviable. In 1993, Horia Sima died in Spain. The Iron Guard lives on in Romania as an obscure troupe. Codreanu's handbook of the leader (*Carticia sefului de cuib*) has been republished again, as have his memoirs, *For My Legionnaires* (*Pentru legionarii*)[372]

The Romanian king was rewarded with high distinctions from both the Soviet and American sides after the war. Yet none of this took away the fact that he was forced to leave the country in 1947 and defected to Switzerland. During British Crown Princess Elisabeth's marriage to Philip Mountbatten, he met Anne of Bourbon-Parma, whom he married in Greece and had five daughters. The marriage was not blessed by the Pope because Michael could not promise to raise the children Catholic (Anne was Catholic). This violated the Romanian constitution. The couple lived in Florence, Lausanne and Hampshire before moving to Versoix in Switzerland in 1956. Three years after the upheaval in eastern and central Europe, the king returned to his country. A restoration of the monarchy proved impossible and he rejected a career in politics. When he returned for a visit to Romania in 1992, it brought a huge crowd to its feet. From a hotel, he addressed nearly a million assembled Romanians.

The king's popularity worried Romanian president Ion Illiescu. Several times, the king was refused entry to the country. In 1997, under the government of Emil Constantinescu, the policy was relaxed again. The king then lived partly in Switzerland and partly in Romania, where he alternately moved into *Savarsi Castle, Elisabeta Palace* as well as *Peles and Pelisor Castle*. The monarch's popularity was variable. In 2007, a poll showed that about 14% of Romanians wanted the monarchy restored. Michael did not impose himself on the people, but did carry out diplomatic missions for the country in the background, which gained him international prestige. As the years climbed, his popularity rose again. When he gave a speech in the Romanian parliament for his 90th birthday in October 2011, Romanians considered him the most trusted representative of their country. On 1 August 2016, his wife Anne died at age of 92 and in June the following year, Michael stepped down from the public domain. On 5 December 2017, the king died in Switzerland and on 13 december, the remains were flown back to the homeland by a military aircraft of the Romanian Air Force. The body was laid to rest at *Peles Castle* in the Carpathians, then continued to the royal palace in Bucharest. On 16 December, Michael was interred in the *Curtea de Arges cathedral*, next to his wife Anne.

For the Romanian people, a new episode began after the war. One had fallen within the Soviet sphere of influence. Churchill had written it out for Stalin in October 1944: 90% and 10%. This meant: Romania fell 90% within Moscow's sphere of influence and 10% under other (Western) influence. The communists proceeded with a certain tact, in that it would take until 1947 before the People's Republic was proclaimed. However, the governments before that were unable to push through a Romanian policy of their own, and the power of the monarch was also limited. Prime Minister N. Radescu had to find refuge in the British embassy, defected to the US and started a government in exile. The communists, with Moscow-backed Ana Pauker as a central force, undermined the existing structures until things imploded and the people's republic took its rise. To this end, the king had to step down and so it happened. Pauker, who became foreign minister, was a typical example of a communist career. This daughter of a rabbi from Moldova had spent much of her life in Russia. Her ex-husband Karl Pauker had been shot as a trotzkist and she herself too, according to good custom and years of loyal service, ended up in the suspect box of the communist secret services. She was put under house arrest in 1950, which remained in force until her death in 1960.

In the West, the communist period that followed is best known for the period of Nicolai Ceaucescu. He effortlessly linked mind-numbing Marxism to his own delusions of grandeur. From 1970, Ceaucescu even allowed himself to be called Conducator (leader), the same term that Antonescu had used at the time. The Romanian people showed that the spark of freedom was still not extinguished and toppled the regime in the tipping year of 1989. For years, people had been ravaged by hunger and Ceaucescu had even put people on rank-and-file for *'eating too much'*. The reality was that Romania, which had always been a big agricultural country, was not producing enough for its own people under communism.

Endnotes

1 Johan Fabricius' comment that Antonescu would be a *'willing Romanian lackey'* who *'bowed'* to Hitler is certainly not correct. Johan Fabricius, *Een wereld in beroering*, Leopold Publishing House, 1952, p. 67
2 Albrecht Penck, *Politisch-Geographische Lehren des Krieges* In: *Meereskunde, Sammlung volkstümlicher Vorträge* heft 106, Berlin: Ernst Siegfried Mittler und Sohn, 1915, p. 9 /Perry Pierik, *Karl Haushofer en het nationaal-socialisme. Tijd, werk en invloed*, Soesterberg: Uitgeverij Aspekt 2006, introduction
3 Richard Hennig/Leo Körholz, *Einführungen in die Geopolitik*. Leipzig: B.G. Teubner Verlag, 1935 p. 89
4 Ibid p. 90
5 Bernd Martin, *Weltmacht oder Niedergang? Deutsche Grossmachtpolitik im 20. Jahr-hundert*, Darmstadt: Wissenschaftliche Buchgesellschaft 1989, pp. 17-19
6 Jan Romein, *Machten van deze tijd*, Amsterdam/Antwerpen: Wereldbibliotheek 1950, p.p. 117-128
7 Haushofer, *Weltpolitik von Heute* p. 34
8 Erich Obst p. 207
9 Albrecht Penck, *Politisch-Geographische Lehren des Krieges* In: *Meereskunde, Samm- lung Volkstümlicher Vorträge* Heft 106, Berlin: Ernst Siegfriend Mittler und Sohn, 1915, p. 9
10 Artur Phleps, *Memoire über die Wahrung Deutscher Belange in Rumänien am 2. Dezember 1940* In:https://www.academia.edu/31300674/Bio-bibliografisches_Handbuch_deutscher_Volksgruppen_S%C3%BCdosteuropa_P
11 Rolf-Dieter Müller, *Hitlers Ostkrieg und die Deutsche Siedlungspolitik*, Frankfurt am Main: Fischerverlag 1991, pp. 83-96, For the position of the 'Auslanddeutschen' through the centuries see Klaus J. Bade/Jochem Oltmer, *Zwischen Aus- und Einwan- derungsland. Deutschland und die Migration seit der 17. Jahrhundert*, In: *Zeitschrift für Bevölkerungswissenschaft* Jg. 28 2-4/2003, p. 816
12 Eric C. Steinhart, *The Holocaust and the Germanization of Ukraine*, Washington: Cambridge University Press 2015, pp. 138, 177
13 Himmler's speech is printed in Rolf Dieter Müller, *Hitler's Ostkrieg*, p. 139 In doing so, Himmler echoed Hitler's speech on 2 October 1939, in which he had already stated that 750,000 Germans from Romania, 600,000 Germans from Yugoslavia and 480,000 Germans from Hungary had to be 'secured'.

14 Dieter Pohl, *Die Herrschaft der Wehrmacht. Deutsche Militärbesatzung und die einheimische Bevölkerung in der Sowjetunion 1941-1944*, Munich: R. Oldenbourg Verlag 2009, pp. 146, 147.
15 German politics towards the 'Volksdeutschen' ran across many discs, fighting each other. At its core, it was party versus SS. Initially, the party had an advantage through the *'Volksdeutscher Rat'*, which Karl Haushofer chaired. This council later merged into the so-called Bureau Kursel, named after Otto von Kursel who later had to give way to Werner Lorenz's 'VoMi'. Hitler's deputy Rudolf Hess later formally restored the party's authority, but Himmler's 'VoMi' remained the driving force. For the 'VoMi' and the balance of power see: Perry Pierik, *Karl Haushofer*, pp. 75-80, for the 'Umsiedlung' of the 'Volksdeutschen' see: *Bundesministerium für Vertriebene, Flüchtlinge und Kriegsgeschädigte, Dokumentation der Vertreibung der Deutschen aus Ost-Mitte- leuropa III, das Schicksal der Deutschen in Rumänien* Munich: Deutscher Taschen- buch Verlag, 1984, pp. 41-47/ http://www.geocities.ws/rausschmiss/S.pdf/ /Valdis O. Lumans, *Himmler's Auxiliaries. The Volksdeutsche Mittelstelle and the German National Minorities of Europe, 1933-1945*, Chapel hill/London: The University of North Carolina Press, 1993 p. 228
16 Antoine Zischka, *De geheime oorlog om petroleum*, Utrecht: Erven J. Bijleveld p. 175
17 Hans-Ulrich Seidt, *Berlin, Kabul, Moscow. Oskar Ritter von Niedermayer und Deut- schlands geopolitik*, Munich: Universitas 2002, pp. 222, 223
18 Dietrich Eichholtz, *War for Oil. The Nazi Quest for an Oil Empire*, Washington D.C.: Potomac Books, 2006, pp. 24, 25
19 Ibid p. 87
20 Perry Pierik, *Karl Haushofer*, p. 97
21 Adina Babes/Alexanderu Florian, *The Beginning of the War in the east and Hastening the Approaches against the Jewish Population*, Academia ed. 2020 p. 98.
22 In *Weltpolitik von Heute*, Haushofer also called this 'Raumuberwindende Wil- le', p. 35
23 *Weltpolitik von Heute* p. 112
24 Ibid p. 36
25 Nicholas M. Nagy-Talavera, *The Green Shirts and Others , a History of Fascism in Hungary and Romania*, Iasi/Oxford/Portland: The Center for Romania Studies 2001, pp. 393, 394
26 *Weltpolitik*, p. 43
27 The term 'Raumschicksal' was introduced by Erich Obst in; Karl Haushofer/ Erich Obst/ Hermann Lautensach and Otto Maull, *Bausteine zur Geopolitik*, Berlin: Kurt Vowinckel Verlag 1928, p. 201
28 Space poilitics sprouted in blood, Haushofer opined in *Weltpolitik von Heute*, p. 35
29 Karl Haushofer, *Weltpolitik von Heute*, Berlin: *Verlag und Vertriebsgesellschaft*

1934, p. 34, 35/Hennig/Körholz, p. 110
30 Erich Obst, *Das Raumschicksal des Russischen Volkes* In: Bausteine zur Politik, p. 201 ev.
31 Gerhard Hirschfeld/Gerd Krumeich/Irina Renz, *Enzyklopädie Erste Weltkrieg*, Paderborn/Munich: Ferdinand Schöningh 2003 p.p. 395, 396/Stephen Pope/Elizabeth-Anne Wheal, *The Macmillan Dictionary of the First World War*, London: Macmillan 1995, p.p. 88, 89
32 Georges Castellan, *Geschiedenis van Roemenië*, 's-Hertogenbosch: Voltaire, 2001, p. 63
33 Ibid
34 Karl Tschuppik, *Ludendorff, die Tragödie des Fachmanns*, Wien/Leipzig: Verlag Hans Epstein, 1931, p. 95
35 Perry Pierik, *Erich Ludendorff, biografie*, Soesterberg: Aspekt Publishers 2017, p. 161
36 Harald Roth, *Kleine Geschichte Siebenbürgens* Köln/Wien: Böhlau Verlag 1996, in- led/ Andras Ronai, *Atlas of Central Europe*, Budapest: Society of St. Steven-Püski Publishing House, facsimile edition numbered copy 0133, 1993
37 Jean Nouzille, *Transsylvania. An Area of Contacts and Conflicts*, Bucharest: Editura Enciclopecica, 1996, pp. 209-211
38 Perry Pierik, *Erich Ludendorff* pp. 164-166
39 Erwin Rommel, *Infanterie greift an*, Potsdam: Voggenreiter Verlag 1942, p.131
40 Perry Pierik, *Erich Ludendorff*, p. 167
41 Ibid p. 167
42 Gebhard Leberecht von Blücher (Rostock, 16 December 1742 - Krieblowitz, 12 September 1819, since 1814 prince Blücher von Wahlstatt, was a Prussian general who led his army against Napoleon Bonaparte at the Battle of Waterloo in 1815
43 T.Schwarzmüller, *Zwischen Kaiser und Führer. Generalfeldmarschall August von Mackensen. Eine politische Biographie*, Paderborn/Munich:Ferdinand Schönigh Verlag 1995, p.136
44 *Dokumente und dienstlicher Schriftverkehr des psychologischen Laboratoriums beim Reichskriegsministerium*, Internal correspondence (05.03.1937) concerning Von Falkenhayn, who was labelled 'very gifted' following the campaign against Romania. GDIR File 500 Findbuch 124632 Act 6
45 M. van der Staal, *On life and death. History of the Great War*, Libertas 1920, p. 71
46 Gerhard Hirschfeld/ Gerd Krumeich/Irina Renz., pp 395, 396/Stephen Pope/Elizabeth-Anne Wheal., pp 88, 89
47 John Keegan, *The First World War*, London: Hutchinson, 1998, p. 330
48 Irina Livezeanu, *Cultural Politics in greater Romania*, Ithaca/London: Cornell University press, 1995, p. 98
49 A.G.M. Abbing, *Het drama Trianon, iets uit de geschiedenis van Hongarije*

	voor onder en na de Wereldoorlog, Amsterdam: Jacob van Campen, 1931 p. 69
50	Hungary also lost territory to other neighbouring countries, such as Burgenland and Vojvodina. Dennis Deletant, *Hitler's Forgotten Ally. Ion Antonescu and the Regime Romania 1940-1944*, Chippenham: Palgrave MacMillan 2006, pp. 8, 9
51	Dennis Deletant p. 14
52	R.Craig, *Nation, Black Earth, Red Star, A History of Soviet Security Policy, 1917- 1991*, Ithaca/ London: Cornell University Press 1992, p. 97
53	Eli WieseL, Tura Friling, Radu Ioanid (ed.) et al, *International Commission on the Holocaust in Romania, Final Report*, Jassy: Polirom 2004, p. 75/ Wilhelmus Petrus van Meurs, *The Bessarabian Question in Communist Historiography*. Utrecht: 1993 (unpublished) pp. 66, 67
54	Wilhelmus Petrus van Meurs, *The Bessarabië Question in Communist Historiografy*. Utrecht: 1993 (unpublished) p. 59
55	For Kun see: Ivo van de Wijdeven, *De spoken van Visegrad. De onbekende geschiedenis van Polen, Hongarije, Tsjechië en Slowakije,*, Utrecht: Spectrum 2018, pp 135-143
56	Wilhelmus Petrus van Meurs, p.p. 60, 61
57	Ibid p.p. 62, 63
58	Z.R. Dittrich/A.P. van Goudoever, *Onafhankelijkheid als wensdroom. De buiten- landse politiek van Roemenië*, Dutch Institute for Peace Issues, NIVV series no.25, Den Haag: Staatsuitgeverij 1980, pp. 86-88/Van Meurs, pp. 70, 71
59	Wiesel p.p. 79, 80
60	Ibid p. 76
61	Costel Coroban, *Playboy King? The Political Thought of Carol II of Romania between Idealism and Realism Before World War II*, In: *Revista Istorica*, tom XXIII, no 3-4, 2012/Michel Sturdza, *The Suicide of Europe*, pp 233, 234. The name Lupescu seemed to be inspired by her real surname Wolff. In her Parisian days she called herself Magda again, possibly partly because in Romania at the time the name Magda was equivalent to the word 'prostitute'
62	Valantin Sandulescu, *Fascism and its Quest fort he 'New Man': the Case of the Romanian Legionary Movement*, In: *Studia Hebraica*, Vol. 4 (2004)
63	Marius Turda, *New Perspectives on Romanian Fascism: Themes and Options* In: *Totalitarian Movements and Political Religions*, 6: 1 2007/ Valantin Sandulescu, *Fascism and its Quest for the 'New Man': The Case of the Romanian Legionary Movement*, In: *Studia Hebraica*, Vol. 4, For developments regarding the völkisch movement and ariosophy see, among others, George L. Mosse, *The Crisis of German Ideology*. New York: Schicken Books, 1964/ Arhtur Herman, *Prophetes des Niedergangs. Der Endzeitmythos im westlichen Denken*, Hamburg: Propyläen Verlag 1998, Michael Prinz/Rainer Zitel-

mann (hg.), National-sozialismus und Modernisierung. Darm- stadt: Wissenschaftliche Buchgesellschaft, 1991, Manfred Kappeler, *Der schreckliche Traum vom vollkommenen Menschen. Rassenhygiene und Eugenik in der Sozialen Arbeit*, Marburg: Schüren 2000, Uwe-K. Ketelsen, *Völkisch-Nationale und Nationalsozialistische Literatur in Deutschland 1890-1845*, Stuttgart: Metzler1956, Nicholas Goodrich-Clarke, *The Occult Roots of Nazism. Secret Aryan Cults and their Influence on Nazi Ideology*, New York: New York University Press 1992, Perry Pierik, *De geopolitiek van het Derde Rijk*, Chapter *3 Reich und Romantik* and Perry Pierik, *Karl Haushofer en het nationaal-socialisme*

64 Dittrich/Van Goudoever, pp. 86, 87
65 Such accusations were common at the time, see Johannes Rogalla von Bieberstein, *Die These von der Verschwörung 1776-1945. Philosophen, Freimaurer, Juden, liberale und Sozialisten als Verschwörer gegen die Sozialordnung* In: *Europäische Hochschulschriften Vol 6 3*, Frankfurt am Main/Bern/Las Vegas: Peter Lang 1978
66 It is unclear who is the author of a detailed letter on this topic dated 27 January 1941: in Klaus Popa, *Voor 70 jaren*, 1941, pp. 11-17. After this issue, the German Embassy relied more on Von Killinger and the newly deployed Dr Hermann Neubacher
67 Raul Carstocea, *Native Fascist, Transnational Anti-Semites. The International Activity of Legionary Leader Ion I. Mota* In: Academia.edu
68 *South-Eastern Europe. A Political and Economic Survey*, London: the Royal Institute for International Affairs 1939, p. 71
69 Letter 01.02.1941 Andreas Rühring from Berlin to SS-Obergruppenführer Lorenz BAB NS 19/3517, published in *Vor 70 Jahren 1941*, pp. 24-26/Olso Klaus file:///D:/Downloads/Bio-bibliografisches_Handbuch_deutscher%20(2).pdf
70 Cristian Alexandru Groza, *The Fascist Phenomenon. National Legionary State between Laws, Journals, Memoirs, and the Jewish Repression between 2-23 January 1941*: In: *Journal of Education Culture and Soceity No 1* 2014, p. 69/ Dennis Deletant, p. 64
71 Groza speaks of 'complete freedom' for Antonescu, p. 71 but Deletant pointed out that this was nowhere evident. Rather, there was some kind of tolerated construction, p. 64
72 Dennis Deletant, pp. 64-65
73 Ibid, p. 66
74 http://www.generals.dk/general/%C5%9Eteflea/Ilie/Romania.html
75 Nicholas Nagy-Talavera, *Reminiscences of Iorga's Murderer: Traian Boeru* In: Kurt W.Treptow (Ed.), *Romanian Civilization Studies Vol. XIII.* 1996/Excavated bones of Codreanu, In: *Nieuwsblad van het Noorden*, 19.11.1940/ Romanian-German *Relations Before and during the Holocaust*,zp.zj.https://www.yadvashem.org/yv/pdf-drupal/en/report/english/1.2_Romanian_German_Relations_before_and_during_the_Holocaust.pdf.For the Iron

Guard's view of developments, they spoke of putsch, see Michel Sturdza, *The Suicide of Europe*, Massachusetts: Western Islands Publishers 1965 chapter 27, p. 211.

76 Dennis Deletant, p. 53/Radu Ioanid, *The Holocaust in Romania. The Destruction of Jews and Gypsies under the Antonescu regime 1940-1944*, Chicago: Ivan R. Dee, 2000, p. 45/Christopher Kshyk, *The Holocaust in Romania: The Extermination and Protection of the Jews under Antonescu's Regime*, Student Pulse Vol.6 No. 12 p. 2

77 For an atmospheric account of the DHM see: *Der Schicksalweg der 13.Panzer-Division 1939-1945* Friedberg: Podzun Pallas Verlag 1986, chapter 2

78 Joachim Drews spoke of *'hardly any industrial development of its own'*, In: Joachim Drews, *Vom Soja-Anbau zum 'Wohlthat'-Vertrag. Der ökonomische Anschluss Rumäniens an das Deutsche Reich*, In: Besatzung und Bündnis, Deutsche Herrschaftsstrategien in Ost- und Südost-Europa In: Beiträge zur Nationalsozialistischen Gesundheits- und Sozialpolitik Band 12 Oldenburg: Verlag der Buchläden 1995, p. 68

79 Übersicht der Heeresstärken der Staaten im Ost- und Südost Raum, In: GDIR: Bestand 500 Findbuch 12450 Akte 50/ Ubersicht der Wehrwirtsschaft Rumäniens, Stand Anfang 1940, DGIR: Bestand 500, Findbuch 12450 Akte 51/OKW Az 3/ WiRüAmt/W III, Vergleich die rumänische Eisenbahn mit den Eisenbahnen Jugoslawien, Ungarn und Deutschland, GDIR bestand 500 Findbuch 12459 Akte 2

80 Drews, p. 74/Helmuth Wohltat, *Der neue Deutsch-Rumänische Wirtschaftsvertrag* p. 560-563 In: Der Vierjahresplan, Zeitschrift für nationaalsozialistische Wirtschafts-politik In: Perry Pierik (hg.), *Der Vierjahresplan, Zeitschrift für Nationalsozialistische Wirtschaftspolitik 1939*, Soesterberg: 2020

81 Avraham Barkai, *Das Wirtschaftssystem des Nationalsozialismus. Ideology, Theorie, Politik 1933-1945*, Frankfurt am Main: 1998, p. 127/Joseph L. Wieczynski, *The Modern Encyclopedia of Russian and Soviet History band 25* s.p.: 1981, pp. 214-219

82 Perry Pierik, *Hongarije 1944-1945, de vergeten tragedie*/Krisztian Ungvary, *Die Schlacht um Budapest 1944/45. Stalingrad an der Donau*, Munich: Herbig Verlag 2001/ Endre B. Gastony, *Hungary and Geopolitics. The Second World War and the Holocaust 1938-1945*, Soesterberg: publisher Aspekt 2019

83 L.M. Taubinger, *Die Entwicklung der ungarischen Erdölindustrie* In: Wirtschaftsdienst 36 (1956) p. 282, Perry Pierik, *Hongarije 1944-21945, de vergeten tragedie*, Manfried Rauchensteiner, *Der Krieg in Österreich*, Wien: Bundesverlag 1984, p. 199, Hans Marsalek, *Die Geschichte des Konzentrationslagers Mauthausen*, Wien 1980 p.109/Joel Hayward, *Too Little, Too Late. An Analysis of Hitlers' Failure in August 1942 to Damage Soviet Oil Production*. In: The Journal of Military History 64 July 2000

84 Hillgruber p. 250

85 Jonathan Morales, *Oil and World war II on the Eastern Front*, 2012 p. 9

86	*Das Ölproblem: Erdölförderung und Erdölausfuhr in Rumänien, Sicherstellung der Bedürfnisse der Wehrmacht mit den Erdölprodukten in den Jahren 1942 - 1943. In: Bestand 500, Findbuch 12450 Akte 145/ OKW Erdölausfuhr Rumäniens nach mengen und Ländern (Vergleich der Jahre 1939-1938) In: Ubersicht der Wehrwirts- schaft Rumäniens stand Anfang 1940, DGIR: Bestand 500, Findbuch 12450 Akte 51*
87	*Hermann Neubacher, Sonderauftrag Südost 1940-45. Bericht eines fliegenden Diplomaten, Göttingen/Berlin/Frankfurt: Musterschmidt Verlag, 1958, pp. 38-42*
88	Oberkommando der Wehrmacht, zu: *Die Wehrwirtschafts Rumänien nach dem Stand von Anfang 1940*: V: B. Erdölwirtschaft In: *Ubersicht der Heeresstärken der Staaten im Ostund Südost Raum*, In: GDIR: Bestand 500 Findbuch 12450 Akte 50
89	*Daniel Dumitran/Valer Moga (ed.),. Papers of the international Conference held in April 15 - 27th 2013, p.p. 352, 353*
90	Neubacher p. 43
91	Ibid p. 44
92	Ibid p.p. 44, 45
93	Ibid p. 46
94	Jonathan Morales, p. 9
95	Pierik/Steeman, Stalingrad p. 57
96	*Pressestelle vertrauliche Mitteilungen, Wochenbericht Südosteuropa, File 500 Findbuch 12450 Act 198*
97	*Das Problem der Ölund Gasleitungen* Bestand 500, GDIR: Findbuch 12451 - Oberkommando des Heeres (OKH) Akte 397/ *Ubersicht der Wehrwirtsschaft Rumäniens stand Anfang 1940*, DGIR: Bestand 500, Findbuch 12450 Akte 51
98	*Deutsche Wehrmission in Rumänien, W-befehl Nr. 5, GDIR Bestand 500, Findbuch 12450, Akte 63*
99	*Oberkommando der Wehrmacht, 26.03.1941* Betr.: *'Barbarossa' Befehl für die Verteidigung des rumänischen Erdölgebietes.* In: *Anweisungen, Anordnungen und andere operative Dokumente des Oberkommandos der Wehrmacht*, In: GDIR: Bestand 500 Findbuch 12450 Akte 82/Richard L. Dinaor, *The German Military Mission to Romania*, 1940-1941 In: *IFQ issue 69* 2nd Quarter 2013
100	*Bericht der Heeresstärken der Staaten im Ost- und Südost Raum*, In: GDIR: Bestand 500 Findbuch 12450 Akte 50 and Akte 51
101	*https://www.newyorker.com/magazine/1996/04/22/blaming-the-germans Dennis Deletant spoke of a 'sovereign politics' in: Review of the book Leon Volovici/ Miria, m Caloianu (ed.), The History of the Holocaust in Romania, Jean Ancel, In: Holocaust and Genocide Studies doi: 10.1093/hgs/dct 044 p. 503*
102	An interesting atmospheric description around the position of the Jews in Romania and the newly acquired territories after 1919 can be traced in

	Prof Dr L.H. Grondijs, *Tussen twee werelden. Studiën over de bewoners van Oost-Europa*. Amsterdam: Elsevier 1944, chapter *Het twee stroomenland tussen Proet en Dnjestr,* pp.160-165
103	Octavian Tiku, *The Molotov Ribbentrop Pact and the Emergence of the 'Moldovan' Nation: Reflections after 70 Years,* In: Almanack of Policy Studies (Politikos mokslų almanachas), issue: 7 / 2010, pp 9-10/ Marina Furima, Moldovianism vs. Romanianism, the Dichotomy of Ethnic Identity. How Moldovia fails at Nation Building, In: Case Study Nation Building in Post Communist Societies, SVNC oo43, 21.05.2018
104	Petru Negura, *From a 'Liberation' to Another. The Bessarabien Writers during the First Year of Soviet Power (1940-1941). Integration Strategies and Forms of Exclusion,* In: Euxeinos 14 (2014/Igor Cașu, Moldova under the Soviet Communist Regime In: Vladimir Tismaneanu and Bogdan C. Iacob, In Remembrance (ed.), History and Justice coming to Terms with traumatic Pasts in Democratic Societies, Budapest-New York: Central European University Press, 2015, p. 350
105	Wiesel p.p. 85-86
106	Ibid p. 114/The outrage in the abattoir made the press in the Netherlands (wedrom) in the Eichman trial, see *Het proces-Eichmann, de Jodenvervolging in Roemenië. Weer een reeks documenten*, In: *Nieuwe Tilburgsche Courant* 24.-05.1961
107	Carp p.139
108	Wiesel p. 127
109	Carp 140,141/The war propaganda also focused on Orthodox Christian themes, saving Europe from godless Bolshevism. People spoke of a *'holy war'*. See: Anton Mioara, *Kriegspropaganda in Rumänin. Die Ostfront, June 1941 - August 1944*, Academia.edu
110	Ibid p. 141
111	Ibid p. 141
112	Ibid p.p. 144-146
113	Ibid p. 142
114	https://www.yadvashem.org/education/educational-materials/lesson-plans/iasi-po- grom.html
115	Wiesel, pp. 120-125
116	Lecture Simon Geissbühler, *Bloody July. Romania and the Holocaust in Summer 1941*, Yad Vashem, Jerusalem 29.10.2015
117	Diana Dumitru, *How Bessaranbiens were perceived by the Romanian Civilian-Military Administration in 1941*, Euxeinos 15/16 (2014)
118	Christian Ingrao, *Hitler's Elite. Die Wegbereiter des nationalsozialistischen massenmords*, Berlin: Propylän Verlag 2012, pp 62, 87, 299/Perry Pierik, Krim, Bestorming, belegering, verovering, bezetting en moord, 1941-1942, Soesterberg: Aspekt Publishers 2014, pp.125-139/For Ohlendorf in Nuremberg see: http://www.world-courts.com/imt/eng/decisions/1948.04.09_United_States_v_Ohlendorf.pdf

119 Steinhart, p. 156/Radu Ioanid, p. 188
120 Simon Geissbühler, *'He spoke Yiddish like a Jew': Neighbors Contribution to the Mass Killing of Jews in Northern Bukovina and Bessarabia, July 1941* in: *Holocaust and Genocide Studies 28* no. 3 (Winter 2014) pp. 430-431/ Steinhart, p. 156
121 Carp p. 142-144
122 Dalia Ofer, *The Ghettos in Transnistria and Ghettos under German Occupation in Eastern Europe. A Comparative Approach* in: Beiträge zur Geschichte des NS 25, Göttingen: Wallstein Verlag, 2009 p. 32/ Svetlana Suveica, *From Heroisation to Competing Victimhoods. History Writing on the Second World War in Moldova*, In: Südosteuropa 65 (2017), no. 2, p. 388/Radu Ioanid, p. 188
123 Ofer, p. 36
124 Ibid p. 33
125 Ibid p.p. 37, 38
126 The 'Altreich' as the Germans said, or 'Binnenrumänien', as Krista Zach calls it, cf: Wolfgang Benz, p. 383
127 Ofer p. 38
128 Hans Schuster, *Die Judenfrage in Rumänien*; Leipzig: Felix Meiner Verlag, pp. 167- 179
129 Kriszta Zach arrived at a number of 211,214 Jews, In Wolfgang Benz, p. 409
130 Benz p. 383
131 John A.S. Grenville, *Neglected Holocaust Victims* In: Michael Berenbaum/ Abraham J.Peck (Ed.), *The Holocaust and History. The Known, the Unknown, the Disputed and the Reexamined*, Bloomington/Indianapolis: Indiana Umniversity Press 1998, chapter 22
132 Peter Gosztony, *Hitlers fremde Heere. Das Schicksal der nichtdeutschen Armeen in Ostfeldzug*, Düsseldorf/Wien: Econ-Verlag, 1976, pp. 76-77 / Rebecca Ann Haynes, *'A New Greater Romania?' Romanian Claims to the Serbian Banat in 1941* In: Central Europe, Vol. 3 November 2005/Zusammenstellung der Grenzzwischenfälle an der rumänischungarischen Grenze. Ungarische Einflüge im Rumänischen Luftraum (vom 22.Juni 1942 bis 22 August 1943, In: GDIR Bestand 500 Akte 111)
133 Ibid, pp. 69-73
134 Ibid, p. 74
135 Ibid, p. 109
136 Deutsche Heeresmission in Rumänien, 12.06.1941, *Memorandum No. 2* In: GDIR Akte 89
137 Ibid 10.06.1941, *Meldungen für Sicherung und Verteidigung der Grenzen Rumäniens gegen Russland* In: GDIR Akte 89
138 Ibid, p. 143
139 Ibid, p. 150
140 Ibid, pp. 151-152

141	Wirtschaftsinstitut für Russland und die Oststaaten E.V. Königsberg (HG.), Die Ukraine und die angrenzenden Gebiete. Wirtschaftgeographische Ubersicht (Nur für Dienstgebrauch), Berlin: Ost Europa Verlag, 1941, pp. 83-88
142	EHRI Online Course in Holocaust Studies. AMR, Armata al IV-a/870 Copy art USHMM archivs, RRG-25.003 reel 12 *The Holocaust in Ukraine*
143	Iulia Padenu, *The Holocaust in Romania. Uncovering a dark Chapter*, pp. 26-28
144	Deutsche Heeresmission in Rumänien 21.10.1941: Allgemeine Weisung Nr. 6 für die D.V.K. der Rumänischen Besatzungsarmee. GDIR Act 108
145	Deutsche Heeresmission in Rumänien, 23.10.1941, An den Kgl.Rumänischen Genertalstab z.Hden.d.Herrn general Palangeanu, GDIR Akte 108
146	Ereignismeldung 52, 14.08.1941
147	For history 170 I.D. see: Samuel W. Mitcham, *Hitler's Legions. German Army Order of Battle World War II*, p. 144
148	Ereignismeldung 38, 30.07.1941
149	Ibid 37 29.07.1941
150	For looting, see e.g. Ereignismeldung 19, 25 and 39 of 11.07.1941, 17.07.1941 and 31.07.1941
151	Armeeoberkommando (OKH), 10.10.1941 Abschrift von Abschrift betr: Verhalten der Truppe im Ostraum, In: GDIR Akte 393
152	Johannes Hütner, *Hitlers Heerführer*, Munich: p. 383
153	Samuel W. Mitcham, *Hitler's Legions. German Army order of battle World War II*, p.118,119. On the release of German units by Romanian troops, see *Deutsche Heeresmission in Rumänien*, 25.01.1942, An den Königliche Rumänischen Grossen Generalstab z. Hd.d. Herrn General Tataranu, in: GDIR Act 108
154	OKH Betr: *Zusammenarbeit mit den Truppen verbündeter Staaten und fremdländischen Freiwlilligenverbänden*, 15.01.1942 In: T312/Roll 158- Von Stauffenberg would later specialise in the Osttruppen, residents of the Soviet Union who collaborated with Nazi Germany. He considered them, according to Nikolaus von Uxkuelll -Gyllenband, (a relative of and commander of the Azerbaijan Legion), as 'his baby'. Perry Pierik, *Neu Turkestan aan het front. Islamitische soldaten uit de Kaukasus en de Balkan in dienst van de Waffen-SS*, Soesterberg: Publisher Aspekt 2019, p.76
155	Zusammenstellung der umgespurten Strecken, NAAR T78/R117
156	Anlage 1 zu Tagesbefehl Nr.45, Soldaten der Ostfront, In: T311/R264
157	Melitopol was captured by the 3rd Romanian Army on 6 October 1941 06.10.1941, KTB Heersgruppe Süd In: T311/R259
158	Perry Pierik, *Krim*
159	Tagesmeldung vom 15.11.1941 In: T311/R257
160	Zwischenmeldung vom 16.11.1941 In: T311/R257
161	1.rum. Gebjgr. Rgt. Sonderbefehl Nr. 111. Der Angriff für den 26 November 1941 In: T311/R1051/KTB 72nd I.D.

162	Tagesbefehl Nr. 109 für den 25.11.1941 T315/R1051/KTB 72nd I.D.
163	Tagesmeldung 18.11.1941 in: T311/R257.
164	Perry Pierik, *Krim*
165	For brief overview of the struggle for *Crimea* see: Perry Pierik, *Krim, bestorming, belegering, verovering, bezetting en moord*, 1941-1942 Soesterberg: Aspekt Publishers 2014
166	Heeresgruppe Süd had already stopped the 1941 summer campaign on 27.10.1941, unlike the other fronts. See: *Oberkommando der Heeresgruppe Süd*, 27.10.1941: Betr: *Führung der Operationen im Winter 1941/21, T311/R263*
167	Gosztony p.p. 291, 292
168	*Kriegstagebuch des Oberkommando der Wehrmacht* 1942 Teilband II d.d. 29 and 30.08.1942
169	KTB OKW reported the capture on 01.09.1942
170	Stephen Walsh, *Stalingrad 1942-1943, the Infernal Cauldron*
171	Note Warlimont to KTB OKW 02.09.1942
172	MS#D-101 (OSS) *Crossing of the Kerch Straits by the 46th infantry division from the Crimea to the Taman Peninsula on 1 and 2 September 1942*, In: www.maparchive.ru
173	Note Warlimont to KTB OKW 02.09.1942
174	Vortragsbericht der Deutschen Heeresmission in Rumänien an Oberkommando des Heeres und an Oberkomamndo der Heeresgruppe A, über Gliederung, Zustand und Führung der rumänischen Verbände der 1. Welle mit den Gliederungsskizzen vom Juli 1942, in: GDIR: File 500 Findbuch 124500 Act 136
175	GDIR, Bestand 500 Findbuch 124500 Akte 136
176	Ibid
177	Ibid
178	Ibid
179	Ibid
180	Lebensraum Europas gewaltig erweitert.02.09.1942. In: Panzerfaust-Nachrichtenblatt einer Panzerarmee Nr.161
181	Oberkommando des Heeres, 03.09.1942, Betr. 'Stab Don' T78/Roll 649)
182	24. Panzer-Division, 03.10.1942, Betrf. Kampfstärkenmeldung T315/ Roll 804
183	Anlage zu 24. Pz. Div. Abt. Ia, Einsatzbereite Panzer (Stand 22.10.1944), T315/ Roll 804
184	Deutsche Heeresmission in Rumanien an den Chef des Königlich Rumänischen Grossen Generalstabes Herrn General Steflea, 02.10.1942, operatives Memorandum No 4, GDIR Akte 77
185	For overview of troop movements at Stalingrad see: Robert Kirchubel, *Atlas of the eastern Front 1941-1945*, Oxford: Osprey 2016, p. 127
186	Gosztony p.p. 305, 306
187	Ibid, p. 306

188 Ibid
189 Ibid pp. 309, 310
190 Ibid p. 312
191 Telex message An OKDO D.H.Gr.DDon, 06.12.1942 T311/Roll 268
192 Frido von Senger und Etterlin, *Krieg in Europa*, Cologne/Berlin: Kiepenheuer & Witsch 1960, p. 73
193 https://de.wikipedia.org/wiki/Armata_a_4-a_Rom%C3%A2n%C4%83
194 Perry Pierik/Peter Steeman, *Stalingrad, de slag en de luchtbrug naar de dood*, Soesterberg: Aspekt Publishers 2014 p. 97-99
195 Ibid p. 104
196 Bullitin article/Tschuikow, W.I. (hg.), *Stalingrad Lehren der Geschichte*, Frankfurt am Main: Rüderberg Verlag 1976, p.p.186/Horst Scheibert, *Ensatzversuch Stalingrad. Dokumentation einer Panzerschlacht 1942*, Neckargemünd: Kurt Vowinckel Verlag,1956 p. 122
197 For dates main developments see: *Gliederung des Ostfeldzuges* (01.10.1942-02.02.1943) 27.05.1943, GDIR Act 68
198 *Chef der Deutschen Heeresmission in Rumänien*, Aktennotiz 28.12.1942 GDIR Bat- dns 500 Findbuch 124500 Akte 77
199 *Zes brieven van Von Manstein aan de Befehlshaber Heeresgebiet Don, aan de Bevollmächtigten General beim rum.AOK 3*, to the Chef des Kgl.,Rum. Grossen Hauptquartiers Herr General Steflea and to the Oberbefehlshaber der 3.Rum.Armee Herrn Generaloberst Dimitrescu, dated 31.12.1942, T 311/Roll 270
200 Ibid
201 Strength report *Armeegruppe Hollidt*, 02.01.1943, T311/Roll 270
202 GDIR, *Bestand 500*, Findbuch 124500, Akte 144, *Angaben über die Verluste der 3. und 4. Rumänischen armeen Am Don und bei Stalingrad*
203 *9.Inf.-Division, betrf.: Beweglichtkeit der Grosswaffen der 3.rum.Geb.Div.* dd 19.03.1943 RH-24/44/140
204 *1.Generalstabsoffizier der 9.Inf.-Division*, dd 28.02.1943, In: RH 24-44/139
205 *Beurteilung der Divisionen*, dd. 09.05.1943, RH 24-44/143, all battalions were listed as weak, except the battalion 'Marincescu'
206 *Deutschen Nachrichtenbüros (DNB)*, no. 38 Eigendienst. 07.02.1943 Blatt 71, Bebooth 500, Findbuch 12463 Akte 71
207 We know of the existence this M.A. club through angry letters and testimonies from the German police attaché Böhme at the German embassy in Bucharest, because he complained about Von Killinger and his contacts with '*the Jewish agent*' Lecca and the functioning of the M.A. club.
208 Böhme, Polizei-Attaché bei der Deutschen Desandschaft in Bukarest nimmt zur 'Dienststellung des polizei-Attaché in Bukarest' Stellung, d. d. 07.01.1943/der Polizei-Attaché bei der Deutschen Gesellschaft in Bukarest, Böhme, äussert sich über den gesandten Freiherrn von Killinger, d.d. 07.01.1943/Der Polizei-Attaché bei der Deutschen Gesandschaft in

Bukarest, Böhme, protokolliert seine 'Besprechungen bei Unterstaatssekretär Luther' am 08.01.1943, 10.30 Uhr In: Klaus Popa, *Vor 70 Jahren. Die NS-'Volksgruppenpolitik'in weiteren Archivdokumenten. Das Jahr 1943*, pp. 1 - 10. For the Mittwochgesellschaft see Pierik, *Erich Ludendorff* pp 183,184

209 Ibid. p. 65

210 *Der Chef des Generalstabes der Heeresgruppe Süd an den Chef des Königlichen Rumänischen Grossen Generalstabes Herrn General Jacobici*, den 23.12.1941 In: T311/ R295/ *Der Chef des Generalstabes der Heeresgruppe Süd an den Chef des Generalstabes des Heeres Generaloberst Halder*, den 21.12.1941 In: T 311/295

211 Uwe Neumärker u.a., *Wolfsschanze, Hitlers Machtzentrale in Zweiten Weltkrieg*, p. 91

212 Silviu Miloiu, *When the West is far away. Romanian attempts to withdraw from World War II (1943-1944).*Finnish Views. In: *The Romanian Journey for Baltic and Nordic Studies*, Vol 6 Issue 2 (2014) pp. 183-205

213 Several letters on this topic can be found in T78/Roll 141. One of the German contacts was a certain Lübbert, delegate for die Türkei der Firma Lassen & Co AG. Hamburg-Berlin *'Umnak Istanbul'* (letter dated 21.07.1943)

214 KTB OKW Band 6 p. 1531-1533

215 https://www.academia.edu/31300674/Bio-bibliografisches_Handbuch_deutscher_Volksgruppen_S%C3%BCdosteuropa_P

216 Valdis O. Lumans, pp. 227-229/Andreas Gilbert, *Waffen-SS, Hitler's Army at War*, Ingram Publishers Services US/George H. Stein, *The Waffen-SS. Hitler's Elite Guard at War 1939-1945*, New York: Cornell University Press, 1984, p.p. 168ff./On loss volunteer concept see: Bernd Wegner, Hitlers politische Soldaten: Die Waf- fen-SS 1933-1945, Paderborn/Munich Ferdinand Schöningh 1997 chapter 17/for collaboation and enlistment Waffen-SS see further Hans Werner Neulen, Euro-Faschismus und der Zweite Weltkrieg. Europa verratene Söhne, Munich: Universitas 1980, p.116 ff /Rolf Dieter Müller, An der Seite der Wehrmacht.Hitlers ausländische Helfer beim 'Kreuzzug gegen den Bolschewismus 1941-1945, Berlin: Ch.Links verlag 2007, p.54 ff.*

217 *Aufstellung des Obergruppenführers-WSS Berger bezüglich die Musterung für die Waffen-SS in Rumänien, unterbreitet dem RFSS Himmler, d.d. 30.07.1943, In: Klaus Popa, p. 49/The numbers of Romanian Volksdeutschen in the Waffen-SS is indicated rather differently. Valdis O. Lumans spoke of a total of 54,000 Romanian Volksdeutschen in the Waffen-SS by the end of 1943. What was certain in any case was that after Stalingrad, the enthusiasm for fighting within the Romanian army waned and there were fewer objections to Volksdeutschen leaving their own ranks to serve in the Waffen-SS. Luman's pp. 230*

218 *Antwortschreiben des RFSS Himmler an SS-Obergruppenführer Berger betreffend Werbung für die Waffen-SS in Rumänien d.d.11.08.1943, In:*

Klaus Popa, p. 52

219 *Perry Pierik, Van Leningrad tot Berlijn, Nederlandse vrijwilligers in dienst van de Duitse Waffen-SS 1941-1945, Soesterberg: 2006, p. 225/ Particularly among the Banat- Schwaben (separate from the unit Brigade 'Netherlands'), desertion frequently occurred, see: Bundesministerium für Vertriebene, Flüchtlinge und Kriegsgeschädigte (hg.). Dokumentation der Vertreibung der Deutschen aus Mitteleuropa band III, das Schicksal der Deutschen in Rumänien, Munich: Deutscher Taschenbuch Verlag, p. 57-e. This would partly be due to ill-treatment of the Volksdeutschen who were seen as 'inferior' (the document uses the word 'Tiere') by other SS personnel, also their (Romanian) military training would be ridiculed. See: Monatsbericht Januari 1944 des Hauptamtes Volksdeutsche Mittelstelle In: Klaus Popa p.p. 87-90. In September 1944 it also came about (outside the Waffen-SS) that so-called Szekler battalions were set up. A letter from the Heeresgruppe Südukraine to the OKH (Guderian) revealed that there was a lot of desertion (700 men were talked about) within these units. Letter Schäfer, Overst i.G. An: Chef des Stabes des Heeres An Herrn Generaloberst Guderian, dd. 18.09.1944, In: GDIR file 500, Findbuch 12469 Akte 53. Friessner also reported the frequent desertion on 17.09.1944, Ibid*

220 Dr. Hans Otto Roth (1890-1953) Vortrag von. Dr. Phil. Florian Roth, Haus des Deutschen Ostens, Munich, 13. Mai 2009, Seite 1 Dr. Hans Otto Roth (1890-1953) - Betrachtungen seines Enkels über den bedeutendsten rumänien- deutschen Politiker des 20. Jahrhunderts Vortrag von Dr. Phil. Florian Roth bei der Kreisgruppe München der Landsmannschaft der Siebenbürger Sachsen im Haus des Deutschen Ostens, Munich, 13. Mai 2009 via: file:///D:/Downloads/ Hans-Otto_Roth_MS.pdf

221 *Traditionsgemeinschaft 50.Infanterie-Division, Die 50. Infanterie-Division 1939-1945, Augsburg: Eigenverlag von der Traditionsgemeinschaft 50. Infanterie-Division, 1965, p. 315*

222 For the evacuation in e.g. March 1943 see; *Unterlagen Ia Heeresgruppe A Bestand 500 Findbuch 12463 Akte 14./*For 13th Pz.D. see; *Generalkommando XXXXIX (geb.) A.K. An Auffrischungsstab-West*, d.d. 08.02.1943 Bundesarchiv-Militärarchiv PG 3576013) Many of the evacuated units assembled at Saporoshje.

223 *Various documents surrounding the 19th Romanian I.D. can be found in the Anlow zum KTB of the 50th I.D. In: T315/Roll 952, including Operationsbefe- hl No.35 (19.09.1943) Sonderbefehl No.40 (25.09.1943), Zwischenmeldung an Gen.Kdo. (28.09.1943) and Morgenmeldung 03.10.1943. more general infor- mation about Romanian units in Kleine Goten-Stellung and the coastal strip behind it see: Unterlagen der Ia Abteilung der Heeresgruppe A, d.d. 26.09.1943, GDIR Bestand 500 Findbuch 12469, Akte 25*

224 *Räumung des Kuban-Brückenkopfes und die Verteidigung der Krim vom 04.09.1943* In: KTB OKW p. 1455

225 *Unterlagen der Ia-Abteilung der Heeresgruppe A, d.d. 08.10.1943, GDIR*

	Bestand 500 Findbuch 12469, Akte 25
226	*Various logistical messages from Befehlshaber Strasse Kertsch and others between 20 43 and 06.08.1943 In: Bestand 500 Findbuch 12469, Akte 19/ Unterlagen der Ia-Abteilung der Heeresgruppe A, d.d. 09.10.1943, GDIR Bestand 500 Findbuch 12469, Akte 25/ Frühmeldung Grenadier Regiment 121 d.d. 27.09.1943 In: T315/ Roll952/* In the Vertrauliche Mitteilungen, Wochenbericht Südosteuropa there was talk of even less losses for the Romanians, 500 men of which 109 were killed. It is possible that this only deals with the moment of dismemberment itself. See: Vertrauliche Mitteilungen. Wochenbericht Südosteuropa, Pressestelle des Reichssicherheitshauptamtes, d.d. 06.11.1943 In: Klaus Popa, p. 73. On defaitis- me at the front see: Document RH 24-441/134 from the Bundesarchiv Freiburg, which reported on a trial of 12 soldiers of the 101st Jäger Division who were tried for 'cowardice in front of the enemy'. The divisional commander of the 101st Jägerdivision threatened with death penalty ('Tod in Schanden'), dated 13.01.1943
227	*Morgenmeldung an den Gen.Kdo. für den 27.09.1943*, In: T 315/Roll 952
228	For analysis of the situation see: Erich von Manstein, *Verlorene Siege*, Bonn: Athenaum Verlag,1955 pp. 512,513
229	*Unterlagen der Ia-Abteilung der Heeresgruppe A, d.d. 09.10.1943, GDIR Bestand 500 Findbuch 12469, Akte 25*
230	There was a small amount of Romanian armoured forces in Crimea around that time, 28 tanks type 38t 'Praga', a now obsolete Czech tank.
231	*Unterlagen der Ia Abteilung der Heeresgruppe A*, d.d. 24.09.1943, GDIR: Bestand 500, Findbuch 12469, Akte 25
232	Die Abwehrschlachten der 6. Armee im Donezbecken und in der Nogaischen Steppe vom 18. 08.- 03.11.*1943/Der Schicksalweg der 13. Panzer-Division 1939-1945*, Friedberg: Podzun-Pallas Verlag 1986, pp. 166-167
233	Peter Dimt, *Die Pantherlinie. Bausoldaten zwischen Peipussee und Finnensee*, Berg am See: Kurt Vowinckel-Verlag 1990
234	Jörn Hasenclever, *Wehrmacht und Besatzungspolitik in der Sowjetunion. Die Befehlshaber der rückwärtigen Heeresgebiete 1941-1943*, Paderborn/Munich: Ferdinand Schöningh 2010, p. 336
235	Brian Taylor, p.106
236	General Stahel for Saporoshje, General Steinbauer for Dniepropetrowsk and General Nehring for Krementschug, In: Fernschreiben 20.02.1943 from Von Manstein to Pz.AO.K.1 and Pz.A.O.K.4 and others, In: GDIR File 500, Findbuch 124659, Act 12
237	Die Winterschlachten der 6. Armee im grossen Djnepr-Bogen im Brückenkopf Nikopol und im Raum Nikopol-Apostolowo-Kriwoi Rog vom 10.01. bis 18.02.1944, bearbeitet durch KTB Führer Major Dr. Franck, Armee-Oberkommando 6 Mai 1944, In: T311/Roll 1469
238	16 Panzer-Grenadier-Division, 04.10.1943 Subject: Zusammenarbeit mit Tiger-Panzern, T315/Roll 808, 04.10.1943
239	Earl Ziemke, *From Stalingrad to Berlin*, Barsnley: Pen & Sword Books

	2014, pp. 222-224
240	Beauftragter d.Reichsmin. f. d. bes. Ostgebiete aan Reichsministerium für die besetzten Ostgebiete, betrift Rückführung der Kaukasier, d.d. 26.01.1944, In: GDIR, Bestand 500, Findbuch 12463, Akte 64/For number of deportees see: Rolf-Dieter Müller (hg.), Die Deutsche Wirtschaftspolitik in den besetzten Sowjetischen Gebieten 1941-1943. Der Abschlussbericht des Wirtschaftsstabes Ost und Auf- zeichnungen eines Angehörgen des Wirtschaftskommandos Kiew, In: Historischen Kommission bei der Bayerischen Akademie der Wisschenschaften (hg), *Deutsche Geschichtsquellen des 19. Und 20. Jahrhunderts, Band 57,* p. 378
241	*Unterlagen der Ia Abteilung der Heeresgruppe A*, Band 3 teil 1, 25.10.1943,
242	Perry Pierik, *Hitlers Lebensraum, de geestelijke wortels van de veroveringstochten naar het oosten,* Soesterberg: Publisher Aspekt 1999, pp. 260-261, later republished under the title *De geopolitiek van het Derde Rijk*
243	*Unterlagen der Ia Abteilung der Heeresgruppe A*, Band 3 teil 1, 25.10.1943, In: GDIR bestand 500 Findbuch 12469 Akte 27.
244	Ibid, Band 3 teil 1, 27.10.1943, In: GDIR Bestand 500 Findbuch 12469 Akte 27
245	KTB OKW band 6, 29.10.1943 p.p. 1228,1229
246	Funkspruch dd. 26.10.1943, Gez. Hansen, General der Kavallerie 219/43, In: GDIR file 500/Findbuch 124500 Akte 175: Schriftwechsel zwischen dem Befehlshaber der Deutschen Heeresmission in Rumänien General der Kavallerie E. Hansen, dem Chef des Generalstabes der Rumänischen Armee Korpsgeneral I.Steflea, dem Ministerpräsidenten Rumäniens Marschall I. Antonescu, dem Führer und Obersten Befehlshaber der Deutschen Wehrmacht A. Hitler über die Verteidi- gung der Halbinsel Krim und Transnistriens, September 1943 - März 1944.
247	Deutscher General b. Obkdo.d.rum. Wehrmacht, to: Chef des gen.Stabes des Heeres, 29.11.1943, In: GDIR file 500/Findbuch 124500 Act 175: Schriftwechsel zwischen dem Befehlshaber der Deutschen Heeresmission in Rumänien General der Kavallerie E. Hansen, dem Chef des Generalstabes der Rumänischen Armee Korpsgeneral I.Steflea, dem Ministerpräsidenten Rumäniens Marschall I. Antone- scu, dem Führer und Obersten Befehlshaber der Deutschen Wehrmacht A. Hitler über die Verteidigung der Halbinsel Krim und Transnistriens, September 1943 - März 1944.
248	Letter dated 02.11.1943 from General Steflea to Marshal Antonescu, In: GDIR file 500/Findbuch 124500 Act 175: Schriftwechsel zwischen dem Befehlshaber der Deutschen Heeresmission in Rumänien General der Kavallerie E. Hansen, dem Chef des Generalstabes der Rumänischen Armee Korpsgeneral I.Steflea, dem Ministerpräsidenten Rumäniens Marschall I. Antonescu, dem Führer und Obersten Befehlshaber der deutschen Wehrmacht A.Hitler über die Verteidigung der Halbinsel Krim und Transnistriens, September 1943 - März 1944.
249	*Letter from Hitler to Antonescu,* early November 1943, in: GDIR file 500/

Find- buch 124500 Act 175
250 *Telegram des Auswärtigen Amts an die Deutsche Gesnadtschaft Bukarest* nr. 3598 vom 16.1.21943, In: GDIR file 500/Findbuch 124500 Akte 175
251 Jenö Ruszkay, *Ungarn und seine Nachbarn im Herbst 1943*, In Klaus Popa, p. 55
252 Die Abwehrschlachten der 6. Armee im Donezbecken und in der Nogaischen Steppe vom 18.08 - 03.11.1943, bearbeitet durtch KTB-Führer Major Dr.Franck, Armee-Oberkommando 6, November 1943, In: T312 R1468
253 KTB OKW band 7 p. 760-763
254 Die Zweite Winterschlacht der 6. Armee zwischen Dnieper, Ingulez und Bug von 3 - 23.03.1944. bearbeitet duch KTB-Führer Mahor Dr. Franck Armee-OP berg-kommando 6 Juni 1944
255 Oberkommando der Heeresgruppe A, Bezug: Ausbau der Festung Krim, which stated: 'Der Führer hat den Ausbau der Krim zur Festung befohlen', dd. 24.05.1943 In: GDIR, Bestand 500, Findbuch 12469, Akte 33. Responsible for this expansion was the Fest.Pi.Stab 5 with headquarters in Simferopol
256 Stand und Kampfkraft der sich auf der Krim befindliche Verbände, GDIR Bestand 500, Findbuch 124500 Akte 189, for Tatarengrab see Zwischenmeldungen der Truppenteile für 03.11.1943, T 315/Roll 952
257 Forsczyk, *Where the Iron Cross Grow. The Crimea 1941-1944* p. 278
258 III./Gebirgsjäger battalion 'Bergmann'.
259 *Forczyk*, pp. 278, 279/There served, according to a document dated 28 December 1943 53,254 'Fremdländische Verbände' in the German Army, see KTB OKW band 6 p. 1483, 1484/BThe Gebirgsjägerregiment 'Krim' unit established in April 1944 served alongside mainly units of the 4th Mountain Division also Cossacks of the 6.(kos.)/Krim- Btl. Upon merging with the mountain regiment, the numbering was changed to 17th Cossack Company. Besides *'Soviet civilians'*, the new unity *'Crimea'* was also equipped with Soviet artillery which had been captured. This was 7.62 cm artillery (Pak 36). See: Generalkommando Vde A.K. Befehl zur Aufstellung des Gebirgsjägerregiments 'Krim' d.d. 03.04.1944 In: File 500, Findbuch 12474, Akte 92
260 David T. Zabecki, *The German War Machine in World War II* p. 67
261 Der Oberbefehlshaber der 17. Armee, 01.10.1943, befehl für den Arbeitseinsatz der Zivilbevölkering auf der Krim, In: GDIR, Bestand 500, Findbuch 12469, Akte 5
262 For details, Jaenecke referred to Von Kleist. *Interrogation record of Colonel-General E.G.Jaenecke, Commander of the 17th Army*, 22.11.1947 in: http://skoblin.blogs-pot.com/2010/07/interrogation-of-colonel-general-e-g.html
263 Gosztony p. 383
264 General zbV beim OKH, d.d. 29.04.1944, Abschlussbericht über die

	Vorgänge auf der Krim im April 1944 In: GDIR Akte 251/Brian Taylor, *Barbarossa to Berlin. A Chronology of the Campaigns of the Eastern Front 1941 to 1945* Vol. Two, Chalford: Spellmount 2008, p.172
265	David T. Zabecki, *The German War machine in Worldwar II* Ii p. 67
266	Various reports in: *Berichte der Schiffahrtstellen in Konstantza, Nikolajew usw., Schriftverkehr und Anweisungen des Reichskommissars für die Seeschiffahrt, Berichte der Schiffskapitäne*, Bestand 500, Findbuch 12463 Akte 233. The above rapports are from February and March 1944.
267	*Der Oberbefehlshaber der Kriegsmarine*, d.d. 19.05.1944, *Die Tätigkeit der Kriegsmarine bei der Verteidigung und Räumung der Krim vom Herbst 1943 ab* In: T1027/ R1907/Admiral Schwarzes Meer, d.d. 23.05.1944, Abschlussbericht über der Festung Sebastopol
268	OKW/WFST Op (M) hat dem Ob.d.M. fernmündlich gemeldet, d.d. 13.05.1944, T1027/Roll 1907
269	Zabecki, p. 67
270	Generalkommando LXXII.A.K. z.b.V. d.d. 05.04.1944, Korpsbefehl zur Verteidigung der Brückenkopf-Stellung Odessa
271	Anniversary of the Liberation of Odessa from the Nazi Occupation, In: https://www.prlib.ru/en/history/619158
272	OKH diary, 09.05.1944 In: T78/Roll 420
273	Heeresgruppe Südukraine an Rum.Verb.Kdo. (Oberst Ivanescu), Betr: Ablösung der ukrainischer, Russischer usw. Einheiten durch rum. Minderheiten-Einheiten, dated 20.07.1944, Bestand 500, Findbuch 12469 Akte 43
274	KTB OKW, band 7 p.764
275	For the Vlassov Army see: Joachim Hoffmann, *Die Geschichte der Wlassow-Armee*, Freiburg: Rombach Verlag 1986, as also Sven Steenberg, *Wlassow, Verräter oder Patriot?*, Köln: Verlag Wissenschaft & Politik, 1968, for Islamic collaboration see Jeloschek/Richter/ Schütte/ Semler, *Freiwillige vom Caucasus. Georgier, Armenier, Aserbaidschaner, Tschetschenen u,.a., auf deutscher Seite. Der Sonderverband Berg- mann und seine Gründer Theodor Oberländer*, Graz: Leopold Stocker Verlag 2003, Joachim hoffmann, *Kaukasien 1942/43. Das deutsche Heer und die Orientvölker der Sowjetunion,* Freiburg: Rombach Verlag 1991, Joachim Hoffmann, *Die Ostlegionen 1941-1943*, Freiburg: Rombach verlag 1981, On Neu-Turkestan and Waffen-SS in the Balkans: Perry Pierik *"Neu Turkestan' aan het front, islamitische soldaten uit de Kaukasus en de Balkan in dienst van de Waffen-SS*, Soesterberg: Aspekt publishers, 2019. On political relations, including around the Grand Mufti see Emerson Vermaat, *Hitler en de arabieren*, Soesterberg: Aspekt Publishing House 2016)
276	*Deutsche Heeresmison in Rumanien, betr. Einstellung von Kriegsgefangenen in die Deutsche Wehrmacht, An: Kommandant Kriegsgefangenen-Stammbezirk Rumänien*, 07.02.1943, In; GDIR Bestand 500, Findbuch 124500 Akte 143. For the deployment of Hiwi's see e.g. the statement 'Personelle Lage' of the 278th

and 305th I.D. on 1 August 1944 with a Hiwi file of 1595 and 1155 troops. T 77 Roll 1142 OKW Wfst. In a letter dated 21.04.1944 Der Vertreter des Reichsministeriums für die besetzten Ostgebiete to The Reichsministerium f.d. besetzten Ostgebiete Herr Ministerinaldirigent Dr.Bräutigam, 30,000 Hiwi's within the German 18th Army on that date were mentioned. DGIR: File 500, Findbuch 12463, Akte 62

277 Der Grosse Rum. Generalstab-Fernschreiben (Steflea) -Ubersetzung- An das Rum. verb.kdo.Oberst Ivanescu, Bestand 500, Findbuch 12469, Akte 43
278 *KTB OKW Band 7 p. 784*
279 Ibid p. 785 / Sean H. Seyer, *The Plan put into Practice: USAAF Bombing Doctrine and the Ploesti Campaign* (2005)
280 Ibid p.p. 785, 790, 791
281 *Ibid p. 787*
282 Ibid p. 791
283 Also referred to in the documents as Hofmeier, but Hoffmeyer is the correct spelling, cf: *SS Verordnungsblatt*, 9. Jahrgang 09.11.1943 Nummer 4a
284 KTB OKW band 7 p.p. 787, 788
285 Ibid p. 789
286 *The 'VoMi' was responsible for the resettlement of ethnic Germans (Volksduits/ Volksdeutschen) living outside Germany's borders. In addition, the head office was concerned with the resettlement of Volksduit descendants of Germanic settlers in the Soviet Union and Eastern Europe.*
287 For detailed correspondence, dated 27.07.1944, 29.07.1944, 04.08.1944, 06.08.1944, 09.08.1944, 15.08.1944 and 18.08.1944 see Klaus Popa., *Vor 70 Jahren. Die NS-Volksgruppenpolitik in weiteren Archivdokumenten, das Jahr 1944*
288 *KTB OKW band 7 p. 790*
289 *Ibid p. 797*
290 A nice insight into the Romanian 'spirit' of those days was given in: *Pressenstelle, vertrauliche Mitteilungen. Wochtenbericht 268, 275 - 277 and 278 period 11 to 18 June 1944, 30 July to 20 August 1944 and 20 August 1944 to 27 August 1944, In: Wochentliche Zusammenstellungen der vertraulichen Mitteilungen über die politischen, wirtschaftlichen und militärische Lage.* GDIR: Betsand 500 Findbuch 124500 Act 198
291 This played out in early August 1943 in the defence of the 'Hagen-Stellung', Panzerarmeekommando 2 dated 03.08.1943, T313 Roll 172
292 *Friessner p.p. 31-34*
293 GDIR Bestand 500 Findbuch 12469, Akte 43
294 Letter Schörner 20.07.1944 in two copies GDIR File 500 Findbuch 12469, Akte 43
295 *Der Oberbefehlshaber der Heeresgruppe Südukraine, An die Generale einschl. Div.-Führer, d.d. 23.07.1944, GDIR Bestand 500, Findbuch 12469, Akte 43*
296 Friessner p.p. 30-33

297 'Schematische Kriegsgliederung der Heeresgruppe Süd' in: Hans Friessner, *Verratene Schlachten. Die Tragödie der Deutschen Wehrmacht in Rumänien und Ungarn*, Hamburg: Holsten Verlag, p. 253

298 Fernschreiben Heeresgruppe Südukraine to OKH dated 29.07.1944, GDIR Bestand 500, Findbuch 12469, Akte 43/Revocation of Decision: Fernschrieben H.Gr.Südukraine d.d. 19.08.144, GDIR File 500, Findbuch 12469, Akte 51

299 Bemerkungen zum Besuch des O.B. beim LVII.Pz.Korps und IV.A.K., 31.07.1944, GDIR Bestand 500, Findbuch 12469, Akte 43

300 Anlage 7 Abschlussmeldung über das Unternehmen 'Michael', Bestand 500, Find- buch 12469, Akte 51

301 Various entries Unternehmen *'Michael'* in KTB.Heeresgruppe Südukraine, dated 16.07.1944, 22.07.1944, 23.07.1944, GDIR File 500, Findbuch 12469, Akte 40, as well as the Abschlussmeldung über das Unternehmen *'Michael'*, File 500, Findbuch 12469, Akte 51

302 KTB Heeresgruppe Südukraine dd.29.087.1944, GDIR File 500, Findbuch 12469, Act 40/the defectors were mostly Moldavians: (Telex) Bericht An Heeresgruppe Südukraine dd.19.07.1944, Nach Meldung der Gruppe Mieth sind vom rum. 7.I.D. zum Feind übergelaufen. This involved four men on the night of 13-14 July and six men on the night of 17 or 18 July 1944. The men were from the 3.Company of I.R. 16, GDIR: file 500, Findbuch 12469, Akte 43

303 Bemerkungen zum Besuch des O.B. beim LVII.Pz.Korps und IV.A.K.

304 Ibid Samuel W.Mitcham, *The German Defeat in the East 1944-45*, Mechanicsburg: Stackpole Books, 2001, p. 192/On 14.07.1944 it came to a ban on visiting *'foreign brothels'*. On 10 August, the Heeresgruppe Südukraine announced an investigation into public and secret brothels in Romania, Anlage KTB Heeresgruppe Südukraine, 14.07.1944 and 10.08.19844, GDIR File 500, Findbuch 12469, Akte 44

305 KTB Heeresgruppe Südukrain d.d. 29.07.1944, GDIR: Bestand 500, Findbuch 12469, Akte 40

306 'Schematische Kriegsgliederung der Heeresgruppe Süd' in: Hans Friessner, *Verratene Schlachten. Die Tragödie der deutschen Wehrmacht in Rumänien und Ungarn*, Hamburg: Holsten Verlag, p. 253/ Tagesmeldung Heeresgruppe Südukraine 28.07.1944, GDIR Bestand 500, Findbuch 12469, Akte 39, KTB Heeersgruppe Südukraine 29.07.1944, GDIR Bestand 500, Findbuch 12469, Akte 40, the large number of Sturmgeschützen with the 1st Romanian Pz.D. were possibly from the H.Sturmgeschützbrigade 905, which was in assigned to the division around 16.07.1944, see Tagesmeldung 16.07.1944, GDIR Bestand 500, Findbuch 12469, Akte 39/

307 See Letter Steflea GDIR: Grosser Rumänischer Generalstab an das Oberkommando der Heeresgruppe Südukraine, 04.08.1944, GDIR: File 500 Findbuch 12469, Act 51. The issue on 02.08.1944 was followed by apologies from the LVII.th Corps to the Romanians. In: *Grosser Rumänis-*

cher Generalstab an das Oberkommando der Heeresgruppe Südukraine, Letter from Steflea on behalf of Antonescu, GDIR: Bestand 500, Findbuch 12469 Akte 51. Regarding remark around commandant 1st Romanian Pz.D. see Bemerkungen zum Besuch des O.B. beim LVII. Pz.Korps und IV.A.K/For apologies see: Armeegruppe Wöhler Betr.Schreiben Gr.Rum. Gen.Stab. 05.08.1944, Stellungsnahme, In: GDIR, File 500, Findbuch 12465 Akte 51

308 KTB Heeresgruppe Südukraine 10.08.1944, T311/R158/
309 Friessner's letter to Hitler and Guderian, dated 03.08.1944, In: GDIR: File 500, Findbuch 12469, Act 51
310 Besprechung des Chefs d. Gen.St. der H.Gr.Südukraine mit dem Chef der G.Rum. Gen.St. am 09.08.1944 In: GDIR File 500, Findbuch 12469, deed 51
311 Vorläufiger Gefechtsbericht der 79. Infanterie-Division über die Kämpfe von, 20.08.1944 - September 1944, In: T78/R140
312 Hillgruber p. 211
313 Walther Rehm, *Jassy, Schicksal einer Division oder einer Armee?* Neckargemünd: Scharnhorst Buchkameradschaft 1959, p. 38
314 Der Oberbefehlshaber der Heeresgruppe Südukraine, An Alle deutsche und rumänischen Kommandeure, d.d. 18.08.1944, GDIR: Bestand 500, Findbuch 12469, Akte 51/Besprechung mit den Chefs d. Gen. St. der 6. Und 8. Armee und dem Chef d.D.V.V.St. 3 am 19.08.1944 in Slanic, In: GDIR Bestand 500, Findbuch 12469, Akte 51
315 KTB Heeresgruppe Südukraine, 20.08.1944 T311/Roll 158/Mitcham, *The German Defeat in the East*, p. 173
316 KTB Heeresgruppe Südukraine 20.08.1941
317 Rehm, pp. 42, 43
318 Ibid, p.p. 44-48
319 Friessner p. 75, report from army group Dumitrescu: Gruppe Ic/A.O., An Abteilung Ia d.d.21.08.1944 GDIR Bestand 500, Findbuch 12469, Akte 54
320 Ibid, p. 73
321 Ibid, p. 75
322 KTB Heeresgruppe Südukraine 21.08.1944
323 Ibid 24.08.1944
324 Hillgruber p. 215
325 Anca Oltean, *The Importance of the Act of 23 August 1944 in the Geopolitical Context of the Second World War*, In: Analele University in Oradea, Seria Relatii Internationale si Studii Europene, Tom IX, p. 7-14/ (*Hillgruber p. 216)
326 Details on the 376th I.D. come from the division's 15 page Gefechtsbericht, prepared on 22 January 1945: OKH/Abwicklungsstab Gruppe F, Gefechtsbericht für die 376.Inf.Div. vom 18.08.1944 - 29.08.1944, In: T78/Roll 139

327 Schlagregen, Leutnant, Betr. takt. Erlebnisbericht des Lt. Schlagregen (106.I.D.) Bezug: OKH, T78/R139
328 OKH/Abwicklungsstab Gruppe F, Gefechtsbericht für die 376.Inf.Div. vom 18.08.1944 - 29.08.1944, In: T78/Roll 139
329 Geschichte der 258. Inf.Div. und Gefechtsbericht für die Zeit von 20.08 bis 30.08.1944. Zusammengestellt durch den Sachbearbeiter Oblt. Schalke, T87/Roll 140
330 Niederschrift über die Vernehmung des Rückkämpfers Lt. Lange, 370.I.D.,d.d. 15.09.1944 GDIR Bestand 500, Findbuch 12469, Akte 53
331 KTB Heeresgruppe Südukraine, 24.08.1944, GDIR: File 500, Findbuch 12469, Act 49
332 Ibid 23.08.1944
333 Anca Oltean, *The Importance of the Act of 23 August 1944 in the Geopolitical Context of the Second World War*, In: Analele Universitatii din Oradea, Seria Ralatii Internationale si Studii Europene, Tom IX, p. 7-14
334 KTB Heeresgruppe Südukraine 27.08.1944
335 Ibid 23.08.1944
336 Friessner p. 92
337 KTB Heeresgruppe Südukraine, 23.08.1944, GDIR: File 500, Findbuch 12469, Act 49
338 Walter Warlimont, Im Hauptquartier der deutschen Wehrmacht 1939-1945. Grundlagen, Formen, Gestalten. Band 2, November 1942 - Mai 1845, Weltbildverlag: z.j., p. 500/ The OSS (predecessor of the CIA) reported the flying in of the British agents, in a top secret document in the CIA.gov./Library/Reading room, document CIA-RP-D13x00001R000100140011-7
339 T78/R140
340 Silviu Miloiu, *When the West is far away: Romanian Attempts to withdraw from World War II 1943-1944*), Finish views, In: *The Romanian Journal for Baltic and Nordic Studies*, Vol 6 issue 2 (2014) p. 203
341 Andreas Hillgruber, *Hitler, König Carol und Marschall Antonescu. Die Deutsch-Rumänischen Beziehungen 1938-1944* Wiesbaden: Franz Steiner Verlag 1954, p. 210
342 Heeresgruppe Südukraine had been renamed Heeresgruppe Süd on 24.09.1944, see e.g. T312/Roll 429
343 Vor 70 Jahren. Die NS-Volksgruppenpolitik in weiteren Archivdokumenten, das Jahr 1944, p. 91/Mitcham, *The German Defeat in the East*, p. 190
344 ibid, p. 90/Mitcham p. 192
345 Besprechung des Oberbefehlshabers mit den Oberbefehlshabern der 6. Und 8. Armee u.a. Am 15.09.1944 in Szatmar Nemety, GDIR Bestand 500, Findbuch 12469 Akte 35
346 Obkdo.d.Heeresgruppe Südukraine, betr. Panzerbekämpfung, d.d. 15.09.1944 GDIR 500 Findbuch 12469, Akte 53
347 Panzerjäger-Sturmgeschütz 38 T (Hetzer), Führungsgrundsätze Inf.Stur-

	mgesch. Kp. attached to letter from OKH to Heeresgruppe Südukraine dated 06.09.1944. GDIR File 500, Findbuch 12469, Act 53
348	Obkdo.d. Heeresgruppe Südukraine an: Armeegruppe Fretter Pico, 8.Armee and others.
	dated 19.09.1944, GDIR Bestand 500, Findbuch 12469, Akte 53
349	Besprechung des Oberbefehlshabers mit den Oberbefehlshabern der 6. Und 8. Ar- mee u.a. am 15.09.1944 in Szatmar Nemety, GDIR Bestand 500, Findbuch 12469 Akte 35
350	Grzegorz Rossolinksi-Liebe called these the 'ínter-fascist' conflicts: Grzegorz Rosso- linksi-Liebe, *Inter-Fascist Conflicts in East Central Europe: The Nazis, the 'Austro- fascists', the Iron Guard, and the Organisation of Ukrainian Nationalists*, Oxford: Berghahn 2017
351	Abschrift des Fernschreiben nr. 835 des Majors der Schutzpolizei Suchanek an den Chef der Sicherheitspolizei und des SD, SS-Gruppenführer Dr. Kaltenbrunner, betreffende Führende Legionäre im Sonderlager Fichtenhain, In: Klaus Popa, Vor 70 Jahren, p. 16
352	Klaus Popa, *Vor 70 Jahren 1945*, quoted *from Lagebricht Südosteuropa Folge 296*
353	Hillgruber *227, 228/ http://www.geocities.ws/rausschmiss/S.pdf*
354	For life history of Andres Schmidt see Klaus Popa (Hg.) Völkisches Handbuch Südosteuropa via: http://www.geocities.ws/rausschmiss/S.pdf
355	1. Jänuar 1945 Abschrift des *'Bericht aus Rumänien'* von Ing. Kurz, besorgt vom SS-Hauptamt, Amtsgruppe D am 24.1.1945 in Berlin-Wilmersdorf, In :https://www.academia.edu/41117971/Documents_concerning_the_ Deutsche_Volksgruppe_in_Rum%C3%A4nien_-_the_German_Ethnic_ Group_in_ Romania_-_in_the_year_ 1945Volker Knoop, *Himmlers letztes Aufgebot. Die NS-Organisation 'Werwolf'*, Köln/Weimar/Wien: Böhlau Verlag 2008, pp. 122- 136/Perry Pierik, *Sicherheitsdienst! Friedrich Knolle bekentenissen van een SD-officier*, Soesterberg: Aspekt Publishers 2011, p. 127 ff. Werewolf hysteria after the war gave the Soviets an excuse to silence any opposition by putting away and arresting ' troublesome' civilians as 'Werwolf agents', see Volker Knoop p. 207 et seq.
356	*https://www.academia.edu/31300674/Bio-bibliografisches_Handbuch_deutshttps://www.academia.edu/31300674/Bio-bibliografisches_Handbuch_deutscher_Volksgruppen_S%C3%BCdosteuropa_P/file:///D:/Downloads/Biobibliografisches_Handbuch_deutscher%20(2).pdf*
357	Besprechung des Oberbefehlshabers mit den Oberbefehlshabern der 6. Und 8. Armee u.a. am 15.09.1944 in Szatmar Nemety, GDIR Bestand 500, Findbuch 12469 Akte 35
358	*Fernschreiben O.K.H. an Heeresgruppe F, Betr.: Rettung deutscher Volksgruppe in Rumänien, d.d. 01.09.1944, Fernschreiben an Reichsführer-SS, Feldkommandostelle by SS-Obergruppenführer Phleps, d.d. 01.09.1944 In: GDIR Bestand 500, Findbuch 12469, Akte 54/ Valdis O. Lumans, p.p. 220, 221*
359	*Das Schicksal der deutschen in Rumänien*, p.p. 75-80

360 Ibid p. 77
361 *Ibid p. 99*
362 Ibid p.p. 94, 95
363 Perry Pierik, *Hungary 1944, 1945, the forgotten tragedy*, Nieuwegein: publisher Aspekt 1995
364 *11. Januar 1945 Abschrift des 'Bericht aus Rumänien' von Ing. Kurz, besorgt vom SS-Hauptamt, Amtsgruppe D am 24.1.1945 in Berlin-Wilmersdorf, In: Klaus Popa, Vor 70 Jahren Die NS-'Volksgruppenpolitik' in weiteren Archivdokumenten Das Jahr 1945*
365 Rsadu Ioanid, *The Holocaust in Romania*, p. 178
366 Krista Zach pointed out that there was mostly a perception that the majority of Romanian Jews had gotten off well, In: Wolfgang Benz (Hg.), Dimensionen des Völkermords. *Die Zahl der jüdischen Opfer des Nationalsozialismus*, München Deutscher Taschen Buch Verlag 1991, p. 381
367 Diana Dumitru, *The Evolution of Holocaust Studies in Moldovan Historiography 1991-2017*, in: Dapim Studies of the Holocaust
368 *An overview on Romanian historiography can be found in: Hildrun Glass, Der Holocaust in Rumänien. Wege der Forschung, In: Einsicht 11, Frühjahr 2014, supplementary see also Simon Geissbühler, 'He spoke Yiddish like a Jew': 'Neighbors' contribution to the Mass Killing of Jews in Northern Bukovia and Bessarabia, July 1941, In: Holocaust and Genocide Studies 28, No 3 (winter 2014)*
369 p. 246-251
370 p. 257, 258/The execution was filmed: https://www.youtube.com/watch?v=Ak-6jwsLS9Sk
371 *Letter from historian Visan Miu Tudor to author, outlining historiography Romania in relation to World War II, dated 04.05.2020. For book Kiritescu deals with the title Romania in al doilea razboi mondial (Romania during World War II)*
372 *On current influence of the Legionaries movement see: Cecilie Endresen, 'The Legionaries rise! The neo-Legionary movement in post-Communist Romania. In: Südost-forschungen 69, October 2011 The Romanian community in Germany after the war comprised some 3,400 people, 1,200 of whom were ethnically Romanian (the rest were Volksdeutscher). A majority of ethnic Romanians adhered to the legionary movement. Some had served in the SS, such as V. Dobrescu of the section in north-west Germany, Vasile Barbulescu, in southern Germany Freiburg, and Grigore Scopochirja at the Munich war veterans' organisation. See: Rumanian Refugee Organisations in Germany, February 1955 Cia. gov/library/reading room)*
372 *On current influence of the Legionaries movement see: Cecilie Endresen, 'The Legionaries rise! The neo-Legionary movement in post-Communist Romania. In: Südost- forschungen 69, October 2011 The Romanian community in Germany after the war comprised some 3,400 people, 1,200 of whom were ethnically Romanian (the rest were Volksdeutscher). A majority of ethnic Romanians*

adhered to the legionary movement. Some had served in the SS, such as V. Dobrescu of the section in north-west Germany, Vasile Barbulescu, in southern Germany Freiburg, and Grigore Scopochirja at the Munich war veterans' organisation. See: Rumanian Refugee Organisations in Germany, February 1955 Cia. gov/library/reading room)

Literature:

Babes, A., / Florian, A., *The Beginning of the War in the east and Hastening the Approaches against the Jewish Population,* Academia .edu 2020

Bade, K.J. Oltmer, J., Zwischen Aus- und Einwanderungsland. Deustchland und die Migration seit der 17.Jahrhundert, In: *Zeitschrift für Bevölkerungswissenschaft Jg. 28* 2-4/2003

Barkai, A., *Das Wirtschaftssystem des Nationalsozialismus. Ideology, Theory, Politics 1933-1945,* Frankfurt am Main: 1998

Benz, W., (Hg.), *Dimensionen des Völkermords. Die Zahl der jüdischen Opfer des Nationalsozialismus,* Münich Deutscher Taschen Buch Verlag 1991

Berenbaum, M. Peck, A.J. (Ed.), *The Holocaust and History. The Known, the Unknown, the Disputed and the Reexamined,* Bloomingrton/Indianapolis: Indiana University Press 1998

Bieberstein, J.R. von, *Die These von der Verschwörung 1776-1945. Philosophen, Freimaurer, Juden, liberale und Sozialsiten als Verschwörer gegen die Sozialordnung* In: *Europäische Hochschulschriften Vol 63,* Frankfurt am Main/Bern/Las Vegas: Peter Lang 1978

Bundesministerium für Vertriebene, Flüchtlinge und Kriegsgeschädigte (Hg.), *Dokumentation der Vertreibung der Deutschen aus Mitteleuropa band III, das Schicksal der Deutschen in Rumänien,* Munich: Deutscher Taschenbuch Verlag

Carstocea, R., *Native Fascist, Transnational Anti-Semites. The International Acti- vity of Legionary Leader Ion I.Mota* In: Academia.edu

Castellan, G., *Geschiedenis van Roemenië*, s-Hertogenbosch: Voltaire, 2001

Caşu, I., Moldova under the Soviet Communist Regime In: Vladimir Tismaneanu and Bogdan C. Iacob, 1 Remembrance (ed.), *History and Justice coming to Terms with traumatic Pasts in Democratic Societies*, Budapest-New York: Central European University Press, 2015

Craig, R., *Nation, Black Earth, Red Star,. A History of Soviet Security Policy, 1917- 1991*, Ithaca/ London: Cornell University Press 1992

Het proces-Eichmann, de Joden vervolging in Roemenië. Weer een reeks docu- menten. *Nieuwe Tilburgsche Courant 24.-05.1961*

Deletant, D., Review of the book Leon Volovici/Miriam Caloianu (ed.), *The History of the Holocaust in Romania*, Jean Ancel, In: *Holocaust and Genocide Studies* doi: 10.1093/hgs/dct044 p. 503

Deletant, D., *Hitler's Forgotten Ally. Ion Antonescu and the Regime Romania 1940- 1944*, Chippenham: Palgrave MacMillan 2006

Der Schicksalweg der 13.Panzer-Division 1939-1945, Friedberg: Podzun-Pallas Verlag 1986

Dimt, P., *Die Pantherlinie. Bausoldaten zwischen Peipussee und Finnensee*, Berg am See: Kurt Vowinckel-Verlag 1990

Dinaor, R.L., The German Military Mission to Romania, 1940-1941 In*: IFQ issue 69* 2nd Quarter 2013

Drews, J., Vom Soja-Anbau zum 'Wohlthat'-Vertrag. Der ökonomische Anschluss Rumäniens an das Deutsche Reich, In: Besatzung und Bündnis, Deutsche Herrschaftsstrategien in Ost- und Südost Europa In: *Beiträge zur Nationalsozialistischen Gesundheits-und Sozialpolitik Band 12* Oldenburg: Ver- lag der Buchläden 1995

Dumitran, D. / Moga, V., (ed.), *Economy and Soceity, Consumption and Eastern Europe. Papers of the international Conference held in Alba Iulia* April 15 - 27th 2013.

Dumitru, D., How Bessarabiens were perceived by the Romanian Civilian-Military Administration in 1941, *Euxeinos 15/16* (2014)

Dumitru, D., *The Evolution of Holocaust Studies in Moldovan Historiography 1991-2017*, in: Dapim Studies of the Holocaust

Eichholtz, D., War *for Oil. The Nazi Quest for an Oil Empire*, Washington D.C.: Potomac Books, 2006

Endresen, C., 'The Legionaries rise!'. The neo-Legionary Movement in post-Communist Romania. In: *Südostforschungen 69*, October 2011

Fabricius, J., *Een wereld in beroering*, Leopold Publishing House, 1952

Forsczyk, *Where the Iron Cross Grow. The Crimea 1941-1944*

Friessner, H., *Verratene Schlachten. Die Tragödie der deutschen Wehrmacht in Rumänien und Ungarn*, Hamburg: Holsten Verlag z.j.

Furima, M., Moldovianism vs Romanianism, the Dichotomy of Ethnic Identity. How Moldovia fails at Nation Building, In: *Case Study Nation Building in Post Communit Societies, SVNC oo43, 21.05.2018*

Gastony, E.B., *Hungary and Geopolitics. The Second World War and the Holocaust 1938-1945*, Soesterberg: Aspekt Publishers 2019

Geissbühler, S., *'He spoke Yiddish like a Jew'*: Neighbors Contribution to the Mass Killing of Jews in Northern Bukovina and Bessarabia, July 1941 in: *Holocaust and Genocide Studies 28* no. 3 (Winter 2014)

Geissbühler, S., Bloody *July. Romania and the Holocaust in Summer 1941*, Yad Vashem, Jerusalem 29.10.2015

Gilbert, A., *Waffen-SS, Hitler's Army at War*, Ingram Publishers Services US Glass, H., Der Holocaust in Rumänien. Wege der Forschung, In: *Einsicht 11*, Frühjahr 2014)

Gosztony, P., *Hitlers fremde Heere. Das Schicksal der nichtdeutschen Armeen in Ostfeldzug*, Düsseldorf/Wien: Econ verlag 1976

Grondijs, L.H., *Tusschen twee werelden. Studien over de bewoners van Oost-Europa*. Amsterdam: Elsevier 1944

Groza, C.A., The Fascist Phenomenon. National Legionary State between laws, Journals, Memoirs, and the Jewish Repression between 2-23 January 19421: In: *Journal of Education Culture and Soceity No 1* 2014

Hasenclever, J., *Wehrmacht und Besatzungspolitik in der Sowjetunion. Die Befehlshaber der rückwärtigen Heeresgebiete 1941-1943*, Paderborn/Munich: Ferdinand Schöningh 2010

Haushofer, K. / Obst, E.,/ Lautensach, H./ Maull, O., *Bausteine zur Geopolitik*, Berlin: Kurt Vowinckel Verlag 1928

Hayward, J., Too Little, Too Late. An Analysis of Hitlers's Failure in August 1942 to Damage Soviet Oil Production. In: *The Journal of Military History 64* July 2000

Haynes, R.A., 'A New Greater Romania?' Romanian Claims to the Serbian Banat in 1941 In: *Central Europe*, Vol. 3 November 2005.

Hennig, R., / Körholz, L., *Einführungen in die Geopolitik*. Leipzig: B.G.Teubner Verlag, 1935

Hillgruber, A., *Hitler, König Carol und Marschall Antonescu. Die deutsch-rumänischen Beziehungen 1938-1944,* Wiesbaden: Franz Steiner verlag 1954

Hirschfeld, G. / Krumeich, G./ Renz, I., *Enzyklopädie Erste Weltkrieg*, Paderborn/Munich: Ferdinand Schöningh 2003

Ioanid, R., *The Holocaust in Romania. The Destruction of Jews and Gypsies under the Antonescu regime 1940-1944*, Chicago: Ivan R. Dee, 2000

Ingrao, C., *Hitler's Elite. Die Wegbereiter des nationalsozialistischen Massenmords*, Berlin: Propylän Verlag 2012

Kirchubel, R., *Atlas of the Eastern Front 1941-1945*, Oxford: Osprey 2016

Knoop, V., *Himmlers letztes Aufgebot. Die NS-Organisation 'Werwolf'*, Köln/ Weimar/Wien: Böhlau Verlag 2008

Kshyk, C., The Holocaust in Romania: The Extermination and Protection of the Jews under Antonescu's Regime, *Student Pulse Vol.6 No. 12*

Livezeanu, I., *Cultural Politics in greater Romania*, Ithaca/London: Cornell University press, 1995

Valdis O. Lumans, *Himmler's Auxiliaries. The Volksdeutsche Mittelstelle and the German National Minorities of Europe, 1933-1945*, Chapel Hill/London: The University of North Carolina Press, 1993

Manstein, E. von, *Verlorene Siege*, Bonn: Athenaum Verlag, 1955

Marsalek, H., *Die Geschichte ders Konzentrationslager Mauthausen,* Wien 1980 Martin,

B., *Weltmacht oder Niedergang? Deutsche Grossmachtpolitik im 20.Jahr-hundert*, Darmstadt: Wissenschaftliche Buchgesellschaft 1989

Meurs, W.P. van, *The Bessarabian Question in Communist Historiography*. Utrecht: 1993 (unpublished)

Miloiu, S., When the West is far away: Romanian Attempts to withdraw from World War II 91943-1944), Finish views, In: *The Romanian Journal for Baltic and Nordic Studies, Vol 6 issue 2* 2014

Mioara, A., *Kriegspropaganda in Rumänien. Die Ostfront, June 1941 - August 1944*, Academia.edu

Mitcham, S.W., *Hitler's Legions. German Army Order of Battle World War II*

Mitcham, S.W., *The German Defeat in the East 1944-45*, Mechanicsburg: Stackpole Books, 2001

Müller, R-D., (Hg.), Die deutsche Wirtschaftspolitik in den besetzten sowjetischen Gebieten 1941-1943. Der Abschlussbericht des Wirtschaftsstabes Ost und Aufzeichnungen eines Angehörgen des Wirtschaftskommandos Kiew, In: Historischen Kommission bei der bayerischen Akademie der Wisschenschaften (hg). *Deutsche Geschichtsquellen des 19. Und 20. Jahrhunderts, Band 57*

Müller, R-D., *Hitlers Ostkrieg und die deutsche Siedlungspolitik*, Frankfurt am Main: Fischerverlag 1991

Müller, R-D., *An der Seite der Wehrmacht.Hitlers ausländische Helfer beim Kreuzzug gegen den Bolschewismus 1941-1945,* Berlin: Ch.Links verlag 2007

Nagy-Talavera, N., *Reminiscences of Iorga's Murderer: Traian Boeru* In: Kurt W.Treptow (Ed.), *Romanian Civilization Studies Vol. XIII.* 1996

Nagy-Talavera, N., *The Green Shirts and Others, a History of Fascism in Hungary and Romania*, Iasi/Oxford/Portland: The Center for Romania Studies 2001

Negura, P., From a 'Liberation' to Another. The Bessarabien Writers during the First year of Soviet Power (1940-1941). Integration Strategies and Forms of Exclusion, In: *Euxeinos 14* (2014)

Neubacher, H., *Sonderauftrag Südost 1940-45. Bericht eines fliegenden Diplomaten*, Göttingen/Berlin/Frankfurt: Musterschmidt Verlag, 1958

Neulen, H.W., *Euro-Faschismus und der Zweite Weltkrieg. Europa verratene Söhne*, Munich: Universitas 1980

Neumärker, U., u.a., *Wolfsschanze, Hitlers Machtzentrale in Zweiten Weltkrieg*

Ofer, D., *The Ghettos in Transnistria and Ghettos under German Occupation* in *Eastern* Europe. *A Comparative Approach in: Beiträge zur Geschichte des NS 25*, Göttingen: Wallstein Verlag, 2009

Penck, A., Politisch-Geographische Lehren des Krieges, In: *Meereskunde, Sammlung Volkstümlicher Vorträge Heft 106*, Berlin: Ernst Siegfriend Mitt- ler und Sohn, 1915

Pierik, P., *Hongarije 1944-1945, de vergeten tragedie*, Soesterberg: Uitgeverij As- pekt 1995

Pierik, P., *Hitlers Lebensraum, de geestelijke wortels van de veroveringstochten naar het oosten*, Soesterberg: Uitgeverij Aspekt 1999

Pierik, P., *Van Leningrad tot Berlijn, Nederlandse vrijwilligers in dienst van de Duitse Waffen-SS 1941-1945*, Soesterberg: 2006

Pierik, P., *Krim. Bestorming, belegering, verovering, bezetting en moord 1941- 1942*, Soesterberg: Uitgeverij Aspekt 2014

Pierik, P., *Karl Haushofer en het nationaal-socialisme. Tijd, werk en invloed*, Soesterberg: Uitgeverij Aspekt 2006

Pierik, P., *Erich Ludendorff. Biografie*, Soesterberg: 2017

Pierik, P. / Steeman, P., *Stalingrad, de slag en de luchtbrug naar de dood*, Soester- berg: Uitgeverij Aspekt 2014

Pierik, P., *Neu Turkestan aan het front. Islamitische soldaten uit de Kaukasus en de Balkan in dienst van de Waffen-SS*, Soesterberg: Uitgeverij Aspekt 2019

Pierik, P., *Sicherheitsdienst! Friedrich Knolle bekentenissen van een SD-officier*, Soesterberg: Uitgeverij Aspekt 2011

Pohl, D., *Die Herrschaft der Wehrmacht. Deutsche Militärbesatzung und die einheimische Bevölkerung in der Sowjetunion 1941-1944*, Munich: R. Olden- bourg Verlag 2009

Popa, K., *Vor 70 jahren. Die NS-'Volksgruppenpolitik' in weiteren Archivdokumen- ten. Das Jahr 1943*

Pope, S., / Wheal, E-A., *The Macmillan Dictionary of the First World War*, Lon- don: Macmillan 1995

Rauchensteiner, M., *Der Krieg in Österreich*, Wien: Bundesverlag 1984

Rehm, W., *Jassy, Schicksal einer Division oder einer Armee?* Neckargemünd: Scharnhorst Buchkameradschaft 1959

Romein, J., *Machten van deze tijd*, Amsterdam/Antwerp: Wereldbibliotheek 1950

Rossolinkssi-Liebe, G., *Inter-Fascist Conflicts in East Central Europe: The Nazis, the 'Austrofascists', the Iron Guard, and the Organization of Ukrainian Natio- nalists*, Oxford: Berghahn 2017

Schramm, P.E., (Hg.), *Kriegstagebuch des Oberkommando der Wehrmacht 1942 Teilband II*, Munich: Bernard & Graefe Verlag 1982

Schuster, H., *Die Judenfrage in Rumänien*; Leipzig: Felix Meiner Verlag

Seidt, H-U., Berlin, *Kabul, Moskau. Oskar Ritter von Niedermayer und Deutschlands Geopolitik*, Munich: Universitas 2002

Senger und Etterlin, F. von, *Krieg in Europa*, Cologne/Berlin: Kiepenheuer & Witsch 1960

Seyer, S.H., *The Plan put into Practice: USAAF Bombing Doctrine and the Ploesti Campaign*, Saint Louis 2005

South-Eastern Europe. A Political and Economic Survey, London: The Royal Institute for International Affairs 1939

Steel, M. van der, *Op leven en dood. Geschiedenis van de grote oorlog*, Libertas 1920

Stein, G.H., *The Waffen-SS. Hitler's Elite Guard at War 1939-1945*, New York: Cornell University Press, 1984

Steinhart, E.C., *The Holocaust and the Germanization of Ukraine*, Washington: Cambridge University Press 2015

Sturdza, M., *The Suicide of Europe*, Massachusetis: Western Islands Publishers 1965

Suveica, S., From Heroisation to Competing Victimhoods. History Writing on the Second World War in Moldova, In: *Südosteuropa* 65 (2017), no. 2

Taubinger, L.M., Die Entwicklung der ungarischen Erdölindustrie In: *Wirtschaftsdienst 36* (1956)

Taylor, B., *Barbarossa to Berlin. A Chronology of the Campaigns of the Eastern Front 1941 to 1945* Vol. Two, Chalford: Spellmount 2008

Tiku, O., The Molotov Ribbentrop Pact and the Emergence of the 'Moldovan' Nation: Reflections after 70 Years, In: Almanack of Policy Studies (Politikos mokslų almanachas) issue: 7/ 2010

Traditionsgemeinschaft 50.Infanterie-Division (hg.), *Die 50.Infanterie-Division 1939-1945*, Augsburg: Eigenverlag von der Traditionsgemeinschaft 50. Infanterie-Division, 1965

Tschuppik. K., *Ludendorff, die Tragödie des Fachmanns*, Wien/Leipzig: Verlag Hans Epstein, 1931

Ungvary, K., *Die Schlacht um Budapest 1944/45. Stalingrad an der Donau,* München: Herbig Verlag 2001

Walsh, S., *Stalingrad 1942-1943, the Infernal Cauldron*

Warlimont, W., *Im Hauptquartier der deutschen Wehrmacht 1939-1945. Grundlagen, Formen, Gestalten. Band 2., November 1942 - Mai 1945*, Weltbildver- lag: z.j.

Wegner, B., *Hitler's politische Soldaten: Die Waffen-SS 1933-1945*, Paderborn/ Munich Ferdinand Schöningh 1997

Wiesel, E, Friling, T. Ioanid, R., (ed.) et al, *International Commission on the Holocaust in Romania, Final Report,* Jassy: Polirom 2004

Wieczynski, J.L., *The Modern Encyclopedia of Russian and Soviet History, Band 25* s.p.: 1981

Wijdeven, I. van de, *De spoken van Visegrad. De onbekende geschiedenis van Polen, Hongarije, Tsjechie en Slowakije*, Utrecht: Spectrum 2018

Wohltat, D.H., Der neue deutsch-rumänische Wirtschaftsvertrag p. 560-563 In: Der Vierjahresplan, Zeitschrift für nationalsozialistische Wirtschaftspolitik In: Perry Pierik (hg.), *Der Vierjahresplan, Zeitschrift für Nationalsozialistische Wirtschaftspolitk 1939*, Soesterberg: 2020

Zabecki, D.T., *The German War Machine in Worldwar II*

Zischka, A., *De geheime oorlog om petroleum*, Utrecht: Erven J. Bijleveld, 1937

Documents/Archives:

Abschlussmeldung über das Unternehmen 'Michael', Bestand 500, Findbuch 12469, Akte 51

Angaben über die Verluste der 3. Und 4. Rumänischen Armeen Am Don und bei Stalingrad GDIR, Bestand 500, Findbuch 124500, akte 144

Anlage 1 zu Tagesbefehl Nr.45, Soldaten der Ostfront, In: T311/R264 Bemerkungen zum Besuch des O.B. beim LVII.Pz.Korps und IV.A.K.,
 31.07.1944, GDIR Bestand 500, Findbuch 12469, Akte 43

Besprechung des Chefs d. Gen.St. der H.Gr.Südukraine mit dem Chef der G.Rum.Gen.St. am 09.08.1944 In: GDIR Bestand 500, Findbuch 12469, Akte 51

Besprechung des Oberbefehlshabers mit den Oberbefehlshabern der 6. Und 8. Armee u.a. am 15.09.1944 in Szatmar Nemety, GDIR Bestand 500, Find- buch 12469, Akte 35

Besprechung mit den Chefs d. Gen. St. der 6. Und 8. Armee und dem Chef d.D.V.V.St. 3 am 19.08.1944 in Slanic, In: GDIR Bestand 500, Findbuch 12469, Akte 51

Beurteilung der Divisionen, d.d. 09.05.1943, RH 24-44/143 CIA.gov./Library/Readingroom, document CIA-RP-D13x00001R000100140011-7 Das Ölproblem: Erdölförderung und Erdölausfuhr in Rumänien, Sicherstellung der Bedürfnisse der Wehrmacht mit den Erdölprodukten in den Jahren 1942 - 1943. In: File 500, Findbuch 12450 Akte 145

Das Problem der Öl- und Gasleitungen Bestand 500, GDIR: Findbuch 12451 - Oberkommando des Heeres (OKH)Act 397)

Der Oberbefehlshaber der Kriegsmarine, d.d. 19.05.1944, Die Tätigkeit der Kriegsmarine bei der Verteidigung und Räumung der Krim vom Herbst 1943 ab In: T1027/R1907/Admiral Schwarzes Meer, d.d. 23.05.1944, Abschluss- bericht über der Festung Sewastopol

Der Chef des Generalstabes der Heeresgruppe Süd an den Chef des Königlichen Rumänischen Grossen Generalstabes Herrn General Jacobici, den 23.12.1941 In: T311/R295

Der Chef des Generalstabes der Heeresgruppe Süd an den Chef des Generalstabes des Heeres Generaloberst Halder, den 21.12.1941 In: T 311/R295

Der Oberbefehlshaber der Heeresgruppe Südukraine, An die Generale (einschl. Div. Führer, d.d. 23.07.1944, GDIR Bestand 500, Findbuch 12469, Akte 43

Der Oberbefehlshaber der Heeresgruppe Südukraine, An Alle deutsche und rumänischen Kommandeur, d.d.: 18.08.1944, GDIR: Bestand 500, Findbuch 12469, Akte 51

Deutsche Heeresmission in Rumanien, 12.06.1941, Memorandum No. 2 In: GDIR Akte 89

Deutsche Heeresmission in Rumanien an den Chef des Königlich Rumänischen Grossen Generalstabes Herrn General Steflea, 02.10.1942, operatives Memorandum Nr. 4, GDIR Akte 77

Deutsche Heeresmission in Rumanien, 10.06.1941, Meldungen für Sicherung und Verteidigung der Grenzen Rumaniens gegen Russland In: GDIR Akte 89

Deutsche Wehrmission in Rumänien, W-Befehl Nr. 5, GDIR Bestand 500, Findbuch 12450, Akte 63

Fernschreiben H.Gr.Südukraine dd. 19.08.144, GDIR Bestand 500, Findbuch 12469, Akte 51

Fernschreiben O.K.H. an Heeresgruppe F, Betr.: Rettung deutscher Volksgruppe in Rumänien, d.d. 01.09.1944, Bestand 500, Findbuch 12469, Akte 54

Fernschreiben an Reichsführer-SS, Feldkommandostelle by SS-Obergruppen- führer Phleps, dated 01.09.1944 In: GDIR File 500, Findbuch 12469, Akte 54

Generalstabsoffizier der 9.Inf.-Division, d.d. 28.02.1943, In: RH 24-44/139 Generalkomamndo V.A.K. Befehl zur Aufstellung des Gebirgsjägerregiments

'Crimea' dated 03.04.1944 In: File 500, Findbuch 12474, Akte 92

Generalkommando LXXII.A.K. z.b.V. d.d. 05.04.1944, Korpsbefehl zur Verteidigung der Brückenkopf-Stellung Odessa

Gliederung des Ostfeldzuges (01.10.1942-02.02.1943) 27.05.1943, GDIR Akte 68

Heeresgruppe Südukraine an Rum.Verb.Kdo. (Oberst Ivanescu), Betr: Ablösung der ukrainischer, russischer usw. Einheiten durch rum. Minderheiten-Einheiten, d.d. 20.07.1944, File 500, Findbuch 12469 Akte 43

MS#D-101 (OSS) Crossing of the Kerch Straits by the 46th infantry division from the Crimea to he Taman Peninsula on 1 and 2 September 1942, In: www. maparchive.ru

Niederschrift über die Vernehmung des Rückkämpfers Lt.Lange, 370.I.D., d.d. 15.09.1944 GDIR file 500, Findbuch 12469, Akte 53

Oberbefehlshaber der 3.Rum.Armee Herrn Generaloberst Dimitrescu, d.d. 31.12.1942, T 311/Roll 270

Obkdo.d. Heeresgruppe Südukraine, betr. Panzerbekämpfung, d.d. 15.09.1944 GDIR 500 Findbuch 12469, Akte 53

Oberkommando des Heeres, 03.09.1942, Betr. 'Stab Don' T78/Roll 649

Oberkommando der Heeresgruppe A, Bezug: Ausbau der Festung Krim, d.d. 24.05.1943 In: GDIR, Bestand 500, Findbuch 12469, Akte 33

Oberkommando der Wehrmacht, 26.03.1941 Betr.: *'Barbarossa'* Befehl für die Verteidigung des rumänischen Erdölgebietes. In: Anweisungen, Anordnungen und andere operative Dokumente des Oberkommandos der Wehrmacht, In: GDIR: Bestand 500 Findbuch 12450 Akte 82

Oberkommando der Wehrmacht, zu: Die Wehrwirtschafts Rumänien nach dem Stand von Anfang 1940: V: B. Erdölwirtschaft In: Ubersicht der Heeresstärken der Staaten im Ost- und Südost Raum, In: GDIR: Bestand 500 Findbuch 12450 Akte 50

OKH/Abwicklungsstab Gruppe F, Gefechtsbericht für die 376.Inf. Div. vom 18.08.1944 - 29.08.1944, In: T78/Roll 139

OKH Betr: *Zusammenarbeit mit den Truppen verbündeter Staaten und fremdländischen Freiwlilligenverbänden*, 15.01.1942 In: T312/Roll 158

Panzerjäger-Sturmgeschütz 38 T (Hetzer), Führungsgrundsätze Inf. Sturmgesch. Kp. attached to letter to letter OKH to 'Heeresgruppe Südukraine' dated 06.09.1944.GDIR Bestand 500, Findbuch 12469, Akte 53

Pressestelle vertrauliche Mitteilungen, Wochenbericht Südosteuropa, Bestand 500 Findbuch 12450 Akte 198

Räumung des Kuban-Brückenkopfes und die Verteidigung der Krim vom 04.09.1943 In: KTB OKW

Rumanian Refugee Organisations in Germany, February 1955 Cia.gov/library/readingroom

Schlagregen, Leutnant, Betr. takt. Erlebnisbericht des Lt. Schlagregen (106.I.D.) Bezug: OKH, T78/R139

Six letters from Von Manstein to the Befehlshaber Heeresgebiet Don, to the Bevollmächtigen General beim rum. AOK 3, to the Chef des Kgl.,Rum. grossen Hauptquartiers Herr General Steflea Strength report Armeegruppe Hollidt, 02.01.1943, T311/Roll 270

Tagesmeldung Heeresgruppe Südukraine 28.07.1944, GDIR File 500, Findbuch 12469, Akte 39

Telexbericht An OKDO D.H.Gr.DDon, 06.12.1942 T311/Roll 268 Ubersicht der Wehrwirtschaft Rumäniens stand Anfang 1940, DGIR: Bestand 500, Findbuch 12450 Akte 51

Vergleich der rumänischen Eisenbahn mit den Eisenbahnen Jugoslawien, Ungarn und Deutschland, GDIR file 500 Findbuch 12459 Akte 2

Vorläufiger Gefechtsbericht der 79. Infanterie-Division über die Kämpfe von, 20.08.1944 - September 1944, In: T78/R140

Vortragsbericht der Deutschen Heeresmission in Rumänien an Oberkommando des Heeres und an Oberkommando der Heeresgruppe A, über Gliederung, Zustand und Führung der rumänischen Verbände der 1.Welle mit den Gliederungssskizzen vom Juli 1942, in: GDIR: File 500 Findbuch 124500 Akte 136

Zusammenstellung der Grenzzwischenfälle an der rumänisch-ungarischen Grenze. Ungarische Einflüge im Rumänischen Luftraum (vom 22.Juni 19412 bis 22 August 1943, In: GDIR Bestand 500 Akte 111

Zusammenstellung der umgespurten Strecken, T78/R117 Zwischenmeldung vom 16.11.1941 In: T311/R257

Internet links:

https://www.prlib.ru/en/history/619158)

https://www.yadvashem.org/yv/pdf-drupal/en/report/english/1.2_Romanian_ German_Relations_before_and_during_the_Holocaust.pdf)

https://www.youtube.com/watch?v=Ak6jwsLS9Sk http://www.worldcourts.com/imt/eng/decisions/1948.04.09_United_States_v_Ohlendorf.pdf http://www.geocities.ws/rausschmiss/S.pdf

Dr. Hans Otto Roth (1890-1953) Vortrag von Dr. Phil. Florian Roth, Haus des Deutschen Ostens, Munich, 13. Mai 2009, Seite 1 Dr. Hans Otto Roth (1890-1953) - Betrachtungen seines Enkels über den bedeutendsten rumä- niendeutschen Politiker des 20.

Jahrhunderts Vortrag von Dr. phil. Florian Roth bei der Kreisgruppe München der Landsmannschaft der Siebenbürger Sachsen im Haus des Deutschen Ostens, Munich, 13. Mai 2009 via: fi- le:///D:/Downloads/Hans-Otto_Roth_MS.pdf

Phleps, A., *Memoire über die Wahrung deutscher Belange in Rumänien* am 2. De- zember 1940 In: https://www.academia.edu/31300674/Bio-bibliografisches_ Handbuch_deutscher_Volksgruppen_S%C3%BCdosteuropa_P

file:///D:/Downloads/Bio-bibliografisches_Handbuch_ deutscher%20(2).pdf

Abbreviations:

D.V.K = Deutschen Verbindungskommando
FH = Feldhaubitze
GDIR = German Docs in Russia
HSSPF = Höhere SS und Polizeiführer
KOR = Kriegsorganisation Rumänien Korück = Korpsrückwärts
KTB = Kriegstagebuch
MG = Machinegewehr
OKH = Oberkommando des Heeres
OKW = Oberkommando der Wehrmacht
Pak = Panzerabwehrkanone
R = Russia
SD = Sicherheitsdienst
I.D. = Infantry Division
z.b.V. = Zum besonderen Verwendung
P = Panzer
Pz = Panzer
D = Division
Div = Division
Gr. = Grenadier
SS = Schutzstaffel

Wi = Wirtschaft
Rü = Rüstung

A word of thanks

A number of people I would like to thank especially, for helping me to create this book as well as getting to know fascinating Romania more closely.

Adrian Pandea
Aida Minerva Tanasescu
Finn Pierik
Gillis Kersting
Isabel Oomen
Marius Ghilezan
Maurice Becker
Tudor Seicarescu
Tudor Vişan-Mi